Film Music

WITHDRAWN

Film Music

Critical Approaches

Edited by K. J. Donnelly

Edinburgh University Press

© the contributors, 2001

Edinburgh University Press Ltd
22 George Square, Edinburgh

Typeset in 10.5 on 13 Sabon
by Hewer Text Ltd, Edinburgh, and
printed and bound in Great Britain by
The Cromwell Press, Trowbridge

A CIP record for this book is
available from the British Library

ISBN 0 7486 1288 2 (paperback)

The right of the contributors
to be identified as authors of this work
has been asserted in accordance with
the Copyright, Designs and Patents Act 1988.

Contents

List of Illustrations

Acknowledgements

For one reason or another, this book had a very long gestation period. Thanks should go to Jackie Jones at Edinburgh University Press for constant encouragement and endless patience. Thanks also to all friends and people who have provided support in whatever way they could, and to Staffordshire University for easing my teaching burden. Special thanks to Mandy Marler and to Joan and Robert Donnelly who encouraged my youthful interest in film and music.

Grateful acknowledgement is made to the following sources for permission to reproduce material previously published elsewhere. Every effort has been made to trace the copyright holders, but if any have been inadvertently overlooked, the publisher will be pleased to make the necessary arrangements at the first opportunity. Thanks to Bourne Music for allowing the excerpts from Bernard Herrmann's *Citizen Kane* and Leigh Harline's *Isle of the Dead*.

The Hidden Heritage of Film Music: History and Scholarship

K. J. Donnelly

Anyone who has seen films has heard film music in copious amounts. I am not simply referring to songs in film musicals, but more to the music heard in the background in almost every film. Much of the time people have hardly noticed it, and this is perhaps why writers and scholars have paid it such scant attention. On closer inspection, however, film music not only displays a rich breadth and diversity, but it also encompasses some of the most interesting and affecting music produced in the twentieth century. Although it is a central component of cinema, the way it works is a mystery and is little understood. This volume of essays elucidates the operation of film music, celebrating its richness and its fascinating characteristics and provides a number of studies that span the history of music in the cinema. This introductory chapter provides a rundown of the scholarly approaches to film music, going on to supply a general history of film music in mainstream Western cinema, which will include an overview of all the chapters in this collection.

The study of film music has taken place in the margins of academia. While film scholarship has largely ignored film music as a problem it would rather not face, music scholarship has persisted in the prejudice that film music is somehow below the standard of absolute music ('pure', non-functional music, written specifically for the 'respectable' concert hall). It is precisely against attitudes such as these that this book militates. Film music is invariably more than it seems to be. It is often far from simply aural wallpaper: it is vibrant and affecting, a central pillar of cinema's power and charm.

So how can we go about discussing film music? It is by no means easy. There is no solid tradition or single accepted approach. The two principal descriptive tools that have so far been used are semiotics and musicology in varying forms. While I do not propose to provide an introduction to these two disciplines, I will sketch their strengths, weaknesses and differences to distinguish the two traditions. Semiotics is concerned with cultural coding, with the way that film music can communicate with an audience through its recognisable elements within certain contexts. This approach often owes much to pragmatics, the study of meaning in relation to the specific context of its appearance, and is concerned with film music as a functional item that exists within the film purely for its communicational value. Musicology, on the other hand, suggests that there are other contexts in which to situate the music, particularly that of its production and relation to the traditions of orchestral music in the classical concert hall. It might also suggest that music is never a simple transitive communication between 'text' and audience, but a more complex process where the music's 'meaning' is imprecise, always excessive to its context, and can never be seen as finite.

  Musicology's own metalanguage evolved for the study of nineteenth-century art music and is tied heavily to notation as an abstract 'essence' of the music. This is highly evident. There is an overriding concern in musicological analyses, especially notation-based 'Schenkerian' analyses, with the structural underpinnings of harmony (chord changes, simultaneous relationships between notes and the development of these relationships). Musicological analyses can often rely heavily on abstract written notations of music and neglect the materiality of music – its particular context of appearance, its individual instrumental (or vocal) sound, the ethos of rhythm as pulse and the cumulative effect of repetition; and the relation of music to other things, such as history, society or film. An example of these shortcomings is that the paper notation of a guitar tune would differ wildly from its realisation by, respectively, guitarists such as the classical player Segovia and the rock guitarist Jimi Hendrix, even though they were playing the same melody 'on paper' as it were. The humanities commonly know this approach as 'formalism', and its major drawback is that it apprehends its object in a void, losing the sense of living relationship that music has with its surroundings. Audiences internalise the cultural coding of film music to such a degree that they readily recognise the burlesquing of film music's 'meaning' by the use of romantic string music in a moment that does not warrant this in a comic film. To remove the shared understanding of film music and enforce a musicological paradigm derived from

Western art music is thus to lose something fundamental in the translation.

Yet on the other hand, we should remember that much film music, and especially that of Hollywood's heyday in the 1930s and 1940s, has been heavily based on nineteenth-century concert music, precisely what inspired formalist 'Schenkerian' analyses of the relations between notes on manuscript paper. However, the form and the function of film music are not the same as concert-hall music. Film music is usually fragmentary and relies on a logic that is not an organic part of the music but a negotiation between the logic of the film and the logic of the music. Consequently, its analysis has to acknowledge this dual logic in merging the two main approaches.

It is significant to note that film music has had a massive audience, in fact probably the largest audience for music ever. Its concern has almost always been with effect, and having an immediate rapport with the audience; hence is has to be approached as a social phenomenon, although this cannot be to the detriment of investigating its own language and the way that has been mobilised in the production of music. The massified social status of this music should not mean that analyses do not relate it to its traditions of production and relationship to other music, especially other film music.

Semiotics, despite seeming word and image-centred, should analyse film music genres and the ways its codes work more than has been the case. After all, certain music in the wake of illustrative 'programme music' has aimed to produce a 'synaesthesia', where certain musical sounds ('timbre') and styles evoke visual aspects. Sometimes the audio and visual codes are intimately related, as in the horror film's 'stinger', which is a musical blast as an aural equivalent of a visual shock. Semiotics is not at all contradictory to musicology – as witnessed by some of the essays in this volume. Semiotics implicates the social level of music's life, where it is seen as a transaction between the sound and the listener. This primarily social concern should never be forgotten, as film music is a vibrant and living form of music that breathes in harmony with its film, to provide a high degree of emotional impact for mass audiences.

As my discussion suggests, severe constraints have blighted the study of film music. There is little common ground or consensus when it comes to music analysis across academic disciplines. The analysis of music from films proves little problem for musicology when the music is fully divorced from its cinematic context, yet this is only one perspective, one that can sometimes lose sight of the music's function and social existence. The study of film music can become the appraisal of CD recordings or reams of manuscript paper rather than an illumination of the phenomenon of film music itself and what it does. I am perhaps putting into words the endemic suspicion in my own discipline, film studies, that besets much talk about musical analysis. Yet equally, when the film studies tradition is surveyed, it too is found as severely wanting as the musicology tradition, perhaps more so. Considerations of one of the most popular genres of classical Hollywood cinema, the musical, have one thing in common: the almost total lack of any consideration of the music itself. There is concern with narrative, with the visual structure of song sequences, with the genre's themes and history, yet the music, the defining aspect of the films is written out of the proceedings. Rick Altman pointed out in *Genre: The Musical*:

> It seems inconceivable that a collection of the latest and best articles devoted to the musical should be all but devoid of detailed consideration of the soundtrack. To be sure, this failing is far from limited to the present collection; it is in fact one of the fundamental limitations of recent film theory and criticism alike. (Altman 1981: 218)

It is nineteen years later as I write and little has changed in film studies. The discipline has roundly failed to incorporate the study of film music into its schemes. Some of the evidence is damning. The lack of seriousness with which film historians deal with film music is vividly demonstrated by one of the pre-eminent studies of classical cinema, in fact probably the central canonical text on classical cinema: Bordwell, Staiger and Thompson's *The Classical Hollywood Cinema*. This book dismisses film music in a few short paragraphs, and yet in that brief space still managing to misname one of Hollywood's principal musicians. It refers to 'Ernest Newman' (1985: 33), a name that does not tally with any of the extensive Newman dynasty who have been prominent in Hollywood film music.

If I have painted a bleak picture of the state of academic approaches to film music, with the two disciplines failing to collaborate, then there are some beacons in the darkness. The last decade has seen a small number of books that manage to speak the languages of both disciplines as well as bear the fruit of both worlds, namely Claudia Gorbman's *Unheard Melodies*, Kathryn Kalinak's *Settling the Score*, Caryl Flinn's *Strains of Utopia* and Royal S. Brown's *Overtones and*

Undertones. These follow in the wake of a book that still dares us to ignore it. Hanns Eisler and Theodor Adorno's *Composing for the Films* seems, on the surface, to be a practical guide for making film music, yet upon closer inspection it offers much in the way of theorisation about film music. First published in 1947, it is still relevant and is difficult to dismiss despite its age. *Unheard Melodies* by Claudia Gorbman is perhaps the most enduring analysis of film music, focusing on classical Hollywood film music and music in European art cinema. It provides a lucid introduction to the theoretical ideas tied to music in the cinema, yet persists in containing sophisticated and relevant debates for the study of film music. Caryl Flinn's *Strains of Utopia* comprises a heavily theoretical analysis of music in classical cinema, attending to its psychological function as a discourse. *Settling the Score* deals with Hollywood film music in a more historical manner, embracing the processes of production as well as the aesthetic blueprints that have defined film music. *Overtones and Undertones* brings together a selection of writings, some published elsewhere, which approach film music from varying points of view. Each of the books has case studies about specific films, and the precision of their analysis is an aspect that this book also hopes to duplicate. While these books are exemplary, they generally lack a solid historical perspective that this book supplies concisely in the second part of this chapter, and their studies lack the breadth possible in an anthology such as this.

This book embraces a wide range of approaches to film music: the historical, the industrial, the musicological, the cultural and the semiotic. While, as I have outlined, separate traditions of approaches to film music exist in the disciplines of film studies and music studies, I hope that the inclusion of these varied approaches in close proximity will firstly allow multiple and divergent points of view about music in films, and secondly help to unify the field of study.

Following this introductory chapter, there are two further chapters that provide information that will give the reader a solid perspective on music in films. David Neumeyer and James Buhler's chapters review the approaches scholars have taken to film music, looking first at music and then at film and music together. As this book is organised broadly along historical lines, this introductory chapter should elucidate the history of film music further. In what follows I will situate each chapter within a historical framework, attending to key developments in European-American film music and noting how each contributor has addressed relevant questions and moments.

A History of Film Music

Although cinema before the introduction of synchronised sound in the late 1920s is called silent cinema, most people are aware that it was never fully silent. The dominant mode for music in the cinema from 1896 until the late 1920s involved the production of live music as an accompaniment to the film's projection. While many films implied music visually through the showing of dancers or musicians, the music of silent cinema was only fleetingly motivated in the diegesis or film world (thus 'diegetic'). It was thus predominantly 'non-diegetic': emanating from outside the world constructed by the film, as if appearing from heaven. The music provided mood, pace and often directly imitated screen action on an aural level. The latter was known as 'mickey-mousing', and has been decried by both composers and critics despite its persistence to a degree in classical cinema and more recent films. Live music was performed by one or more musicians in the theatre where the film was projected and it usually provided a virtually constant aural fabric that paralleled the film's development, as well as helping to supply it with continuity. The music for silent cinema always retained a large degree of autonomy from the film and was thus a primary element in film exhibition. The lack of full ties to the image track meant that the music was never fully standardised in the manner of music in classical cinema through its use of optical synchronised sound, where it became the strip on the edge of film.

The change from a musical discourse that included anything that the pianist desired (London 1936: 40; Burch 1990: 235) – and often bore no similarity to the internal dynamics or overall mood of the film – to a closer relationship between the two media was noted at the time, with a 1909 review stating, 'A pleasant variation from the eternal ragtime was a refined deliverance of classical music corresponding to the character of the picture'.[1] The construction of music to fit the perceived demeanour of specific films resulted in a compound of classical pieces and popular tunes. At around this time, a surrounding industry quickly developed for the manufacture of 'cue sheets' (Marks 1997: 9). These were either pieces of sheet music already assembled to fit specific films, or blocks of sheet music that could be assembled in different orders to 'fit' a number of films. Later this became a sophisticated art with systematic guides such as Erno Rapée's *Encyclopedia of Music for Pictures* (1925) and Hans Erdmann and Guiseppe Becce's *Allgemeines Handbuch der Film-Musik* (1927), while other libraries of sheet music often developed through business agreements with the film production companies (Hofmann 1970).

The larger and more expensive the cinema, the larger the musical ensemble it had. So while small cinemas had only a piano, the biggest had full orchestras with a full-time musical director arranging the music. The development of a closer relationship between the music and the images came with the release and tremendous success of D. W. Griffith's expensive and prestigious production of *Birth of a Nation* (1915). This had a fixed orchestral score especially written for the film by Joseph Carl Breil with help from Griffith himself. While the score was essentially still a compilation of existing music, Breil had written his own themes and integrated these with music culled from a variety of sources into a continuous piece of music. This particular mode of film music production, the compilation of a composite score, continued and became more widespread until after the advent of synchronised sound and the espousal of high production values in the early 1930s. *Ben Hur* (1926) used an orchestral score compiled by William Axt and David Mendoza that conjoined and made variations on existing pieces of music, while the same musicians scored *The Big Parade* (1928) through much the same technique and added some musical themes of their own to the composite of music.

Generally speaking, the characteristics of silent cinema's musical accompaniments included firstly the use of standard music, usually wrested from another context and sometimes familiar to the audience. Secondly, silent cinema music displayed a certain autonomy from the image track that, before the institution of some standardisation with the cue sheet, meant music could be totally unrelated to image dynamics. Silent film music attempted to become an aural equivalent to screen action through homologising image and narrative dynamics and providing additional information about the diegesis and narrative to the audience.

The advent of sound films saw *Don Juan* (1926) use discs to provide music for the film, while the more celebrated *The Jazz Singer* (1927), starring Al Jolson, concentrated on the synchronised performances of songs and particularly dialogue, also on disc using the Vitaphone system. In one of the first chapters of this book, film historian Michael Allen describes the use of discs for musical accompaniment to films.

He provides hitherto uncharted information about this practice in Britain in the late 1920s, and describes a technique that foreshadows more recent practices of inserting popular music in films.

In the early 1930s, film music consolidated into a blueprint defining the music that would appear in the background in mainstream films. Kathryn Kalinak refers to it as the 'classical film score' (1992: xv–xvi), while Claudia Gorbman refers to the process of 'classical film scoring' (1987: 70). The development of particularity in film music – background scores being constructed for each individual film – has to be seen as the alignment of film music with what is commonly termed classical cinema. In other words, it was only with the advent of specially written scores for films that music became an integrated component of classical cinema. While some commentators view the late 1910s as the critical period for the consolidation of the classical mode of film production and practice,[2] in terms of music this period is characterised by only isolated examples of the particular, context-specific dramatic underscores that gradually became the norm after the advent of synchronised sound (Salt 1992: 213). The move from live performance in silent cinema to the establishment of a consistent paradigm for recorded background music during the 1930s meant fundamental changes in music's role and articulation for films. The early processes of putting music to film used for silent films were adapted in the early 1930s as Hollywood started to institutionalise the process of film-making.

The early 1930s were years of flux for music in films. In 1931 films used almost no non-diegetic music; in the following years, non-diegetic music established itself as a prime component of classical cinema. An example of the paucity of non-diegetic music at this time was *What Price Hollywood?* (1932) which, apart from the title sequences, included only two instances of non-diegetic music. The first is for a dream sequence and the second is for a similar montage sequence. The standardised musical practice of non-diegetic underscores was established by Max Steiner's scores for *Symphony of Six Million* (1932) and *King Kong* (1933), the establishment of an Academy Award for musical (background) score in 1934 and Steiner's Oscar-winning score for *The Informer* in 1935. By the time of the last of these events, the background score had become firmly established in Hollywood films and Steiner's work provided an influential blueprint for Hollywood film music to follow. In his chapter Peter Franklin discusses *King Kong*, attending to the way that the music has something fundamental to say about the relationship between woman and beast, and woman and man.

The model of film music that was established by the mid-1930s comprised dramatic and dynamic underscoring based on orchestral concert music and having an essentially non-diegetic status. These 'symphonic' scores or 'classical film scores' were conceived as a coherent and organic discourse within the film as well as an important component of film narration. Further, the system that was established by the Hollywood studios involved the writing and production of often original music for each individual film, whereas earlier it had been the fashion to weave a pastiche of existing musical pieces into the musical flow of a film's accompaniment.[3] Studio finances as well as aesthetic reasons motivated the changes. The studios decided to integrate the music industries; as composer Dimitri Tiomkin noted, 'The film companies were paying millions of dollars to publishers and composers for the use of published music. They soon found it more profitable to hire composers to write original music and to organise their own publishing houses' (Winkler 1974: 24). It was thus an industrial expedient for Hollywood to shift the film music paradigm and mode of production to a system where the studios employed a number of musical technicians (composers, orchestrators, musicians and so on) who would produce new music for each film as a part of the studio's production line (Prendergast 1974: 30–1). Under the Hollywood studio system, musicians were usually assigned to films once the shooting was over; they then 'spotted' the film, picking moments for music. The music was then written, often matching action with precision through the use of a regular pulsing 'click track'. It was often orchestrated and arranged by other musicians and recorded with a studio orchestra. Finally the finished product was edited into the film by a music editor, after which (occasionally earlier) the music was either accepted or rejected by director and producer. Thus the industrial organisation of the studio system directly dictated the style of film scores, producing music that was written quickly and was usually thought of as a momentary, 'throw-away' product.

From the mid-1930s until the 1950s, there was a 'classicism' in Hollywood film scores that is equivalent to the dominant conceptualisation of a classical cinema. The principal model of a typical, high-quality, classical film score from the 1930s and 1940s can be illustrated by reference to any of the scores of this period written by prominent composers for the cinema such as Steiner or Erich Wolfgang Korngold. Both of these steadfastly used the principle of the leitmotiv (also written leitmotive or leitmotif), a functional theme usually associated with a character on screen, as a building block to give structural unity to the film as well as consolidating the relationship between the music and the action on the screen and its narrative development. This blueprint also included the use of a full orchestra, the provision of a 'wall-to-wall' fabric of music throughout the film, and the general matching of the dynamics on screen (Steiner 1937: 220). William H. Rosar's chapter discusses the music of one of the mavericks of film music, a composer never swamped by the studio system, retaining instead his individual musical voice. This was Bernard Herrmann, probably the best-known composer of film music, and Rosar's chapter investigates the music for Orson Welles landmark *Citizen Kane* (1940). Herrmann's score was influential, and this chapter addresses the interpretation of some of the film's music, looking for origins and intentions. Like Welles film itself, Herrmann's music is perhaps an exception to the classical Hollywood norm. It is more individualistic than much of the music in classical films, resembling that produced for European art films, where there was no musical production line in the Hollywood fashion.

Concerned more with the margins of Hollywood and American film production, Alfred Cochran's chapter is about a composer respected for his experimentation in documentary films. The Second World War encouraged many art music composers (such as Vaughan Williams in Britain and Copland in the USA) to write film music as their own personal war effort, while the proliferation of propaganda films gave them great musical scope. This chapter investigates Gail Kubik's wartime documentary music. While Hollywood film music was a 'classical' art, working within certain well-defined boundaries, there were areas of film production such as the documentary that allowed for experiment outside the aesthetic bounds set by the studio system.

During the 1950s, there were some significant changes in Hollywood film music although the model established by classical cinema broadly remained in place. A new generation of film music composers appeared who were heavily influenced by jazz. This led to the widening of musical vocabularies to include not only the jazz idiom, but also the unresolved dissonance of twentieth-century concert-hall music. In many cases, younger composers also desired to increase further the level of integration between film music and narrative, and, perhaps conversely, were less willing to see film music as a purely secondary phenomenon to the dialogue and images of the film as had been its common status in the 1930s and 1940s.

The 1950s began with a work important for the subsequent history of film music: Alex North's score for *A Streetcar Named Desire* (1951), which made extensive use of the techniques and instrumental styles of jazz, as did Elmer Bernstein's for *The Man With the Golden Arm* (1955), one of the most highly acclaimed scores of the decade. Alongside this current, some of the film music of the 1950s reflected the increased prestige of films: epic films called for epic music, orchestral scores that were not going to sit quietly in the background but would be a major part of the cinematic package of conspicuous consumption. Examples of this are Miklos Rozsa's music for *Quo Vadis* (1951), *El Cid* (1955) and *Ben Hur* (1959) and Alfred Newman's music for *The Robe* (1953). At the same time, the discordant sounds that had been adorning the orchestral concert halls since the early part of the century also made their way into films. Leonard Rosenman's score for *East of Eden* (1955), for example, bore more resemblance to modernist art music than to the film music that had been dominant throughout the previous two decades. Instrumental sounds appeared increasingly prominently as sound effects, catalysed by the increased employment of electronic musical instruments. Following occasional earlier use in films, electronic instruments such as the theremin, ondes martenot and other devices were used as featured sound devices in science fiction films such as *The Day The Earth Stood Still* (1951) and *Forbidden Planet* (1956).[4] Traditional orchestral music's forces also began to 'feature' specific sounds; for instance James Bernard's scores for Hammer horror films tended towards a consistent use of strident and discordant brass, while Bernard Herrmann scored *Psycho* (1960) purely for an ensemble of strings, creating a 'black and white sound' equivalent to the tonality of the film's image. Such film music tended to emphasise music's spatial and atmospheric capabilities more than music in classical cinema. One of the few household names in film music, Ennio Morricone, came to prominence in the 1960s. He has consistently produced outstanding scores that display his penchant for instrumental sonority and texture as much as melody.

Throughout the 1960s and 1970s, more sparse scores, both in terms of the amount of music and the number of instrumentalists, generally superseded large orchestral scores (Darby and Dubois 1990: 38). The more recent system of film music production involved fewer personnel, lacking the ranks of arrangers, subsidiary composers and musical directors of the studio system. The work of a composer such as Jerry Goldsmith has encompassed the changes between the 1950s and today's less opulent modes (Darby and Dubois 1990: 496). His score for *Chinatown* (1974) was very sparse and concerned with instrumental textures in much the same way as contemporaneous art music. Similarly, Richard Rodney Bennett's music for *Figures in a Landscape* (1970) and Jerry Fielding's for *Straw Dogs* (1971) demonstrated a concern with smaller scale ensembles and angular modernist musical style. European art cinema was perhaps even more willing to consort with modernist art music, as well as other kinds of music. Art films such as those discussed by Caryl Flinn in her chapter on music and kitsch in a film by Werner Schroeter, utilise music using myriad strategies, most unlike the Hollywood norm. A further aesthetic development has been the recontextualisation of music by films, whereby established music was taken and inserted into a (new) film. A famous example of this was in Luchino Visconti's art film *Death in Venice* (1971), where excerpts from three of Gustav Mahler's symphonies were used efficaciously. Probably the most celebrated instance of this process was Stanley Kubrick's *2001: A Space Odyssey* (1968), which memorably used excerpts from Richard Strauss's *Also Sprach Zarathustra* and much more besides. It largely retained its 'temp track' – pieces of music taken from commercially available recordings and inserted into the film's 'rough cut' to be shown to studio executives. Kubrick found the reuse of this existing music so pleasing that he discarded the score Alex North had written for the film in favour of the composite of concert-hall pieces. Broadly speaking, this process coincided with the end of studio system production line and industrial procedure of creating film music using teams of specialist composers and musicians, and concluding in an orchestral score that covered much of the film.

Pop songs were also inserted into films to replace especially written musical underscore. My later chapter deals with a film filled to the brim with different types of music used in every possible way. *Performance* (1970) was made at the height of the psychedelic culture of the late 1960s and its musical score by Jack Nitzsche merges the traditions of film music and modernist music with the explosion of interest in rock music and 'ethnic' music. Around this time, the influence of pop music was strong in films with eclectic and multi-faceted music, such as Michel Legrand's for *The Thomas Crown Affair* (1968), while jazz rock was the impetus behind Lalo Schifrin's music for *Magnum Force* (1972) and 'blaxploitation' films used foregrounded soul and funk music that inflected the background scores. This current has been of lasting influence, with a number of composers such as John Barry, Quincy Jones, Graeme Revell and Hans Zimmer having transversed the membrane dividing pop music and scoring films, bringing many of the techniques of pop music with them. At the same time, there has been a dramatic growth in the use of pop songs as the whole or a significant part of the music for films (Smith 1998).

With the advent of John Williams music for the *Star Wars* trilogy starting in the late 1970s, however, there was something of a rediscovery of the sound of the big orchestra and the Romantic-flavoured music that had graced classical cinema (Kalinak 1992: 189; Donnelly 1998). The turn to large-scale orchestral scores in the 1980s was evident in most mainstream Hollywood film productions, with prominent examples being Williams's for *ET: The Extra-Terrestrial* (1982), Alan Silvestri's for *Back to the Future* (1985) and James Horner's for *Willow* (1988). While many of these scores are superficially similar in style, there are plenty of opportunities for experiment and examples of adventurousness in contemporary film music. Robynn Stilwell's chapter discusses the use of film sound as a form of musical discourse, detailing the aural component of *Closet Land* (1990). Ken Garner's chapter also deals with the unconventional use of music in films. He writes about the notable and highly successful use of music in Quentin Tarantino's films, *Reservoir Dogs* (1992), *Pulp Fiction* (1996) and *Jackie Brown* (1997). He investigates the impact of the film's music and its primary role in motoring the elliptical narrative, while attempting to account for its central symbolic and 'authentic' position in constructing the film's cultural status and within its aesthetic processes.

After the stabilisation of film music production in the Hollywood studio system in the early 1930s, there was a relative immutability of classical film scores as a model until the 1950s. From this point there was a gradual influx of new musical languages and techniques. The film music of Hollywood has always proved itself suited to eclectic and adaptable musicians, and the narrative of development is one of assimilation, taking classical art music in the 1930s, jazz and modernist art music in the 1950s and 1960s, and pop music in the 1970s and 1980s. While European art and sometimes popular cinema often followed a different procedure (Donnelly 1997; Egorova 1997), Hollywood provided a model, a quality and style to which films would aspire or from which they would differentiate themselves. This book has a chronological structure, providing a number of case studies across the breadth of film music history. While the background music in films regularly has gone unnoticed, this anthology not only delineates the ways which it has worked in films, but also celebrates the richness and diversity of music and the techniques that have appeared them.

Notes

1. Review, *Moving Picture World*, 13 March 1909, quoted in Hofmann 1970, section entitled 'Music to Fit the Pictures' (no page numbers).
2. Bordwell, Staiger and Thompson identify the classical cinema as being relatively stable from 1917 to 1960. As an aesthetic model, this denies any development in music and marginalises the introduction of sound and the foundation of the film musical. Ellis identifies the period of the 'classic Hollywood film' as dating from 1915 to 1955 (1982: 63).
3. Although cheaply made films and other forms of film production still recycled and joined together music from elsewhere.
4. Rosza had already used the theremin to augment the mental dislocation of the protagonist from *The Lost Weekend* (1945), as well as using it in *Spellbound* (1945).

Bibliography

Adorno, T. W. and Hanns Eisler (1994) *Composing for the Films* (originally published 1947). London: Athlone Press.

Altman, Rick (1981) *Genre: The Musical*. London: British Film Institute (BFI).

Bordwell, David, Janet Staiger and Kristin Thompson (1985) *The Classical Hollywood Cinema: Mode of Production 1917–1960*. London: Routledge.

Brown, Royal S. (1994) *Overtones and Undertones: Reading Film Music*. Berkeley: University of California Press.

Burch, Noël (1990) *Life to Those Shadows*. London: BFI.

Darby, Ken and Wiliam Dubois (1990) *American Film Composers*. Washington: McFarland.

Donnelly, K. J. (1998) 'The Classical film score forever?: *Batman, Batman Returns* and post-classical film music' in Steve Neale and Murray Smith (eds) *Contemporary Hollywood Cinema*. London: Routledge.

Donnelly, K. J. (1997) 'Wicked sounds and magic melodies: Music in 1940s Gainsborough melodrama' in Pam Cook (ed.) *Gainsborough Pictures*. London: Cassell.

Egorova, Tatiana (1997) *Soviet Film Music: An Historical Survey* (trans. Tatiana Ganf and Natalia Egunova). Amsterdam: Harwood.

Ellis, John (1982) *Visible Fictions: Cinema, Television, Video*. London: Routledge.

Erdmann, Hans and Guiseppe Becce (1927) *Allgemeines Handbuch dev Film Musik*. 2 vols. Berlin-Lichterfelde: Schlesinger 'sche Buch-und Muslekhandlung, Robert Lienau.

Flinn, Caryl (1992) *Strains of Utopia: Hollywood Film Music*. Princeton: Princeton University Press.

Gorbman, Claudia (1987) *Unheard Melodies: Narrative Film Music*. London: BFI.

Hofmann, Charles (1970) *Sounds for Silents*. New York: DBS.

Kalinak, Kathryn (1992) *Settling the Score: Narrative Film Music*. London: University of Wisconsin Press.

London, Kurt (1936) *Film Music*. London: Faber.

Marks, Martin Miller (1997) *Music and the Silent Film: Contexts and Case Studies, 1985–1924*. Oxford: Oxford University Press.

Prendergast, Roy M. (1974) *A Neglected Art: A Critical Study of Music in Films*. New York: Proscenium.

Rapée, Erno (1970) *Encyclopedia of Music for Pictures* (originally published 1925). New York: Arno Press.

Salt, Barry (1992) *Film Style and Technology: History and Analysis*. London: Starword.

Smith, Jeff (1998) *The Sounds of Commerce: Marketing Popular Film Music*. New York: Columbia University Press.

Steiner, Max (1937) 'Scoring the film' in Nancy Naumburg (ed.) *We Make the Movies*. New York: W. M. Norton.

Winkler, Max (1974) 'The origin of film music' in James Limbacher (ed.) *From Violins to Video*. Metuchen: Scarecrow.

Chapter 1

Analytical and Interpretive Approaches to Film Music (I): Analysing the Music

David Neumeyer and James Buhler

Introduction

The literature of cinema is large, as one would expect of a medium that has dominated the arts and culture throughout the twentieth century. Nearly every conceivable audience has been served by publishers' offerings ranging from juicily anecdotal (and usually ghost-written) celebrity autobiographies through general and special-interest trade-books to scholarly monographs on film history, theory and aesthetics. Periodicals cover the same range, from those offering popular reviews of current movies to those serving scholarly audiences.

Within this broad expanse of literature, film music remains at best a niche market. (Even the larger topic area of which music is part – the film soundtrack – is a speciality subject.) Furthermore, the readership for film music is by no means monolithic in its interests. In a recent survey of film-music criticism, Claudia Gorbman has distinguished five types of writing according to their goals: 'musical, fan or market, academic, cultural, and mainstream' (1995: 72). The first of these draws attention to film music as music, the second serves the sound-track collector, the third 'examines how a particular score works in the film it was composed for,' the fourth considers film music in a cultural–historical context, and the last 'imagines' a mainstream film critic who includes music in his or her critique of a film. The audiences overlap and so do the style and goals of the writing; for example, the 'musical' and 'fan or market' categories frequently are indistinguish-able, as soundtrack collectors will debate the merits of film scores at length while freely admitting that they have never seen the film from which the music was drawn.

Thus, the meaning we attach to 'analysis and interpretation' in this chapter will vary depending on which of Gorbman's five categories serves as our frame of reference. The mainstream film critic's obligation is to evaluate a film while entertaining his or her readers with a well-written newspaper or magazine column. In that context, interpretation serves evaluation, and music is only relevant as its functions or style might serve that goal. The soundtrack collector is interested in audio quality, the individual performance, completeness of the track list in relation to the original score or effectiveness of the selections made and so on. In what follows, we will focus on the third and fourth of Gorbman's categories because these best represent the activities of the film-music student and scholar. The third category depicts film-music 'analysis', which is a reading or description of music's position and function within a particular film. The fourth category places music within an historical account or a framework of culture criticism. These categories of analysis and history or culture criticism can – and, one might argue, should – overlap considerably, but differences of emphasis reflect the interests of different groups of film and music scholars.

Background

In the most recent edition of the venerable *New Grove Dictionary of Music and Musicians*, the term 'analysis' warranted an essay of nearly fifty pages (Bent 1980: 340–88). In the recently published *Oxford Guide to Film Studies* (Hill and Church Gibson 1998), the term rarely appears and is wholly absent from section labels and titles for the sixty-two individual essays. Instead, one finds 'film interpretation', 'critical approaches', and 'theoretical frameworks'.

This discrepancy may serve to highlight differences between the disciplines of cinema studies and music scholarship (musicology), differences that may be traced in part to the histories of those disciplines, in part to the artworks they study. Cinema studies as a university discipline has evolved out of the work of early theorists and critics (such as Arnheim and Bazin), the writings of film-makers (such as Eisenstein), and the pedagogy of literature instructors who drew film into their teaching and for whom a tight relation between film criticism and literary theory was assumed (structuralism, semiotics, and subsequently neo-Marxism, feminism, and post-structuralism). Only in the past decade have traditionalist attitudes within such disciplines as history and philosophy made serious inroads into cinema studies, the most vocal advocates being David Bordwell and Noël Carroll (Bordwell 1989; Bordwell and Carroll 1996; Carroll 1996; Allen and Smith 1997).

Very much the opposite has been true of musicology. Born out of the historicising interests of nineteenth-century composers and performers (the most spectacular instance being the Bach revival of Mendelssohn, Schumann and others), by the century's end musicology was moving down to two divergent paths, both of which had their source in an unending obsession with Beethoven. The first of these was the detailed study of 'style', which, as Ian Bent puts it, turns analysis into 'a tool for historical inquiry': the musicologist 'uses it to detect relationships between "styles", and thus to establish chains of causality' (Bent 1980: 341). Though this activity sounds neutral, one of its initial applications was as a weapon in nationalist culture wars, in particular as a means of claiming a nation's decisive compositional influences on Beethoven (French, German, Austrian, Italian, depending on the scholar). The second path followed the Romantics' arguments about music's special status as a 'language above language', an 'absolute' art wholly unmediated and untainted (Dahlhaus 1989: 60). Of course, this distinction applies only to 'pure' instrumental music, not to song, stage works or 'programme music' (instrumental music with an associated title or story). Not only did 'the idea of absolute music' offer another way of valorising the great master of symphonies and sonatas, Beethoven, at the expense of the lyrical opera composers of French and Italian traditions, but by the early twentieth century it had coalesced into an aestheticist mode of analysis that focused almost entirely on formal structure and design: Austrian theorist Heinrich Schenker founded an analytical school which made good Edward Hanslick's claim that musical meaning and significance reside wholly in the musical structure. Against these entrenched stylistic and aestheticist modes of analysis ('musicological' and 'theoretical', respectively), analysis informed by critical theory has made only intermittent progress.

Thus, if at one time it seemed reasonable to study film in relation to literature, and therefore to place emphasis equally on style or expression and on social and cultural contexts (ideology), then in music it seemed equally reasonable to focus either on works as they fit into the firmly Beethoven-centred style history or as they embodied aesthetic ideals of sound, progression and form.

How might all this apply to film music and affect its study? The authors of this chapter share a commitment to an historically and critically informed analytic practice that at the same time avoids positing any single account of film (or music) history as central. That having been said, the scope of the present chapter is restricted to outlining analytical approaches that privilege the music itself. (The following chapter adopts a different strategy, assuming that music should be considered first and foremost a component of a film's sonic architecture, or its sound design.) Here we treat issues ranging from the efficacy of analysing 'purely' musical parameters, such as pitch relations and tonal design, to analysis of semantic properties of musical elements, including leitmotiv and style topics. This approach does distort the filmic experience of most viewers, to be sure, but it has the advantage of focusing attention on the extensive work that music performs in shaping the filmic experience. The basic assumption is that music runs parallel to the imagetrack, which, on a theoretical level, can be conceived as a sort of 'super-libretto' to the music. Thus we can focus on music while acknowledging that it (like all of film sound) remains subordinate to the image (Chion 1994: 45).

Pitch Relations; Consonance and Dissonance; Tonality and Atonality

Music analysis is typically directed at pitch relations – or (in tonal music) harmony and voice-leading – and at musical form, or temporal articulations and associated recurrences and thematic networks. Even at the outset, one worries that these emphases miss the bulk of what is at stake in film scores, but traditional modes of analysis are nevertheless indispensable for a thorough musical understanding of individual cues and the higher level structuring of groups of cues. The film-music scholar needs to be vigilant against inherent biases in analytical tools that were developed to study absolute (instrumental) music rather than programmatic music or music for the stage. Beyond that, analytical methods in general are challenged by the wide variety of musical styles employed in film – indeed, nearly every kind of music written or performed in the twentieth century has appeared in the movies. Consequently, it makes a good deal more sense to look to the conventional interplay of stage action, mood and musical *topoi* in the nineteenth century than to look to tonality alone for an explanation of the dramatic functions or the psychological power of music.

Nevertheless, much of the film-music literature is concerned mainly with the symphonic background score, and that is the place where traditional analytical modes work best, at least on the local level, if for no other reason than that the stylistic base of Max Steiner, Erich Korngold and other masters of the 1930s and 1940s was an extension of the late-tonal, post-Romantic idiom of Richard Strauss and Gustav Mahler. In *Overtones and Undertones*, Royal S. Brown discusses concepts of tonality, beginning with the familiar notion of centricity, or a hierarchical scheme built on a single controlling pitch. Departure and return are fundamental to this system: 'Psychologically and aesthetically speaking, tonality sets up a certain order, creates a sense of loss and anxiety in its various departures from that order, and then reassures the listener by periodically returning to that order, which will generally have the final word' (Brown 1994: 3). This description fits well the music of the first Viennese golden age, the last quarter of the eighteenth century, but it misses the fact that this system of tonality, as scale-based melodic forms and harmonic stereotypes derived from figured bass, was transformed into something considerably more complex and subtle by the mid-nineteenth century. This new system, heralded above all in the music of Franz Liszt and Richard Wagner, included the old as one of its possibilities, but also exploited the form-creating (and therefore psychologically and aesthetically motivating) power of motivic (or melodic) organisation and music's 'secondary parameters' of music: dynamics, register and orchestration (Meyer 1989: 208–11).

Two broad categories within the traditional system do, however, remain pertinent: major versus minor and consonant versus dissonant. Paraphrasing Leonard Meyer, Brown says that 'the major mode, in offering fewer potential directions within active anticipation, ties in with a greater sense of stability and order, which are very much a part of the modern Western ethos, than the innately more chromatic . . . minor mode' (Brown 1994: 6). This familiar claim imputes a firmer acoustical foundation to the major mode, even though for all practical purposes tonic centricity works quite as well in the minor. The minor mode is indeed more susceptible to chromaticism, but the notion that chromaticism is always linked to dissolution of key, threatened or real, attempts, once again, to universalise some specialised eighteenth-century practices. What is crucial in the major/minor distinction is affect, not scale form or the diatonic/chromatic dichotomy. In other words, major/minor is another aspect of the 'cultural musical codes' (Gorbman 1987: 3), a coded binary pair originally established and

developed in eighteenth- and nineteenth-century opera and instrumental music. Reading this way, we can see that Brown is on the mark
when he writes that 'the optimistic heroism of a film such as *The Sea
Hawk* [1940] is musically generated in part by dominance of the
major mode in its various cues, making the appearance of the minor
mode in such music as the galley theme and the dirge modification of
the romantic theme all the more dramatic' (Brown 1994: 6).

The consonance/dissonance pair, unfortunately, is linked in the
musicological literature to a confusing variety of purposes with the
pairs diatonic/chromatic and tonal/atonal. Brown echoes this variety
by stating, for example, that 'dissonance often gets used in film music,
much the way the minor mode does, to creative affective backing for
more ominous situations.' And, 'even the most dissonant scores rarely
venture too far from tonality.' But also 'the setting of Maria's theme
[in *The Sea Hawk*] includes dissonant notes . . . no doubt to suggest
the enmity that the Spanish noblewoman bears at the moment towards
her British captor/rescuer' (Brown 1994: 8). These quotations show
confusion between general and particular definitions of consonance
and dissonance. Specific dissonances, such as suspension figures, can
and do appear in music of all affect types – they are not reserved for
'ominous situations' but may add musical and emotional piquancy or
depth to the most rigidly diatonic major-key dramatic *maestosos*,
pastorales or naïve love themes. In its most extreme form, consonant/
dissonant is attached to tonal/atonal, and this latter pair to broad style
distinctions in twentieth-century music, as in the phrase 'even the most
dissonant film scores rarely venture too far from tonality' (Brown
1994: 8). It is true that musical passages predominantly characterised
by dissonant figures and chromatic harmonic progressions were
already part of the affective arsenal of early eighteenth-century
composers and were especially exploited by nineteenth-century composers to make dark/light contrasts. Liszt and Chopin, for example,
often allow a theme to 'emerge', clear and triumphant, out of an
unstable, dissonant and chromatic 'storm' of figuration or the 'mor-
ass' of a moody, dissonance-laden introduction over a prolonged
dominant sonority. It is this phenomenon – again an affective category, culturally constructed – to which Brown is really referring.

The complexity of these several pairings is apparent in the music for
a famous scene in *Casablanca* (1943). Emerging from the back room
of his café, Rick (Humphrey Bogart) sees Ilsa (Ingrid Bergman) for the
first time since they parted in Paris. His shock is mirrored in a

dissonant chord which combines the first six notes of a D minor scale, although they are spaced and orchestrated in a way that produces three clear layers: D in the bass, the tonic triad in the treble and the supertonic (diminished) triad in between. This chord, whose bass and upper layer establish the key of D minor despite the overall dissonance, is held for some time as the two characters absorb the psychological impact of their reunion, and the oboe plays, pathetically (in the key of F major) the opening phrases of *As Time Goes By*. The bass follows the ancient chaconne bass pattern (D–C–B flat–A) reaching a clear and prolonged A major triad (a firm dominant of D minor) as Rick finally adjusts to conversation in the group that also includes Ilsa's husband Victor Laszlo (Paul Henreid) and Captain Renault (Claude Rains). The chord above the bass C would traditionally be an A minor triad, but Steiner 'lowers' it to A flat major, giving an extra twist to the bittersweet mood. This A flat chord has long-term consequences, as the cue moves toward flat keys and the scene eventually ends firmly in D flat major as Laszlo and Ilsa leave the café. This cadence articulates the end of the film's first long café scene, though an abrupt shift to D flat minor, as if an afterthought, hints at subsequent events: the bitter exchanges later that evening when Ilsa returns to the café to find Rick drunk, and Ilsa and Laszlo's interview by the Nazi Colonel Strasser the following morning. Throughout, consonance and dissonance are not slavishly tied to major and minor, and the strongest affirmation of tonality, the cadence in D flat at the end, is ironic: this is exactly the point in the film where the principal characters are least certain of what will happen next.

Such subtleties and complexities are characteristic of the style Steiner inherited from Strauss and Mahler (both of whom were friends of the Steiner family), but there are some broad, systemic differences between tonal and atonal dissonance which do have consequences for film music. Tonal dissonance entails a resolution to a particular consonance (whether or not the expected consonance follows), so that we experience a build-up and discharge of tension in the dissonance–consonance pair in a relatively predictable way; whereas atonal music has 'emancipated' the dissonance from its entailment to a following consonance, so that the dissonance has an identity wholly independent of any 'resolution' that may follow. Tonality functions as a system exterior to the musical material that regulates and directs the flow of musical tension into a series of preformed channels. Atonality, on the contrary, does not presume this exterior system for regulating the flow of tension but must articulate that system within itself; thus, it frequently produces the effect of an open system, of leaving matters unsettled, of not being able to find a point of definitive closure. When tonal music lacks closure it is nearly always experienced as a defiant refusal fraught with dramatic import rather than as the systemic incapacity characteristic of atonality.

Consequently, the preference for closed classical dramatic forms in Hollywood's studio era no doubt underwrote a corresponding preference for tonal composition, however attenuated it may be. It is surely not a coincidence that atonality makes its deepest inroads in suspense, horror and science fiction films, genres less marked by the classical dramaturgical canons of tragedy and comedy. In suspense films, subjective crisis and psychological rupture are often prominent themes, with the character experiencing a debilitating loss of centre, which is figured musically by the absence of a tonal centre. In horror films, the monster often embodies a kind of dystopian projection, a means of figuring unintended consequences of the system, which take musical shape as tonality gone awry to the point of incomprehension. In science fiction the future, like the monster of the horror genre, serves as the site of utopian or dystopian projection, and atonality signifies either positively the supercession of the old order; or negatively the dissolution of that order through its own logic, or, more typically, through its displacement by the imposition of some artificial – often rigidly rational and mechanistic – social order. In each of these cases, atonality, even when figured positively, becomes aligned with alienation, incomprehension and absence, whereas tonality gains associations with the opposite.

Style Topics

Style topics (essentially synonymous with Gorbman's 'cultural musical codes') are the most common analytical categories used in non-specialist writing about film music, and rightly so. Style topics function much like the vocabulary of a rudimentary system of musical signification, and film composers rely on such predictable responses: a gap-scale tune soaring over a widely spaced chord immediately conjurs up images of the untamed West; an anguished atonal cluster portends the monster behind the door: while the sultry wail of a lonely saxophone inevitably marks the entrance of the *femme fatale*. Deciding which style topic will best fit the cinematic moment is often a crucial element of effective film composition; pitch relations become a secondary aesthetic (and so presumably interpretive) consideration. In other words, pitch relations do not so much constitute the central musical event in film music as they serve as the technical means of articulating the style topic (though it goes without saying that a composer's execution of a style topic can be done well or poorly).

Film inherits the bulk of its style topics from concert and theatrical music. The topic of the American Indian used frequently in Westerns appears in numerous compositions at the turn of the century with all the significant features of its archetypal statement in *Stagecoach* (1939). Much important historical work remains to be done tracing the transmission and stabilisation of such topics, though it seems clear that most of the topics derive from nineteenth-century opera, programme music and incidental music. Still, until the rise of the silent film, the cataloguing of style topics consisted mainly in a few musical rules of thumb to guide the composer in producing an effective sonic image of stock scenes: a storm, a battle, a Spanish folk dance, and so on. It was the musicians of the early silent film who codified the practice of style topics. Detailed catalogues such as Erno Rapée's *Encyclopedia of Music for Pictures* (1925) and Hans Erdmann and Guiseppe Becce's *Allgemeines Handbuch der Film-Musik* (1927) derive their indisputable value and influence from the effective way they order the standard repertory according to rubrics such as 'love theme,' 'storm', 'hurry', 'neutral', 'dramatic *maestoso*', and so forth. The contribution of such books transcends the actual pieces catalogued, however. The decisive intervention is the way these books organise musical thought: they were highly influential not only because musical directors, pianists and organists of the early cinema turned to them to locate specific pieces but also because those pieces helped delimit or confirm boundaries of topics, fitting newly composed music into them as well a substantial percentage of the standard repertory after roughly 1850.

The analysis of style topics in film scores operates on three distinct levels: the traits characteristic of a topic in general; the degree and manner in which a particular cue invokes the topic; and how the topics are deployed dramatically in a film. The first mode is as much theoretical as analytical and is concerned with identifying the features that define a topic in general; the second mode is concerned more with the particular realisation of a style topic; whereas the third mode is concerned with such issues as the appropriateness of matching a style topic with a particular sequence in a film. Though conceptually distinct, these modes are often difficult to separate in practice. By way of example, consider the motto from Bernard Herrmann's music for Hitchcock's *The Trouble with Harry* (1955) – a four-note figure (E flat – C flat – A flat – D) that follows a pattern of alternating ascending and descending intervals, a so-called 'cross' motif often used in the baroque era (several of Bach's fugues contain it) as a figure of deep pathos. A rather more arcane reference than is typical of Hollywood, this motto is announced in strangely enigmatic form. For one thing, the large, angular leaps of the motto, though a property of the 'cross' motiif in general, are actually rendered rather abstractly: the horns emphasise the individual pitches more than the intervals between them, an effect especially pronounced through the timbral shift from open to stopped tone for the final note. If pathos is not the first thing that comes to mind when we hear this motto, this is because it estranges its relation to the baroque pathos topic even as it invokes it. The resulting distance from the topic renders its pathos ironic, an irony achieved only because it relates at some level to the underlying style topic; without that underlying strata of signification, the semantic shift to irony would not have been possible.

In the sound-film era, style topics blur significantly with genre in the sense that certain collections of topics became closely associated with particular film genres, which can often be divined from the title music alone (as in *The Magnificent Seven* [1956], *Ben Hur* [1959], *Breakfast at Tiffany's* [1961], and many others). The appropriateness of Korngold's title music for *Kings Row* (1940), for instance, has been questioned exactly because its topic seems at odds with the genre of the film (Murphy 1997: 119–43). Today, topics may well refer as much to earlier film-scoring practices as to specific topics. Thus, a theme such as the one John Williams devised for the Indiana Jones trilogy seems to conjure up the spirit of the old serials (which relied on standard repertory orchestral music or a music library of composed cues rather than original music) as much as anything particular to the action-adventure genre, though the theme obviously also invokes the general topic of the heroic. Even so, the effect of a style topic can be quite pronounced, altering significantly our understanding of the visuals. In *Raiders of the Lost Ark* (1981), for instance, the dark filmic ambivalences of Indiana Jones' character in the prologue, ambivalences reinforced initially by music that gestures and percolates, mixing with the other mysterious sounds of the jungle without really clarifying anything, are forgotten the moment the score breaks into bright tonal sounds of the theme as Indy runs toward the plane. The music here proclaims Jones' fundamental heroism long before this is evident from the narrative itself. In the next sequence the government agents refer to Jones as an 'obtainer of rare antiquities' rather than an archaeologist *per se*. The very strength of the heroic style topic, however, makes it difficult to recall those initial forebodings about his character.

Tonal Design

Tonal design, the patterning of succession and relationships of key centres, has traditionally held a privileged place in the analysis of music for concert and can claim broad formal and affective (or sometimes other referential) dimensions. (Consider, for example, the potency of Beethoven's substitution of the mediants for the dominant and tonic, respectively, in the second-theme areas of the *Waldstein Sonata*, first movement.) The possibility of large-scale key relations in film music has received only limited study (Rodman 2000).

Early Hollywood composers were, by and large, trained in the theatre (or radio), where lyricism, brilliant scoring and dramatic timing were more highly valued than were niceties of syntax. Consequently, early technical manuals on film take tonal relations into consideration only on the most local level. The so-called 'fifteen-second rule' cited by Gorbman states that 'if music has been absent for more than fifteen seconds, the composer is free to start a new music cue in a different and even unrelated key, since the spectator/auditor will have sufficiently forgotten the previous cue's tonality' (Gorbman 1987: 90). Yet during the 1920s music directors routinely drew on the concert repertoire for music to accompany silent films. Film composers, then, were faced with a number of overlapping and potentially conflicting models for tonal design: the unified hierarchical schemes of instrumental music, simple 'chaining' of key regions (as in popular theatre such as operetta), the seemingly radical disunity of the fifteen-second rule, and such later nineteenth-century practices as associative tonality (key symbolism) and double-tonic complexes. Composers' choices were further complicated by the fact that music is generally used intermittently rather than continuously in film; by a lack of unilateral power to dictate where music would be used; and by source music already incorporated into the film as part of the production work. And of course, the results were also influenced by post-recording editing of sound and imagetrack, where the mixing levels of the various soundtrack elements fell outside a composer's control.

Given these constraints, especially the intermittent quality of film music, it seems reasonable to assume that any large-scale tonal designs found in film scores will be abstract and symbolic rather than functional. The large-scale tonal coherence of Herrmann's score for *The Trouble With Harry* serves a symbolic function. Relying on those cues where the tonality is relatively unambiguous, we can arrive at a key scheme for the score that looks something like Figure 1.1 (see p. 35). If it is true, as Royal Brown has written, that 'one thing Herrmann obviously fathomed . . . in Hitchcock and his art was the perfect ambivalency' (Brown 1994: 149), Herrmann expresses this 'ambivalency' here on a structural level with a double-tonic complex of traditional relative keys, E flat minor and G flat major (or F sharp major), the two beamed open notes labelled 'Harry' in the figure. At the most general level, the double-tonic complex itself marks the dramatic situation: the 'trouble' that Harry's body presents to the four main characters. As might be expected, the minor key is used in the more serious and threatening situations (the four-note motto from the beginning that shows up each time a new complication arises in disposing of the body, for instance); whereas the major key underscores the more whimsical or comedic scenes. Half-step relations, which are depicted with closed notes in the figure, fan out on either side of the principal centres. In broad terms, it might be argued that the two half-steps about E flat represent the situation as it is, whereas those about G flat/F sharp the plot as it progresses. D major, for instance, is reserved primarily for the bumbling doctor, who is given one of the most distinctive scherzando themes in the score and whose profession reminds one constantly of the medical – and legal – problems of having a corpse lying about. This key is also used to accompany the sight gag of a closet door that opens ominously without human aid. E minor (often expressed modally), on the contrary, serves as one of two keys to express the environment and time of year, a gentle pastoral effect for a New England autumn. G major (a minor second above F sharp just as E minor stands a half step above E flat minor) is the other pastoral key and makes its first appearance in connection with the Captain as he walks through the woods in the film's opening scene. Subsequently, the key of G is associated with the Captain himself, with the unfolding romance between him and Miss Gravely, with Miss Gravely herself and – by transposition to the other couple – with the developing romance between Sam and Jennifer. For this reason, the key of G major has been labelled 'Solutions' on the figure. In one sense, the pairings of Jennifer with Sam and Miss Gravely with the Captain are the solution to the film's main subplot: the coupling of the film's primary characters. Indeed, one of the film's narrative pleasures is the uncertainty about whether this subplot or 'the trouble with Harry' is the primary driving force of the film. And, at the very end, G major rudely supplants F sharp for the concluding cadence, as the problem of Harry is swept aside and the new romantic attachments are in a position to grow unhindered. Finally, F major, used sparingly, is associated specifically with romantic feeling, as when Miss Gravely goes to Mrs Wiggs' general store to buy a coffee cup in advance of the Captain's visit to her house; or when Sam first tells Jennifer that he loves her.

As this brief sketch of the tonal structure makes clear, the score of *The Trouble With Harry* is not in E flat minor or G flat major – or even G major for that matter, despite its assertion of primacy at the end of film; nor does it really make sense to trace functional progressions of keys across the several cues in the way we might do through the parts of a concert overture, especially since cues are often separated by large stretches of non-musical sound. On the other hand, the symbolism of the key scheme is hard to ignore once identified: among other things, it allows insight into some of the less obvious aspects of the composer's craft and also potentially into the composer's own 'reading' of the film to which he has attached his music (cf. Stilwell 1997: 552).

The Leitmotiv

A more overt symbolic device than tonal design is the leitmotiv, the most common musical device for structuring a film score on a large-scale level. The practice began in the silent era, but it is especially characteristic of Hollywood composers during the first decades of the sound era, in particular Steiner, Korngold and Alfred Newman, but also to a slightly lesser extent Franz Waxman, Victor Young, Miklos Rosza and Herbert Stothart. Scores relying heavily on leitmotiv treatments have been somewhat less typical of European cinema composition.

Without doubt leitmotiv lends a score a semblance of unity, as the recurrence, elaboration and transformation of motifs allow musical connections to be drawn over the whole span of a film (or in the case of sequels, over the span of the series). The unity that the leitmotiv delivers is somewhat analogous to the melodic/motivic networks of a concert work, except that the film composer can draw on the image-track as a means of motivating the introduction a leitmotiv into the musical texture at any given moment. Perhaps it is exactly this that suggests a brute-force quality about the unity the leitmotiv delivers: a unity posited rather than won. The practice does have its critics. It has been claimed that the use of leitmotiv in films is inflexible, that if is not well suited to the discontinuities of the filmic medium and even that the deployment of leitmotiv in film does not coincide with Wagnerian practice (Adorno and Eisler 1994: 4–6; Paulin 2000). All of these objections have at least limited validity, and they would certainly need to be answered in any comprehensive theory of film music; but none accounts for the prevalent use of leitmotiv scores in film – Adorno and Eisler can really only point to it as a 'bad habit' – nor for the fact that scores quite frequently succeed, sometimes despite a rather too mechanical matching of music and image (Adorno and Eisler 1994: 3; Buhler 2000).

Leitmotiv analysis can be applied on two distinct levels: the musical characterisation in the leitmotiv itself and its pattern of recurrence in the film. The first mode is very much concerned with technical analysis of musical detail, showing, for example, how a motif relates to a particular style topic (which can say something important about the character with which it is associated). The second deals with how the recurrence of a motif marks shifts in character and articulates large formal spans in the film; it is this mode that allows one most readily to tie the musical score into a narrative analysis. Of course, these two modes are not mutually exclusive, and they can seldom be cleanly separated in analytical practice. Often the formal dramatic significance of motivic recurrence, for instance, can only be properly evaluated by assessing how the musical details of the motive are altered from one appearance to the next. A motif whispered softly by winds in one passage and blared out fortissimo by the brass in another obviously shifts from membership in one style topic to another (here, perhaps, from the pastoral to the heroic) even if all the other musical parameters remain unchanged (cf. Darby and Dubois 1990).

Few film composers can entirely resist using leitmotiv. Even Bernard

Herrmann, who generally eschews leitmotiv scores, deploys one in *The Trouble with Harry*, albeit ironically. Here, the motto used to mark the body recurs very much like a leitmotiv, with a sardonically witty result that matches the overall tenor of the film. Yet Herrmann is slyly critical of the practice as well. The motto does not so much clarify the cinematic situation – the music really tells us no more about Harry than does any other parameter of the film – as it marks the body as an enigma. Tonally, the motto seems to absorb the energy of the music leading up to it, stopping the music in its tracks whenever it appears, and therefore it does not so much refer to the body as suggest a musical analogue to the way the latter's unintelligibility animates the action. In this sense the motto becomes a kind of musical 'blot,' a musical dead spot that nevertheless organises a system of musical signification (Žižek 1991: 90).

Timbre

Themes and leitmotiv can derive meaning as much from timbral qualities as from pitch sequences and their tonal associations. Thus, a motif played tenderly by an oboe may shift the associations of the music toward the style topic of the pastoral; whereas the same theme played by a solo violin, all things being equal, may sound nostalgic and sentimental. In other words, the recurring identity of the thematic material serves as the ground by which the significance of the timbral variant can be interpreted. Sometimes timbral change and leitmotiv identity can combine to deliver a rather definite musical meaning that seems almost linguistic in its specificity. The *Imperial March*, played serenely by flute and harp as Darth Vader dies near the end of *Return of the Jedi* (1983), seems laden with meaning, due in great part to its timbral distance from the model, which is nearly always pounded out by brasses from the moment it is introduced in *The Empire Strikes Back* (1980).

Although it often seems on the cusp between a purely musical parameter and issues of semantics and meaning, timbre itself, especially a particularly striking instrumental colour, occasionally assumes a structural importance much like a leitmotive. In Franz Waxman's score to Hitchcock's *Rebecca* (1940), the sound of a harmonium (an organ-like instrument), rather than a specific theme, establishes the aural image of the title character, and, in this case, attention to timbre would probably result in a richer interpretion of the absent character's musical portrait than would a more typical analysis of pitch structure. Similarly, in the 1951 version of *Showboat*, the disembodied sound of the choir becomes associated with the river, endowing it with a symbolic import of mythic grandeur that far exceeds the stage version and the earlier film version, both of which locate the choir in a specific river community. Finally, in a manner typical of Hollywood teenpics, *Clueless* (1995) associates various popular musics with different characters. Here, clear timbral distinctions among various styles of popular music are used as a means of quickly developing character: we intuit much about Cher's Mr Knightly, Josh, simply because the soundtrack associates him with alternative rock.

Under many conditions film music, like much music for the theatre, will disregard syntax to achieve a certain colouristic effect. As noted above, the erosion of the distinction between syntactic elements and colouristic ones was already quite pronounced by the end of the nineteenth century, even in concert music. But unlike concert music, which requires a syntactic or structural payoff for colouristic effects in order to ensure musical coherence, film music (as with theatrical music in general) receives its dividends from the interaction of the effect with the narrative. For instance, the sound of a particular instrument in a specific register can determine key selection even if that key makes little syntactic sense with respect to large-scale design: Frank Skinner, who worked for Universal Studios for nearly thirty years, relates how he would transpose a theme from, say, E flat to C simply because a leitmotiv to be played by the brass sounded more effective in that key (Neumeyer forthcoming). Similarly, modulation (or change of key), which nearly always serves definite syntactic functions in instrumental music, often has a primarily colouristic rather than syntactic function in film music, brightening or darkening the mood rather than coherently shaping the large-scale tonal motion. A surprising modulation is deployed for its dramatic effect, for the way it tips the music off-balance; a series of modulations, for the way it produces the sensation of churning (Buhler 2000).

Musical Form and Filmic Form

A system of themes or leitmotivs, restated, varied and developed, is the traditional foundation of a music score's unity, but such a system is hardly a requirement: the reoccurrence of a mood or affect can make connections between scenes with or without close thematic relations, as happens, for instance, with the several scherzandi and the three distinct 'love' themes in *The Trouble With Harry*. The latter link the old-fashioned courtship rituals of Miss Gravely and the Captain with the decidedly unconventional wooing of Jennifer Rogers by Sam, and they confirm the idea of parallel romances as important elements in the plot. Likewise, the four-note motto contributes substantially to the articulation of filmic form, chiming the stages of the plot: each time Harry's appearance interrupts the quartet's romancing, a shift in the plot occurs, usually occasioning a burial or disinterment.

The standard practice of the spotting session creates the musical form of the film in the most basic sense: the composer, sound editor or director watches a print of the film and make decisions about where and what kind of music should be used. Thus, empirically, the 'form' of a cue begins as an entrance timing (or even frame number) and a duration. More theoretically, the proximity of musical and filmic form rests on the fact that both are temporal arts: form in music, as in film, is a structuring of time. The impression of filmic unity – the sense that the film coheres into something more than an indifferent juxtaposition of disparate images – is dependent on how time is structured by image and sound (including music) working in tandem. Bernard Herrmann knits these two strands of empirical and theoretical form together in his comment that film music functions 'to fuse a piece of film so that it has an inevitable beginning and end. When you cut a piece of film you can do it perhaps a dozen ways, but once you put music to it, that becomes the absolutely final way' (Manvell and Huntley 1975: 244). Music, like the other components of the soundtrack, lends the flow of images a sense of necessity, helps it assume a distinctive and definitive shape.

The mere fact of multiple cues – the pattern of music's occurrence, absence and recurrence – already means that music has the potential to affect filmic form as substantially as any other structuring opposition: shot and reverse shot, indoor and outdoor location, day and night, dialogue and action, dramatic and comedic and so forth. In *Casablanca*, for example, the oscillation between non-diegetic orchestral score and diegetic dance-band music is essential to articulating the underlying filmic form. On this basis, the first third of the film unequivocally falls into three parts: introduction and scene setting, the evening life and local problems of the refugees, and the relationship of Rick and Ilsa. The orchestral main-title music segues into music under the prologue, finally going out shortly after the first scene begins. During the prologue's voiceover narration, the tone is one of high pathos, suggesting something of world historical import; the music is committed to this narration, confirming its truth as it were, as it helps us 'read' the images of the refugees as mythic rather than individual. From the end of the prologue until roughly thirty minutes into the film, the dance-band music of Rick's *Café americaine* floods the soundtrack, so much so that in terms of sheer number of performances an argument could be made for interpreting the film as a musical. Yet what makes such an interpretation obviously inadequate is the indifferent tone of this music with respect to the narrative: musical performance in a musical is rarely if ever indifferent. With the possible exception of *Tango della Rose*, the upbeat, even perky performances of music in the café grate with what we see, especially the desperate plight of the characters trying to escape Casablanca (Marks 2000). The indifferent tone of this music likewise coincides with Rick's initial cynicism: he is cynical because the world seems indifferent to him. Thus the dance-band music marks a musical antithesis to the pathos of the prologue: where the opening music had been committed to the plight of the refugees, if only abstractly, the café music is indifferent even as it is highly concrete. Forging a workable synthesis of these two musics proves to be the task of the remainder of the score: it must come to terms with *As Time Goes By* just as Rick must come to terms with the shock of seeing Ilsa again (the exact point at which orchestral music re-enters with the start of *As Time Goes By*). The resulting synthesis is a music that is both committed and concrete. On the one hand, even the music of the café begins to take on a committed tone, as becomes clear in the musical battle between the anthems *La Marseillaise* and *Die Wacht am Rhein*. On the other hand, orchestral music dominates the remainder of the soundtrack, displacing the café music to the margins; the apotheosis on *La Marseillaise* at the end returns to the original tone of world historical importance, albeit this time with a more hopeful tone.

Music can also exaggerate or impose small-scale unity on a sequence, especially when a cue is tonally closed or structured by frequent thematic recurrence; and music is commonly called on to give structure to a montage sequence as well. Likewise, music following a 'cumulative' design such as an ostinato or a passacaglia not only helps build and sustain an underlying dramatic tension, but the repetitive pattern can also give a sense of coherence to the sequence it underscores, as in the passacaglias written by Waxman and David Raksin, respectively, for murder scenes in *Sorry, Wrong Number* (1948) and *Force of Arms* (1951). Frequently structured around an ostinato (or other short, repeated phrases), music for action sequences such as chases or battles lays down a 'temporal perspective' (Widgery 1990) or a defined frame of reference within which the chaotic actions can intelligibly unfold: William Walton's battle music for Olivier's *Henry V* (1944) is a good example. The mere presence of music can also add a sense of motion – of physical or temporal direction – to an otherwise static segment. And it can do the reverse: by removing a clear pulse from the music, an effect of suspended time (or perhaps inner or psychological time in counterpoint to the image) can be articulated, as George Burt describes in connection with Leonard Rosenman's music for *Fantastic Voyage* (1966), for example (Burt 1994: 124–6). Thus, music can speed up or slow down the flow of a sequence, intensifying or attenuating rhythms already present in the image. Flexibly – and rapidly – shifting the musical flow in response to fluctuations in the flow of the narrative is a function of the 'melodramatic cue,' a term that refers less to the film melodrama than to the source of the technique in the stage melodrama of the eighteenth and nineteenth centuries (Neumeyer 1995: 61–4). In melodramatic cues, the rise and fall of musical lines helps shape the dramatic flow of a sequence. For example, a strong dynamic rise, usually with broadened registral span as well, often signals a moment of action, elevation or emotional and psychological climax. Famous instances include Scarlett's 'I'll never be hungry again' soliloquy which closes Part I of *Gone With the Wind* (1939) and, in *Casablanca*, Ilsa's last confrontation with Rick over the letters of passage. Steiner's scores are especially rich in the use of such devices as a way of underscoring dialogue.

Unlike ostinati, passacaglias and short song forms, other formal schemes common in instrumental and vocal music – sonata movements, rondos, arias, dance movements and so on – are not generally transferable to film composition, because the structuring of musical time in film cannot proceed oblivious to the unfolding of the narrative without coming to seem strangely indifferent. This is not to say that music never dictates the filmic form, but it does so only in special cases, for example, where the performance is itself diegetic, that is, part of the narrative (as in the song performances in *Casablanca* or the notorious 'Aria from *Salaambo*' in *Citizen Kane* [1941]). Likewise in musicals, especially for production numbers, musical form becomes filmic form as the main articulations in a scene tend to follow the form of the music (which is always recorded prior to shooting). Not only are shots cut to coincide with musical rhythms, but the beginning of a new section (chorus) of music typically also initiates a new phase in the presentation of the images. Similarly, the use of a familiar piece will gather together the events in a sequence, as for example when the *Blue Danube* waltz underscores the arrival at the space station in Kubrick's *2001: A Space Odyssey* (1968).

Short cues, often of somewhat indeterminate musical character, are occasionally used as transitions between scenes. These have their sources in nineteenth-century melodrama and were exploited especially in radio and, later, television. Bernard Herrmann, who began his media-composition career in radio, uses such transition cues extensively in *Citizen Kane*, but they do not play a prominent role in his Hitchcock film scores from the 1950s. In *The Trouble With Harry*, for instance, most cues stay within the bounds of the scene, which can perhaps be explained by the fact that the film's plot is essentially static. Indeed the opposite was needed: 'characterising' cues that focus the listener's attention on a trait or affect, such as the clumsiness and social ineptitude of the doctor or the romantic motivations hidden behind Miss Gravely's purchase of a coffee mug.

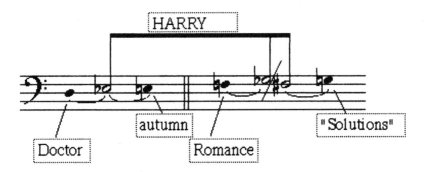

Fig 1.1: Bernard Herrmann: Music for *The Trouble With Harry*.
Summary of tonal relationships and symbolism.

Finally, music serves as a formal frame, a function inherited from the traditions of the theatre, especially operetta and melodrama. Main-title and end-credit cues separate the film's time from its surroundings and thus ease the viewer/listener into and out of the alien temporality of the filmic narrative. As Gorbman puts it, main-title music announces genre, mood and setting, and the finale provides 'musical recapitulation and closure [to reinforce] narrative . . . closure' (Gorbman 1987: 82). In the studio era, symphonic main-title music often includes an opening flourish and the first statement of a theme associated with the principal action or protagonist; this is followed by a more lyrical theme, usually associated with the female lead or romantic situation. In most instances, main-title music overlaps with the beginning of the film's first scene and then fades out (music, indeed sound in general, rarely ends on an image-cut or dissolve except to mark significant formal boundaries). End-credit music in the studio era tended to be brief, sometimes nothing more than a short flourish into the title followed by a cadence. When cast titles are used, the music for the cast title often has no connection to the rest of the score at all. By the 1960s, the traditional main-title sequence was varied more often. Frequently, as with the James Bond films, the titles appear only after an opening action prologue. *Raiders of the Lost Ark* similarly begins *in media res*, but the atmospheric action prologue subsumes the role of the main-title sequence as well, as the principal titles overlay the sequence. The latter solution – combining the titles with the opening scene – becomes quite common once the bulk of the credits move to the end. Today, end credits can easily extend five minutes or more, and composers have sometimes exploited this generous amount of 'undisturbed' time to write extended pieces based on material from the film.

Conclusion

The type of musical analysis that underlies the topics discussed above is not new: rather, it is the traditional method used to study the interactions of music and text in opera, operetta, melodrama or song. And the topics themselves are familiar: major/minor contrasts are distinctive guides to shifts in narrative trajectories in Schubert *lieder*, for example. Leitmotiv originated in nineteenth-century opera and subsequently became basic to the study of the genre's music. Formal patterns reflect or organise units of text and plot. *Topoi* have been shown to be central to the music of the Viennese golden age. And symbolic or associational key schemes are a common feature of opera after Wagner. Although we conceded early on that the soundtrack (music, dialogue and effects) is subordinate to the imagetrack in narrative film, throughout most of this essay we have resisted that subordination deliberately in order to highlight parallels between film-music and concert-music composition. That resistance was artificial, to be sure, but it showed some productive results, and it did suggest ways in which one can seek to reveal connections and continuities between the practices of composers in cinema and concert.

Placing music more firmly in the soundtrack and examining its function there is the subject of the next essay.

Bibliography

Adorno, T. W. and Hanns Eisler (1994) *Composing for the Films* (originally published 1947). London: Athlone Press.

Allen, Richard and Murray Smith (eds) (1997) *Film Theory and Philosophy*. Oxford and New York: Oxford University Press.

Bent, Ian (1980) 'Analysis' in Stanley Sadie (ed.) *The New Grove Dictionary of Music and Musicians*. Washington: Macmillan.

Bordwell, David, Janet Staiger and Kristin Thompson (1985) *The Classical Hollywood Cinema: Film Style and Mode of Production to 1960*. New York: Columbia University Press.

Bordwell, David (1989) *Making Meaning: Influence and Rhetoric in the Interpretation of Cinema*. Cambridge, MA: Harvard University Press.

Bordwell, David and Noël Carroll (eds) (1996) *Post-Theory: Reconstructing Film Studies*. Madison: Wisconsin University Press.

Brown, Royal S. (1994) *Overtones and Undertones: Reading Film Music*. Berkeley: University of California Press.

Buhler, James (2000) 'Star Wars, Music, and Myth' in James Buhler, Caryl Flinn and David Neumeyer (eds) *Music and Cinema*. Middletown, CT: Wesleyan University Press.

Burt, George (1994) *The Art of Film Music*. Boston: Northeastern University Press.

Carroll, Noël (1988) *Mystifying the Movies: Fads and Fallacies in Contemporary Film Theory*. New York: Columbia University Press.

Carroll, Noël (1996) *Theorizing the Moving Image*. Cambridge: Cambridge University Press.

Chion, Michel (1994) *Audio-Vision: Sound on Screen* (trans. Claudia Gorbman). New York: Columbia University Press.

Dahlhaus, Carl (1989) *The Idea of Absolute Music* (trans. Roger Lustig). Chicago: University of Chicago Press.

Darby, William and Jack Du Bois (1990) *American Film Music: Major Composers, Techniques, Trends, 1915–1990*. Jefferson, NC: McFarland.

Erdmann, Hans and Guiseppe Becce (1927) *Allgemeines Handbuch der Film-Musik*, 2 vols. Berlin-Lichterfelde: Schlesinger'sche Buch- und Musikhandlung, Robert Lienau.

Gorbman, Claudia (1985) The state of film music criticism. *Cineaste* vol. 21, nos. 1–2.

Gorbman, Claudia (1987) *Unheard Melodies: Narrative Film Music*. Bloomington: Indiana University Press.

Hill, John and Pamela Church Gibson (eds) (1998) *The Oxford Guide to Film Studies*. New York: Oxford University Press.

Manvell, Roger and John Huntley (1975) *The Technique of Film Music*. New York: Hastings House.

Marks, Marty (2000) 'Music, Drama, Warner Brothers: The Cases of *Casablanca* and the *Maltese Falcon*,' in James Buhler, Caryl Flinn and David Neumeyer (eds) *Music and Cinema*. Middletown, CT: Wesleyan University Press.

Meyer, Leonard (1989) *Style and Music: Theory, History, and Ideology*. Philadelphia: University of Pennsylvania Press.

Murphy, Scott (1997) 'Korngold and Kings Row: A semiotic interpretation of Film Music'. MM thesis, University of Kansas.

Neumeyer, David (1995) Melodrama as a compositional resource in early Hollywood sound cinema. *Current Musicology*, no. 57.

Neumeyer David, Tonal design and narrative in film music: Bernard Herrmann's *A Portrait of Hitch* and *The Trouble With Harry*. *Indiana Theory Review*, forthcoming.

Paulin, Scott, 'Richard Wagner and the fantasy of cinematic unity: The idea of the *Gesamtkunstwerk* in the history and theory of film music' in James Buhler, Caryl Flinn, and David Neumeyer (eds) *Music and Cinema*. Middletown, CT: Wesleyan University Press.

Rapée, Erno (1970) *Encyclopedia of Music for Pictures* (originally published 1925). New York: Arno Press.

Rodman, Ronald (2000) 'Tonal design and the aesthetic of pastiche in Herbert Stothart's *Maytime*,' in James Buhler, Caryl Flinn, and David Neumeyer (eds) *Music and Cinema*. Middletown, CT: Wesleyan University Press.

Stilwell, Robynn (1997) 'I just put a drone under him . . .': Collage and subversion in the score of *Die Hard*'. *Music and Letters*, vol. 78, no.4.

Claudia Widgery (1990) 'The kinetic and temporal interaction of music and film: three documentaries of 1930s America'. PhD diss., University of Maryland at College Park.

Žižek, Slavoj (1991) *Looking Awry: An Introduction to Jacques Lacan Through Popular Culture*. Cambridge, MA: MIT Press.

Chapter 2

Analytical and Interpretive Approaches to Film Music (II): Analysing Interactions of Music and Film

James Buhler

The previous chapter outlined ways in which traditional analytical modes for concert and stage music might be adapted (or resist adaptation) to the context of film music. It showed how careful musical analysis can contribute to a richer understanding of what music, considered in its own terms, can accomplish in a film. Certainly articulating the full effectiveness of music within film requires recourse to insights opened up by purely musical analytical techniques such as those presented in the previous chapter. Yet interpretation cannot stop at this stage without falsifying its object as film music. As Claudia Gorbman succinctly puts it, 'to judge film music as one judges "pure" music is to ignore its status as a collaboration that is the film. Ultimately it is the narrative context, the interrelations between music and the rest of the film's system, that determines the effectiveness of film music' (Gorbman 1987: 12). Evaluating the effectiveness of music with respect to the 'narrative context' requires moving analysis beyond the purely musical.

This chapter presents a set of alternatives to analysing music as a relatively autonomous element of film. It gives priority to understanding music in film rather than for film (Altman, Jones and Tatroe 2000), that is, to understanding music as it works within a general filmic system. I begin by offering, somewhat programmatically, a series of critical analytical sketches of how the engagement of music with image and narrative might be productively interpreted. Following Michel Chion, I argue for interpreting music as an element within the overall sound design, but with Rick Altman and against Chion I argue that the three elements of the soundtrack (dialogue, music and effects) do indeed constitute an integral, parallel track to the images; that indeed the two tracks, image and sound, are most fruitfully interpreted as in a dialectical tension, each track structured in turn by its own internal dialectic. The aim is to treat music as an important but subsidiary element in the sound design. The purpose here is not to undermine the undeniably important role that music plays in film but to treat it as subsidiary element in order that a musical sensibility can thus be extended to the soundtrack as a whole.

Music, Narrative, and the Analytical Distinction between Diegetic and Non-diegetic Music

The development of a critical interpretive practice of film music began with Gorbman's groundbreaking *Unheard Melodies*, which argued the efficacy of making the informal industry distinction between source and background music more systematic. Drawing on narrative theory, Gorbman imported the terms diegetic and non-diegetic and applied them to music, the former being roughly equivalent to source music, the latter to background scoring.[1] Yet the most important contribution of Gorbman's distinction, which has not always been fully appreciated, lies where it departs from the earlier one. Diegetic and non-diegetic define music in relation to narrative rather than image; for Gorbman, the primary question is not so much whether we see the musical performers, the key to the industry distinction, which is motivated by rates of remuneration (Buhler, Flinn and Neumeyer 2000), rather, Gorbman is interested in whether the music belongs to the diegesis, the world of the narrative. Not all diegetic music is source music. In *Grand Hotel* (1932), for instance, the source for the music is only rarely shown, though the music clearly seems to be part of the ambient sound of the hotel, the unconvincing sound levels notwithstanding. Likewise, in musicals, the source accompaniment often dissolves into a background orchestra. Under special circumstances non-diegetic music can even be source music, as in *There's Something About Mary* (1998), where a singer occasionally strolls through a scene commenting on the action much like a Greek chorus.

Since Gorbman introduced the distinction, it has become a basic analytical tool for studying interactions between music and image. Still, theoretical interest tilts overwhelmingly in favour of non-diegetic music, probably because diegetic music appears theoretically more straightforward than the background score, at least with respect to its relation to narrative. Precisely because it is an object of the narrative, diegetic music does not generally narrate (compare with Abbate

1991). Consequently, there is little need to devise theoretical explanations for the existence of diegetic music: its motivation is patently obvious. No one wonders much about the physical source of Doris Day's *Que sera, sera*, in *The Man Who Knew Too Much* (1956), even when her voice begins to float about the embassy in a strangely disembodied fashion, because the film clearly binds the sound of that voice to her body at the very start of the sequence (cf. Chion 1999: 117). The justification of the voice on the soundtrack is simply the image of the singing body.

Real to Ideal: The Audio Dissolve

Yet diegetic music comes in many gradations, and these gradations raise many interesting theoretical problems that have not yet been adequately addressed. Musicals especially often render a strict binary opposition between diegetic and non-diegetic music moot by means of an audio dissolve from source accompaniment, typically a piano, to background orchestral accompaniment. In *For Me and My Gal* (1942), for instance, Harry (Gene Kelly) and Jo (Judy Garland) try out the title song at the piano. A dissolve from diegetic piano to extra-diegetic orchestral backing allows them to move into a dance routine, and as they do Jo – and the audience – completely forget just what a cad Harry has been, indeed so much so that she agrees to become his partner. Rick Altman suggests that such audio dissolves mark a transition from the real to the ideal realm, a displacement that Altman says is a thematic constant of the musical genre. The diegetic sound source serves as a 'bridge between time-bound narrative and the timeless transcendence of supra-diegetic music[; it] exists only to be silenced, suppressed and left behind' (Altman 1987: 67).

Though dramatic films typically draw a clear distinction between diegetic and non-diegetic music due to their stronger commitment to the aesthetic of realism, audio dissolves can be found in these films as well under certain, albeit highly contained, circumstances. For instance, a particularly striking audio dissolve initiates Rick's famous flashback sequence in *Casablanca* (1942); the dissolve marks the flashback as a perhaps overly idealised past. Another example is the *Non nobis domine* sequence from Branagh's *Henry V* (1989). Patrick Doyle's musical setting begins with a diegetic vocal solo before the tune is taken up by the non-diegetic orchestra and choir. Presumably this audio dissolve, which accompanies a magnificent, long tracking shot of Henry crossing a blood-strewn battlefield, invokes the 'timeless transcendence' of music to help universalise the sentiment of the sequence.

Interpreting an Audio Dissolve: The Case of *Showboat*

The *Ol' Man River* sequence from the 1951 version of *Showboat* makes especially effective use of an audio dissolve, one with unusual narrative implications. While Joe sings the tune at an oppressively slow, dirge-like tempo, the camera remains fixed on him as wisps of white fog float by, half obscuring him at times. Unlike the stage show, where the black community gathers around Joe as he sings, and they join him after his first chorus, the black community of the 1951 film is pushed to the margins (though not without marks of erasure: the backgrounds are continually filled with blacks working on the docks and in the fields); Joe is consequently reduced to something of an archetype. Thus, his performance in the film does not receive the confirmation of a diegetic community as it does in the show.[2] Instead, it is followed by an audio dissolve to a non-diegetic orchestra and wordless choir as the Julie–Steve plot line is resolved, and the ship prepares to leave dock. Only at this point does Joe sing again, now beginning with the bridge of the song. But the camera is here distracted by plot developments as it seeks out the disappearing Julie and Steve. On the one hand, the sequence unites *Ol' Man River* with the injustice of Julie's forced departure; on the other, it pushes Joe even more to the margins than is already the case in the stage version, further isolating him. The fate of the song in the film is identical to the fate of the black community: the miscegenation scene and the song become excuses for pathos; the real plight of the black community is metaphorically displaced by the pathetic ordeal of Julie, who looks white enough to pass for white (and who is, of course, played by a white actress).

Yet for all that, the isolation and displacement of the blacks in the 1951 film is perhaps a more truthful depiction of the marginalising consequences of racial oppression than is the idealised diegetic community of blacks in the often valorised stage version, which tends toward the depiction of 'happy darkies' whenever the chorus begins to sing. The musical effect of the film, therefore, is highly ambivalent, because the community has been displaced to the transcendent and universalising non-diegetic register: for the mythic community thus engendered remains that – not real, not yet actual. The film mirrors society: where society pushes the black community to the side, so too does the film. Everything comes back to that single pathos-filled moment when Julie's world comes crashing down because the rule of law is rigidly enforced at the expense of justice. As she drives away in her buggy with Steve, she looks back to see the water rolling in the paddles of the *Cotton Blossom*. Interestingly, this shot mirrors an especially striking one at the end of the film: the paddle-wheel on the boat goes mechanically around as Joe sings about being 'tired of living' and the song dissolves into the non-diegetic chorus and orchestra. All this feels very much like a metaphor, the wheels of fate that bring about the recurrence of the same. This metaphor of mythic recurrence remains sublime, even somewhat unintelligible. In the final scene Julie appears to weep as she watches the ship, not only because she has given Ravenal back to Nollie, her 'Dear Nollie'; but also because Julie cannot herself reclaim what Nollie now has and what was once her own – life, the community aboard the *Cotton Blossom* – but is still denied her by the unjust rule of law. Her tears flow, like Ol' Man River, bittersweet. What is troubling about the symbolic work here – and the audio dissolve contributes to it in crucial ways – is that the forceful symbolic closure runs dangerously close to making Julie's fate universal, thus rendering the marginalisation of the black community in general eternal and unalterable.

The Value of Diegetic Music

Until the 1960s, the non-diegetic score was commonly orchestral, drawing primarily on the resources of art music, but the diegetic score usually consisted of popular song. This distinction was reinforced institutionally and still survives in the separation of credits for composers and songwriters. Hence, no small part of the lack of theoretical and analytical interest in source music is a lingering cultural élitism: orchestral music is where the art is. The result has been a heavy interpretive bias toward the symphonic non-diegetic score, a bias that distorts interpretive practices by drawing tacitly on a linked set of binary oppositions that inscribe a hierarchy of covert cultural values in the practice and interpretation of film music. If non-diegetic music is opposed to diegetic, then a symphonic sound is opposed to the dance band, 'classical' music to popular (jazz, or later, rock), and, therefore, high art and aesthetic values are set against low art and commercial value.[3]

Yet cinema music's tradition of stylistic variety and its fluid movement between the diegetic and non-diegetic tend to break down the status of the latter pair as the principal category for film-music interpretation. The linkage of the non-diegetic to the symphonic, and thus (potentially) to classical high art is certainly not intrinsic to any demands of cinematic technology or any generalisable demands of narrative or production style. Nor is symphonic music stylistically monolithic: imitations of the Viennese classical style of Mozart and Beethoven were relatively uncommon even in the silent era – the traditional orchestra was used as often for the 'light classics' of French and Italian theatrical styles, Viennese operetta and Broadway shows, as it was for that lingua franca of underscoring, the symphonic-operatic style of Wagner and Strauss. The popular song style also found its way early into underscoring, as in the jazz-inflected tune Steiner wrote for the female lead in *The Informer* (1935) or Gershwin's background cues for *Shall We Dance?* (1937), or Victor Young's many scores based on standards of his own composition.

The use of non-diegetic popular songs has become commonplace in films today. A film such as *Clueless* (1995) is hardly unusual in deploying various styles of popular song to define character; in such films popular music in the underscore functions very much like style topics in a traditional orchestral score (indeed, directors from Nora Ephron to Woody Allen have made references to popular songs a distinctive feature of their work). Thus, even if it is statistically true that in feature films of the 1930s and 40s symphonic music predominates in the background and popular music prevails onscreen, this does not mean that the distinction between source and background must necessarily be tied to simplistic dichotomies of musical styles, narrative functions or hierarchies of value. (For the same reasons, it cannot be reasonably maintained that the sound design of dramatic feature film, which has relied most heavily on underscoring and most consistently enforced a distinction between source and background music, should be privileged over that of the film musical – or that of the teenpic, for that matter.)

Two Theories of the Non-Diegetic Score: Synchronisation versus Counterpoint

Still, the major debate on interactions between music and narrative has taken place, for better or worse, on the terrain of the background score. In this debate, interactions between music and narrative fall into two broad categories, both extrapolations from theories of sound design in early sound film: synchronisation and counterpoint. One of the central preoccupations of early sound film was obtaining a convincing synchronisation of image and sound, especially dialogue and lip movement. Synchronisation is important to a perception of dialogue and sound effects as 'spatially anchored' to the diegesis, to the physical world of the narrative. However, music in film, especially in the products of classic Hollywood, is only exceptionally diegetic (exempting, of course, the special case of the musical). Yet what is called the 'synchronisation' theory of film music holds that even such non-diegetic music should, as Max Steiner put it, '[fit] a picture like a glove' (Steiner 1940). By this, Steiner means music should take its impetus wholly from the narrative: it should not stray from the images but reinforce them. The technique of closely synchronising music and image has become known as 'mickey-mousing', a somewhat pejorative term that recalls the music of cartoons; but the technique does have a venerable history in the sound feature film. An especially effective example occurs in Steiner's score for *Mildred Pierce* (1945), during the early sequence where Wally is trapped in the beach house. Wally, basically a comic character who has been duped by Mildred, looks a bit of a fool as he crashes about the house trying to find a way out, an effect that is reinforced by an uncannily close synchronisation of image and music (Steiner actually wrote detailed descriptions of the action into every bar of his musical sketch). Under the theory of synchronisation, music may occasionally extend beyond what the narrative presents in order to clarify what would otherwise be ambiguous, but its guiding aesthetic is one of restraint, with the music allowed to depart from the image only if it effectively enhances narrative clarity.

The opposing theory of film music takes its point of departure from the technological separation of soundtrack and imagetrack. Synchronisation is simply one possible solution to the relationship of image and sound and arguably the least interesting. Indeed, many who resisted the introduction of sound film did so especially because they reasoned that synchronised sound contributes rather little to film, especially when compared to the more autonomous musical sound that accompanied the silent cinema. Those sympathetic to such arguments but also interested in the possibilities of sound film sought ways in which sound and image could enter into a relationship that was neither redundant (as with synchronised sound) nor simply arbitrary (as when sound and image each simply goes its own way with no consideration given to the other). In this way, sound might add something not already present in the image. Applied to film music, this approach to sound became known as the 'counterpoint' theory of film music. Adorno and Eisler give the theory a sociological twist, one that has proved influential in subsequent attempts to theorise film music:

> The alienation of the media from each other reflects a society alienated from itself, men whose functions are severed from each other even within each individual. Therefore the aesthetic divergence of the media is potentially a legitimate means of expression, not merely a regrettable deficiency that has to be concealed as well as possible. And this is perhaps the fundamental reason why many light-entertainment pictures that fall far below the pretentious standards of the usual movie seem to be more substantial than motion pictures that flirt with real art. Movie revues usually come closest to the ideal of montage, hence music fulfils its proper function most adequately in them. Their potentialities are wasted only because of their standardisation, their spurious romanticism, and their super-imposed plots of successful careers. They may be remembered if the motion picture is ever emancipated from the present-day conventions. (Adorno and Eisler 1994: 74)

In actuality, synchronisation and counterpoint are ideal types only rarely encountered in pure form. Synchronised sound, though clearly a guiding norm, is hardly an absolute in classic cinema, even for dialogue. Like the offscreen look, offscreen sound (a device nominally borrowed from the theatre but with markedly different implications in film [Chion 1999: 22–3]) expands the diegetic world beyond the edges of the screen, and thus hearing what was not seen became an important means of motivating filmic action, of moving the camera. In short, the synchronising of offscreen sound with an image – an instance of what Stephen Heath calls 'metonymic lock' (1981: 45) – is as basic to the syntax of sound film as the eye-line match or the shot/reverse-shot sequence. The choreographed unveiling of the physical source of an ambiguous sound is thus a technique that expands on the critique of synchronised sound, though admittedly it turns that critique on its head by simply reinscribing the norm of synchronisation as primary and natural. Dialogue, too, is occasionally non-synchronous (some directors, such as Sergio Leone, for example, deliberately use a slightly dis-synchronous overdubbing to create a distancing effect not unlike dubbing in a foreign language), and both dialogue and effects are frequently used in semi-sync for the generic sound of groups, crowds, races or battles.[4] With respect to background music, too, extensive synchronisation, such as in Steiner's remarkable score for *The Informer* or in many cartoons, is the exception rather than the rule; and music without an occasional sync point would seem strangely indifferent to the narrative rather than its dialectical counterpoint, as even advocates for contrapuntal treatment of music such as Adorno and Eisler are clearly aware (1994: 117).

Clarity, not Fidelity

Still, synchronisation in non-absolute form does represent well the scoring practice of the classic film, probably because it conforms to Hollywood's guiding ideology of clarity while minimising conflicts with the prevailing aesthetic of realism. In radical form, however, synchronisation itself can turn critical. Steiner's score for *The Informer*, for instance, nearly obliterates realism altogether, the manneristic melodramatic tone often producing the effect of what Chion rightly calls 'spoken opera' (1994: 52). What is distinctive about the score is not so much the musical presences – the much ridiculed mickey-mousing of Gypo's walk, for instance – but the musical absences, the way, as Chion puts it, music 'often gets interrupted bluntly and suddenly, in mid-phrase, producing a silence in which the subsequent dialogue resonates strangely' (1994: 54). The music, as it were, finds expression in the silences between the notes, underscoring the dialogue by refusing to come to its rescue.

Although *The Informer* is an extreme case, it effectively demonstrates how the very unreality of the musical score allows it to break open the narrative and radically transform what the audience sees and hears. The music grants insight into what must otherwise remain unseen and unsaid: psychology, mood, motivation. This symbolic function would become the principal justification for the non-diegetic score. Leonard Rosenman, for instance, valorises music for its lack of spatial anchoring, arguing that this lack is a 'dramatic necessity for the intrusion of an 'unreal' or illusory element for the purpose of creating a new and imaginative reality. Music should illuminate the deepest well of inner life within the character and situation' (Rosenman 1955: 3). The visual metaphor should not pass unnoted: it points to the supplementary status of music in Rosenman's account. If the model of *The Informer* never took hold, this is perhaps because the score does not behave as a proper supplement to the image: its intervention runs too deep, it does not merely 'illuminate' but admits to structuring and reconstituting the image, which would not be what it is without the music. The extreme synchronisation of the music with Gypo's gait, for example, is as much allegory as an instance of mickey-mousing. It represents the weight of the community and Gypo's isolation from it: Gypo cannot shake this music because he cannot shake his guilt.

Interpretive Clarity and Effaced Musical Symbols

Where the allegorical music of *The Informer* thus makes us continually aware of the structuring properties of music, the more common approach is to efface any symbolic work of music as much as possible. Devices such as mickey-mousing that draw attention to this symbolic work are generally held in disfavour because their relative 'crudity' imperils effacement. The symbolic function of enhancing clarity even as that function is effaced stems from the ideology of the apparatus, which has always been definition rather than fidelity (Doane 1985: 58–9; Chion 1994: 98–9). The point of classical sound recording technique, derived from radio, is clarity and purity of sound in the reproduction, a clarity that is masked by noise and sonic distortion in the real world. In studio-era films especially, a departure from clarity either opens a gap to be closed, as with the acoustic 'metonymic lock' when an ambiguous sound is later clarified by synchronising it to the image of its physical source; or it carries a semantic charge, generally as a sign of distance and mediation: the telephone, the radio and the phonograph. In the latter case the lack of clarity in the reproduction emphasises by means of contrast the immediacy of the cinematic representation. When this distancing effect is not used, the resulting clarity usually underscores a cinematic point.

Hence, in *A Song is Born* (1948), the overwhelming presence of Honey Swanson's voice on the phonograph poignantly reminds the professors of their loss. Likewise, near the end of *My Fair Lady* (1964), Professor Higgins wallows nostalgically in the sonic clarity of his recording of Liza, hoping to preserve an element of what he has lost. While both films use the phonograph to accentuate a sense of loss, marking the structuring presence of an absence, the difference between the two is striking. The power of Honey's spectral voice is more than the professors can take in *A Song is Born*, and they rush to turn off the infernal clarity of the machine's reproduction. Higgins, on the contrary, takes solace in the machine and its reproduction, using the simulacrum to regress to an earlier state; Liza's materialisation becomes a kind of wish fulfilment of the machine's promise to arrest the temporal flow, to recover what has been lost.

Another way in which music offers interpretive clarity is by reading an image against the grain, revealing a surplus in the image, a surplus in need of interpretation. Counterpoint theorists had suggested that music not immediately concordant with the image invokes our critical interpretive faculty. This insight is appropriated by Hollywood composers, not for its critical value but because it can increase interpretive clarity. George Burt, hardly a dialectician, notes that if an image of a person running down the street is accompanied by hurrying, churning music, the audience will interpret the running more or less at face value as flight; but if that same scene is scored with lyrical music, music at odds with the image, this indicates that there is more to the image than meets the eye: 'The music interacts with the intrinsic meaning of the sequence, as distinct from a surface-level meaning; it is addressed to what is implicit within the drama, not to what is explicit . . . that is, to what you cannot see but need to think about' (Burt 1994: 7). Music is especially prominent at such moments because it has a tangible effect on what we see. Yet, unlike mickey-mousing, the symbolic work of music, if not the music itself, remains effaced at such moments. It transparently urges us to interpret the image rather than the music (Chion 1994: 144). Music, like the recording apparatus, remains deferential, letting the symbolism accrue to the image.

False Clarity: The Case of *Amistad*

Caryl Flinn makes the important point that music grants film a clarity unobtainable in the real world, making the world seem impoverished by comparison (Flinn 1992: 109). This clarity is false and illusory not because it does not coincide with the existing world – the critical force of film lies in its ability to show that the world might be otherwise – but rather because the means by which the clarity is obtained are effaced. The ability of music to offer unrivalled interpretive clarity is apparent in the Supreme Court Chamber sequence from *Amistad* (1997). Here, John Quincy Adams is reading aloud from an article written by his nemesis Senator Calhoun, an article that draws an argument in favour of slavery out of the Old Testament. As Adams reads from Calhoun's article, John Williams' music darkens, becoming more dissonant and much less tonally coherent; indeed the music here stops progressing for the bulk of Calhoun's arguments, as it simply rearticulates one dissonant chord and a descending motive that seems unable to escape the musical quagmire. The moment Adams shifts to his own oral arguments linking the abolition of slavery with the ideals of the Founding Fathers, the music shifts tone: when Adams says the word 'freedom', Williams places a kind of musical halo around the word, as the music brightens, opening up into expansive harmonies reminiscent of Aaron Copland (the sound Hollywood has adopted for an 'American' style topic). The effect of the music in this scene encourages audience identification with the second argument: we have faith in Adam's claims, in their truth even, because the music seemingly has faith with them. But the association of non-tonal dissonance and tonal ambiguity with argumentative sophistry is as troubling as it is effective: it reinforces a link between complication and intellectual intricacy on the one hand and artificiality, evilness and falseness on the other. In other words, an analysis of the relation of the music to the narrative here unveils a rhetoric of anti-intellectualism driving the scene. The right and true gain their force in this scene through an association with the beautiful. Yet this has the effect of placing the situation today safely outside the arguments offered: we can congratulate our society for having moved beyond accepting such arguments as Calhoun mounts while we honour the film for having the integrity to reveal the horrors of the past, which are apparently no longer with us. It is music that allows this false clarity of the past. What is lost is any sense of the 'evil' argument as compelling, why it might have once been convincing. Because the film never makes us face the argument, it remains a latent danger, a danger the music conceals but does not mitigate: since the music makes it unnecessary to deal with the argument, it may well return. The moral clarity that the music conjures up veils an underlying moral ambiguity: Adam's argument carries the day for us not through the force of reason, as the film wants to imply, but through persuasive (musical) rhetoric. Music thus ensures our 'proper' identification within the scene, determining in a significant way how we comprehend it.[5]

Presence of an Absence: The Musical *Acousmêtre*

If music can affect what we see in an image and how we interpret it, it is also well suited to showing us what is not in the image. A disembodied voice, whether a voice-over narrator in a documentary or what Chion calls an *acousmêtre* (acoustical being) such as the mother in *Psycho* (1960), acquires a kind of power and authority by means of its ability to resist becoming an object of the camera's gaze, to resist synchronisation (Chion 1999: 140–51). Non-diegetic music, too, appropriates this power to speak from a transcendent realm beyond the image, nowhere more so than when music represents the structuring presence of an absence: the force of the dead on the living. In films such as *Rebecca* and *Laura* (1944), the title characters are first of all musical entities. Through music we sense the extent to which these characters determine the action in the diegesis even when the image can detect only their fragmentary traces. The constant presence of the kitschily haunting theme in *Laura* belies something obsessive about the diegetic world. The theme for the title character in *Rebecca*, by contrast, is rather indefinite, recognisable more by the instrumental timbre of the harmonium than the thematic material *per se*. The sound of the harmonium itself, which, because of its close resemblance to the organ, might at first be taken as signifying something like saintliness and purity, is an effective choice in that it inscribes on a musical level the idea of misrecognition that guides the film as a whole. Only near the end of the film do we learn that this sound is not so much transcendent as gaudy. As so often in Hitchcock's films, music here does not offer clarity but deepens the ambiguity.

Narratological Issues and the Soundtrack

As noted in passing above, the basic dichotomies of diegetic and non-diegetic, on the one hand, and synchronisation and counterpoint, on the other, may be related to dialogue and sound effects as well. Dialogue (even when overdubbed) is normally diegetic and synchronous, but voice-over narration is extra-diegetic and may occupy the same narrative plane as non-diegetic music if the narrator cannot readily be placed in the physical world of the story (as in documentaries). Most narrators in fiction films, however, are closer to that physical world than is typical of background music, and this undermines their discursive authority. Such is the case, for instance, in

Double Indemnity (1944), where the narrator is one of the main characters. Non-diegetic music, on the contrary, always speaks from a position of discursive authority on a narrative plane (Buhler and Neumeyer 1994: 378–81), which is probably one reason its 'servitude is . . . enforced with special vigor' (Flinn 1992: 14).

Effects, by contrast, are only rarely non-diegetic, as when a cut or dissolve is emphasised by means of an effect not locatable in the diegesis (the use of non-diegetic sound is less common in film than television, where the non-diegetic effect serves occasionally as a sound bumper distinguishing story threads – as in *The Practice* and *The X-Files*). Non-speech sounds heard by a character subjectively, in connection with a point-of-view shot or sequence, are at some level diegetic because they are associated with a physical entity in the story-world (the character) and a location (that character's mind).

Modern sound design, however, has eroded these boundaries. In some cases (especially in science fiction films or thrillers), effects may be integrated into the rhythms of an ongoing non-diegetic musical cue. Or, in a sound bridge (a favourite device of Robert Altman's films), an effect or dialogue will begin not just offscreen but before a cut or dissolve. The initial lack of spatial anchoring is considerably greater than a simple offscreen sound, though the filmic syntax in both cases works to dramatise the eventual movement to synchronised sound. (Likewise, a music bridge reverses the syntax of an audio dissolve, moving from non-diegetic to diegetic music; this is not only possible, but actually relatively common, especially over establishing shots.) Similarly, many effects in films today are designed with only cursory thought given to achieving fidelity of diegetic sound: for example, a car door slamming shut might have the hollow metallic ring of a prison door snapping into place. A related technique, a special case of a stinger, underscores a sound effect with an orchestral hit. Both techniques have the potential to 'denaturalise' the synchronised sound effect; but denaturalisation in such cases is generally attenuated if not rendered moot by requiring that such departures from fidelity, much like non-diegetic orchestral music, serve some narrative function: that, for instance, they clarify a dramatic or psychological point. Finally, some sounds may hover between effect and music. In the *Terminator* series, the mechanical sound associated with the Terminator, like music, is pitched and only loosely synchronised with the image; yet the sound is mechanistic, oppressively repeating over and over without variation or musical development. Similarly, the sound of helicopters in *Apocalypse Now* (1979) serves an almost musical function, recurring like a leitmotive that drapes a mythic veil around the whole film.

The Ontology of the Soundtrack

The soundtrack is usually divided, as above, into three basic components: dialogue, sound effects and music. The ontological status of the soundtrack rests on whether these components, in the absence of the image, are merely, as Chion puts it, the empirical, 'end-to-end aggregation of all sounds in a film'; or whether they combine to articulate 'an internally coherent entity on equal footing with the imagetrack' (Chion 1994: 40). One way of thinking about this question is to ask whether we can reconstruct the narrative from the soundtrack alone. Chion thinks not, making the radical claim that 'there is no soundtrack'. Whereas he thinks the imagetrack is 'a valid concept,' that of the soundtrack is 'inert and with no autonomous meaning' (Chion 1994: 39). Indeed, 'a film's aural elements . . . are immediately analysed and distributed in the spectator's perceptual apparatus according to the relation each bears to what the spectator sees at the time' (Chion 1999: 3).

We relate the sounds to the image, he suggests, through a process of 'perceptual triage', where the sounds are attributed to either the physical space implied by the image or to an imaginary place, akin to the proscenium in the theatre. Moreover, 'it is the image that governs this triage, not the nature of the recorded elements themselves.' Because the visual field thus determines the aural, the soundtrack is always in some sense supplemental to the imagetrack.

Chion's polemic against the soundtrack is perhaps best understood in the context of calls, such as that once put forward by Noël Burch, for 'the creation . . . of a coherent, organically structured soundtrack in which the forms of interaction between sound and images will be closely tied to other interactions between the three basic types of film sounds' (Burch 1985: 203). A unified soundtrack, Burch suggests, becomes possible by exploiting affinities among dialogue, music and sound effects, so that these basic types dissolve into one another. Where, in Burch's account, classical sound design tends to enforce boundaries between basic sound types because such demarcation ensures clarity, Burch emphasises a sound design where such boundaries are continually transgressed and subverted. Fluid boundary conditions for sound design, he says, unsettle a spectator's relation to film and thus make the viewer self-conscious of the means by which sound in particular contributes to film's illusion of coherence.

Burch is no doubt correct in his assessment that classical sound design is relatively impoverished because its emphasis on clarity rules out many productive uses of sound. Yet the price Burch pays for a unified soundtrack is too dear: on the one hand, Burch's unity erodes the distinctiveness of the individual components, blunting whatever critical edge each component might have in its own terms; but on the other hand, it surrenders the possibility of forging an internal dialectic of sound. We might ask, for instance, whether underscoring is 'a totally discredited convention' because it maintains its identity as music (as Burch implies with his call for music that more closely resembles noise)[6] or because its place within the sound design has become too comfortable and predictable. By confusing the first question with the second Burch vacates the dialectic of the soundtrack even as he insists on its unity; the unified soundtrack must therefore stake everything on its interaction with the image because its own internal dialectic has been dissolved by fiat. What is lost is not just various possibilities of using sound critically, but also the potential of forging the conflicts among the components into a productive tension.[7] Without this tension, moreover, much of the dialectical potential of sound *vis-à-vis* image disappears, because sound becomes subservient to image. The structural use of sound thus reverts to a simple and rather conventional supplemental binarism of image plus sound.

If, as Chion notes, one difficulty with the unified soundtrack is that it tends conceptually toward reduction to this simple binarism, where 'all the audio elements recorded together onto the optical track of the film are presented to the spectator as a sort of bloc or coalition, across from the other bloc, a no-less-fictive "imagetrack"' (Chion 1999: 3), sound also remains supplemental to the image in Chion's account, which merely accepts uncritically the suspect, though admittedly pervasive notion that sound film is essentially a visual medium. Ultimately Chion, like Burch, reduces film to image plus soundtrack; and it remains unclear why, in Chion's account, the supplemental status of the soundtrack should obviate rather than reproduce the danger of binarism.[8] As Chion himself frequently reminds us, sound affects our impression of an image every bit as much as the image affects our impression of a sound. With respect even to closely synchronised sound (the limit case of sound determined by the image), he argues that 'the creators of a film's sound . . . know that if you alter or remove these sounds, the image is no longer the same' [emphasis in original] (Chion 1999: 4). Indeed, Chion's analyses of film sound often undermine his theoretical claim against the ontology of the soundtrack: his nuanced and always informative analyses testify to the fact that the soundtrack, like the imagetrack, is structured by a series of oppositions that gives each film a distinctive sonic shape or soundscape.

Music of the Soundtrack: *Mise-en-bande*

Recently Rick Altman and several of his students have looked at the issue of the soundtrack from a historical perspective. They have found that, while the individual components of a soundtrack are admittedly intermittent, this does not mean that a soundtrack does not have an overall coherence of its own, a coherence they suggestively dub the '*mise-en-bande*' of the film (Altman, Jones and Tatroe 2000). Through a series of analyses of early sound films, Altman and his students show how the sound conventions of Hollywood film only gradually coalesced and that the relationship of the soundtrack to the image was less important to the development of these conventions than balancing competing demands of the separate audio elements. This suggests, contrary to Chion, that an internal dialectic does in fact structure the soundtrack, which is consequently to some extent an autonomous entity *vis-à-vis* the imagetrack.

Still, a theory of the *mise-en-bande* – an object of which is to uncover the technological and aesthetic obstacles to implementing a self-critical sound design – must remain cognisant of Chion's critique of the unified soundtrack even as it seeks to move beyond that critique; to proceed otherwise would be to regress to a pre-critical understanding of the soundtrack, whose unity, if it indeed exists, emerges dialectically with respect to the internal structuring tensions among its components on the one hand and to the way these components engage the imagetrack individually and collectively on the other. This is to say that Chion's claim against the soundtrack might be redeemable at some level, but only to the extent that the imagetrack is de-essentialised by insisting on its likewise fictive status, a possibility that Chion hints at but does not pursue. For the power of the imagetrack too derives not from some mystical unity but from the way editing in particular productively structures the tensions among the various components of the imagetrack – *mise-en-scène*, lighting, framing, blocking and so forth. By refusing to grant either image- or soundtrack a more secure ontological status *vis-à-vis* film (or, more properly, narrative) would permit articulating the relation between the two tracks as thoroughly dialectical rather than a supplemental binarism.

On the Structural Use of Music

In terms of music, such a dialectical interpretive framework requires first of all evaluating the particular contribution of music to the '*mise-en-bande*' (much as we might ask about the specific contribution of lighting is to the *mise-en-scène*). *The Jazz Singer* (1927), for instance, somewhat crudely juxtaposes two distinct approaches to the *mise-en-bande*. The family melodrama follows the sound design of silent film with ubiquitous music not synchronised in any rigorous way to the images, whereas the sound design of the performances, whether secular or sacred, is one of synchronised sound. The sound design itself thus articulates the central dramatic conflict of the film, marking performance as a special register where the proper place of Jackie/Jack's voice, synagogue or stage, is contested. Likewise music is the sound of the fantastic in *King Kong*; the presence of music in the soundtrack places Skull Island worlds apart from the early sequences in New York, where a lack of music emphasises its 'mundane' character (Gorbman 1987: 79–80; Kalinak 1992: 71–2; Brown 1994: 41). As mentioned in the previous chapter of this book, an opposition between diegetic and non-diegetic music similarly articulates the dramatic structure of *Casablanca*. (Perhaps not coincidentally, both of the latter two scores are by Steiner.)

Impromptu (1991), a film account of the affair between Frédéric Chopin and George Sand, likewise deploys its music structurally; that is, music generally serves more than an atmospheric function in the film. Nowhere is this more evident than in Sand's frantic ride through the woods, which uses music to underscore the complex way culture and nature intersect in her rebellious character. At first, Sand's shooting of the lame horse, adoption of male dress and frequent recourse to expletives mark her as someone who refuses the cultural imperative to live as a proper lady and who chafes against the categories set down by culture. In terms of narrative, the ride figures her refusal as an uncontrolled flight from culture to nature, a nature that is as wild and undomesticated as the horse she mounts despite the warning of the Duke. Sound initially reinforces this binary division into culture and nature, adding a gendered dimension to the division. As the sound of Sand's horse fades into the distance, the Duchess insists on Sand's feminine nature: 'Madame George Sand, dear, the authoress.' Ironically, Sand's gender is thus reinscribed and essentialised the moment she attempts to leave culture behind. This bit of dialogue is directly followed by a curiously intrusive ambient birdsong, which is in turn displaced by the non-diegetic entrance of Chopin's G sharp minor *Prelude*. The sequence of sounds here allies Chopin's *Prelude*, a sound of culture, with the sound of nature; the musical presence here thus already alerts our ears that Sand's attempt to use nature to escape culture is in some sense untenable and even illusory, as it must proceed as though nature were not already a cultural category. The next brief sequence of sounds serves to introduce Chopin into this increasingly problematic opposition of nature and culture. First, the sound of Chopin's carriage fills the soundtrack, analogous to the sound of Sand's horse although oriented toward culture rather than away from it. Next, Chopin coughs in audible close-up, a sound positioned, like Sand's expletive, on the cusp between nature and culture, here perhaps hinting that, *contra* the apparent intent of her ride, uncontrolled eruptions of nature into culture can be as unhealthy as culture itself. Moreover, the insertion of the short sequence with Chopin here demonstrates the extent to which her flight from culture remains indifferent to her desire, which is to meet Chopin.

The remainder of the sequence centres on the ride, as horse's hooves and music fuse into a sonic image of nature. Yet the film does not even allow this mediated image of nature to stand unchallenged. As the horse halts before the ditch and throws Sand, this sonic image is itself denatured as it dissembles into a rapid antiphonal chorus of separate soundtrack elements. The music punctuates the fall with a reverse stinger as Sand moans 'Ugh' and the horse whinnies and runs off.[9] The following lap dissolve intensifies the thematic reversal here; ambient sounds of nature now flood the soundtrack with a sort of super-realistic sound design, but the image presents Sand, in long shot, walking toward the house. In other words, the sound design returns to a 'natural' state the moment Sand herself returns to culture, here figured as the house.

In the house too, elements of the preceding sequence recur as if to underscore the point that a flight from culture remains always caught within the enclosure of culture, that nature is but a cultural category. Malfi, a former lover, confronts Sand and tries to trap her in her room (another attempt to hold her in a 'proper' place for a lady). Sand escapes, this time fleeing not to nature, as with the ride, but following the sound of the music, which this time is anchored diegetically, to Chopin. Here, in an intriguing reversal, Chopin's music serves not as an analogue to nature as in the ride but as an analogue to culture: Chopin plays within the house. Successful flight, the soundtrack helps us hear, occurs not from culture but through it.

Conclusion

As this and other examples in this chapter suggest, an emphasis on understanding music in the sound design allows interpretation to probe the rich tensions, complexities and contradictions that music helps articulate in sound film. Yet attention to sound design permits more than this. If music is a structuring of sound in time, as many twentieth-century aestheticians have claimed, then conceptually the *mise-en-bande*, with its the complex interplay of music, dialogue, ambient sound, effects, silences and so forth, can be understood – indeed is perhaps best understood – as a kind of musical 'composition'. At this point, aural analysis (including both technical musical analysis and Schaeffer's 'concentrated hearing'), along with a specifically musical sensibility, can be brought to bear on the soundtrack as a whole, its relation to the image, and its contribution not just to the narrative, but to the act of narration itself. Interpreting a film in this way is perhaps the most 'musical' way of reading it, more so than treating the score as a relatively independent component of the film, an analytical strategy that necessarily takes as its object music for film rather than music in film.

In this context, whether music used in a film is as effective as music outside the cinematic environment has little bearing on evaluating its success within the film: everything depends on the dialectic the music establishes with the imagetrack on the one hand and with dialogue and effects in the soundtrack on the other hand. A composer can use the most advanced compositional techniques (atonality, serialism, electronics and so forth) to write a score where this 'advanced' material is used very conventionally, as Adorno and Eisler warn in their treatise.[10] Equally, an effective score can be created using only traditional materials as, for instance, in Kieslowski's *Trois Couleurs:*

Bleu (1993), where the music is oddly decentred despite the conventional material. This being the case, it can be argued that a film score should be evaluated according to Adorno's general dicta: first, how well it solves the musicodramatic problem it poses for itself (Adorno and Eisler 1994: 88, 121, 127); and second, that categories once problematised do not return unproblematised (Adorno 1997: 36; Adorno 1992: 269–322; Jameson 1990: 246–7; cf. Buhler 1994: 139–63). Music in film would then need to be evaluated in terms of whether and how productively it problematises its own conditions of possibility; that is, its relation not just to the imagetrack but also its place in the sound design.

Notes

1. The usual term opposed to diegetic in narrative theory is extra-diegetic, meaning 'external to (not part of) any diegesis'; that is, extra-diegetic is external to 'the (fictional) world in which the situations and events narrated occur' (Prince 1987: 20, 29). Gorbman's 'non-diegetic', however, has become the standard in film-music literature.
2. The 1936 film version closely follows the stage show in this respect.
3. See David Neumeyer (forthcoming). It is in order to dissolve some of these oppositions that we advocate a shift to historically informed interpretive practice where music is considered in relation to its place in the overall sound design.
4. Indeed, such scenes are nearly always shot silent, with the sound dubbed in later.
5. A similar argument could also be mounted against Eisler's score for *Hangmen Also Die* (Cf. Adorno and Eisler 1994: 27–8).
6. Burch erroneously calls this kind of music 'serial,' perhaps confusing the attack of serialism on tonality with the attack of the musical avant-garde on the concept of the musical as a world apart. Serialism is a formal means of rationally controlling the compositional material, whereas the incorporation of noise in avant-garde music tends to be figured compositionally as the opposite: either as an outburst of anti-music and irrationality; or as a kind of revelation of the musicality of mundane life. On another level, Burch's call for music to become sound effect is oddly not all that far removed from the mickey-mousing practice of Steiner.
7. It is true that eroding the distinctiveness between the components is one way of articulating such tension; our concern here is to avoid positing it as the only means of such articulation. Under Burch's scheme, for instance, there is little room for music qua music to assert itself as a filmically critical force. But if music did not possess the potential of such critical force, it seems highly unlikely that film theory would have spent such energy trying to domesticate it, seeking to hold it to its 'proper' role.
8. In this sense, Kaja Silverman's charge that Chion makes 'uncritical' recourse to metaphors of gender (sound as inscribed with the maternal, image and meaning with the paternal) is not entirely misplaced (1987: 73–8). (The claim that Chion's gendered language is 'uncritical' is made on p. 49.) Cf. Gorbman 1999: xii.
9. The actual sequence of the soundtrack is as follows: first, the music stops abruptly on the reverse stinger; second, the horse whinnies; third, George utters

a brief 'Ugh!' as she falls; fourth, she hits water at the bottom of the ditch; fifth, she utters 'Oh, uhh'; sixth, hoof noises sound briefly as the horse runs off.
10. 'A hair-raising, "thrilling" accompaniment to a murder scene will be essentially the same even if the whole tone scale is replaced with sharp dissonances' (Adorno and Eisler 1994: 80).

Bibliography

Abbate, Carolyn (1991) *Unsung Voices*. Princeton: Princeton University Press.

Adorno, T. W. (1997) *Aesthetic Theory* (trans. Robert Hullot-Kentor). Minneapolis: University of Minnesota Press.

Adorno, T. W., and Hanns Eisler (1994) *Composing for the Films* (originally published 1947). London: Athlone Press.

Adorno, T. W. (1992) 'Vers une musique informelle' in *Quasi una Fantasia: Essays on Modern Music* (trans. Rodney Livingstone). London: Verso.

Altman, Rick (1987) *The American Film Musical*. Bloomington: Indiana University Press.

Altman, Rick, McGraw Jones and Sonia Tatroe (2000), 'Inventing the cinema soundtrack: Hollywood mulitiplane sound system' in James Buhler, Caryl Flinn and David Neumeyer (eds) *Music and Cinema*. Middletown, CT: Wesleyan University Press.

Buhler, James (1994) Review of translations of Adorno's *Alban Berg: Master of the Smallest Link*; *Mahler: A Musical Physiognomy*; and *Quasi una Fantasia*. *Indiana Theory Review*, vol. 15, no. 1.

Buhler, James and David Neumeyer (1994) Review of Caryl Flinn's *Strains of Utopia*, and Kathryn Kalinak's *Settling the Score*. *Journal of the American Musicological Society*, vol. 47, no. 2.

Buhler, James, Caryl Flinn and David Neumeyer (eds) (2000) *Music and Cinema*. Middletown, CT: Wesleyan University Press.

Brown, Royal S. (1994) *Overtones and Undertones: Reading Film Music*. Berkeley: University of California Press.

Burch, Noël (1985) 'On the structural use of sound' in Elisabeth Weis and John Belton (eds) *Theory and Practice of Film Sound*. New York: Columbia University Press.

Burt, George (1994) *The Art of Film Music*. Boston: Northeastern University Press.

Chion, Michel (1994) *Audio-Vision: Sound on Screen* (trans. Claudia Gorbman). New York: Columbia University Press.

Chion, Michel (1999) *The Voice in the Cinema* (trans. Claudia Gorbman). New York: Columbia University Press.

Doane, Mary Anne (1985) 'Ideology and the practice of editing and mixing' in Elisabeth Weis and John Belton (eds) *Theory and Practice of Film Sound*. New York: Columbia University Press.

Flinn, Caryl (1992) *Strains of Utopia: Gender, Nostalgia, and Hollywood Film Music*. Princeton: Princeton University Press.

Gorbman, Claudia (1987) *Unheard Melodies: Narrative Film Music*. Bloomington: Indiana University Press, 1987.

Gorbman, Claudia (1999) 'Editor's note' in Michel Chion *The Voice in the Cinema*. New York: Columbia University Press.

Heath, Stephen (1981) *Questions of Cinema*. Bloomington: Indiana University Press.

Jameson, Fredric (1990) *Late Marxism: Adorno, or, the Persistence of the Dialectic* London: Verso.

Kalinak, Kathryn (1992) *Settling the Score: Music and the Classical Hollywood Film.* Madison: University of Wisconsin Press.

Neumeyer, David, 'Performances in early Hollywood sound films: Source music, background music, and the integrated sound track'. *Contemporary Music Review*, forthcoming.

Neumeyer, David, Caryl Flinn and James Buhler (2000) 'Introduction' in James Buhler, Caryl Flinn and David Neumeyer (eds) *Music and Cinema*. Middletown, CT: Wesleyan University Press.

Prince, Gerald (1987) *A Dictionary of Narratology*. Lincoln: University of Nebraska Press.

Rosenman, Leonard (1955) 'Notes on the Score to *East of Eden*'. *Film Music*, vol. 14, no. 5.

Silverman, Kaja (1987) *The Acoustic Mirror: The Female Voice in Psychoanalysis and Cinema*. Bloomington: Indiana University Press.

Steiner, Max (1940) Interoffice memo to Carlyle Jones, Warner Bros. Pictures, 11 March. Quoted in 'Introduction' in James Buhler, Caryl Flinn and David Neumeyer (eds) *Music and Cinema*. Middletown, CT: Wesleyan University Press, 2000.

Chapter 3

'In the Mix': How Electrical Reproducers Facilitated the Transition to Sound in British Cinemas

Michael Allen

It is widely acknowledged that the coming of sound from mid-1926 onwards revolutionised the film industry, first in America and then the rest of the world. The immediate impact was felt by exhibitors in the United States, with the following year or eighteen months marked by frenetic activity as manufacturers tried to satisfy demand for equipment from exhibitors who, in turn, were trying to satisfy their audiences' demands for sound and talking pictures.

The situation in Britain was slightly different. Awareness of the advent of sound films by British exhibitors, production workers and, to a lesser though increasing extent, spectators, grew as it took place in America. However, the immediate chances of British exhibitors getting their hands on relevant equipment was slim, at least in the short term; the resultant gap between first awareness and acquisition being eighteen months and two years. But while in America this time period signalled the gap between first appearance and large-scale installation of theatres with sound equipment, in Britain the time-frame was between first awareness of sound films in America and the appearance of any significant American apparatus in Britain. It is this two-year gap in the British situation regarding the coming of sound films – roughly from early 1927 to the end of 1928 – which forms the time-frame of this chapter. Its central argument is that a specific kind of audio technology – the electrical reproducer – was developed to 'plug the gap', and, by using recorded music on commercially available records, provided British audiences with some semblance of sound and talking picture experience until the appearance of the American equipment.

Robert Murphy is dismissive of the part played by electrical reproducers in British cinemas between 1927 and 1929. He notes that:

the most successful [gramophone company], British-Brunswick, which marketed the 'Panatrope' developed by Brunswick–Balke–Collender and General Electric in America, claimed to have installed gramophones in over a thousand British cinemas by mid-1928, despite stiff competition from rival models such as the 'Celebritone', the 'Phanestra' and the 'Ethatrope', and that British Phototone, associated with the Brunswick concern, was initially to market a synchronising device which would enable the 'Panatrope' to be used to play sound films. (Murphy 1984: 145)

But having done so, he refuses to explore the implications of these developments, even though 'over a thousand' constituted between a quarter and a third of Britain's cinemas at that date. Rachel Low is equally dismissive; note the tone of her brief summary description:

About August 1928, Electramonic, a gramophone grandly called a 'sound reproducing device', was oversubscribed ten times. The Celebritone Company, registered at about the same time, with a capital of £160,000, was also heavily oversubscribed; it seems to have been an amplifying system. Filmophone was registered at about the same time, with a capital of £225,000, to market a synchronisation system for discs. And early in 1929 a studio in Leeds was said to be turning out Electrocord shorts which, again, sound like films with discs. (Low 1971: 204)

Low's strangely lethargic style, depending more on hearsay ('seems', 'was said to be' 'sound like') than hard evidence, sums up the general refusal to pursue the significance of these sound systems.

This chapter describes the brief but significant history of recorded music and sound, using electrical and mechanical devices, in British cinemas between 1927 and 1929. It traces the development and adaptation of the technology as it emerged from the gramophone industry; the commercial and economic relations between gramophone and film industries; and the variety of uses to which the devices were put in supporting and supplementing the exhibition of films in Britain during the transition to sound of the late 1920s.

The Gramophone Industry, Electrical Recording and Reproduction

Electrical reproducers were a product of the gramophone industry. It might therefore be useful to give an historical overview of the industry as a means of placing the emergence of electrical reproducers within a broader context. That context will be partly industrial, partly cultural and partly aesthetic.

The second decade of the twentieth century saw an exponential growth in the number of gramophone record manufacturers. In 1912, there were only the big three – Victor, Columbia and Edison. By 1914, there were eighteen, producing 500,000 records a year. This increase was sparked, amongst other things, by a dance craze which erupted in the States in 1913, to be followed, post war, by a jazz craze beginning in 1919:

> The jazz craze of 1919–24 coincided with the fattest years of the record. 110 million records produced in 1922 and most of that jazz or dance or both. Any band worth a fig had to be under contract. Victor had Paul Whiteman; Columbia, Ted Lewis; Okeh, Vincent Lopez.
> We've seen some of the reasons why jazz caught on. But another important one was that jazz bands – loud, brassy, blarey, recorded well . . . Recording horns trapped some of the ODJB [Old Dixieland Jazz Band]'s glorious moments and turned millions on to jazz all over the world. (Whitcomb 1986: 97)

By 1919, there were 200 manufacturers, making over 2 million records. By 1921, over 100 million records were being produced annually. The massive increase in new companies was the result of the lapsing of patents owned by the Victor and Columbia Gramophone companies.

America became identified as a country of low-brow rather than refined taste – of popular music rather than classical; classical music was Europe's province. While American companies built up catalogues of short jazz and popular song titles, European manufacturers, with Germany at the forefront (Deutsche Grammophon was established in 1921), pioneered full-length orchestral works.

In 1923 America experienced a radio boom. The gramophone manufacturers combated the threat by producing combination phonograph and radio units: Brunswick went in with RCA to install RCA Radiolas in Brunswick phonograph players; Victor announced plans to built its Victrolas with an empty space into which owners could install a radio of their choice.

Electrical recording, using a microphone (instead of a conical horn) to convert sound waves into an electrical signal and a loudspeaker to do the opposite at the receiving end, had been in development throughout the first half of the 1920s. It became a commercial reality by April/May of that year. Gelatt describes electrical recording as 'staggeringly loud and brilliant [when compared with recordings made by the old method], it embodied a resonance and sense of "atmosphere" never before heard on a phonograph record, and it sold in the thousands' (Gelatt 1956: 174–5).

Developments were, however, slow. 'By the end of 1925, Victor had issued a smattering of electrical Red Seals, enough to whet the musical appetite but not to satisfy it' (Gelatt 1956: 175). These were short pieces – jazz and popular dance music – on single records, rather than multi-disc classical symphonic pieces. 'To England went the distinction of pioneering in the area of full-length works', with the HMV release, in December 1925, of Tchaikovsky's *Fourth Symphony*. Both of the largest British record companies acquired the rights to Western Electric's recording system through their American affiliates (Gelatt 1956: 175).

In early November 1925, Brunswick unveiled an electrical reproducer which it had developed in collaboration with the General Electric Company. Named the Panatrope, it was intended for use in the home, and came in various models (with or without radio) for £350 and upwards.[1] By the summer of 1926, the Brunswick Panatrope was being used to make electrical recordings. This is a crucial date. At the same time, Warners were preparing to release their first synchronised music-and-effects feature film, *Don Juan* which premiered on 6 August 1926. That is to say, by the time electrical recording for domestic records and reproduction machines had become a reality, Warners had developed the Vitaphone as a commercially viable film-sound system.

Electrical recording temporarily rejuvenated the record industry. In 1927, 1 million phonographs and 100 million records were sold in America. But the recovery was short lived, and the combination of the Great Crash in 1929, the continued and even increased popularity of radio (which was free – an attractive feature in times of financial difficulty) caused the record market to plummet again over the following years. '[T]he national economy began to contract, and the phonograph and record business withered as if frozen in full bloom by a bitter Arctic frost. Everything went into a decline, but the phonograph went into a tail spin' (Gelatt 1956: 189). By 1932 only 6 million records were sold in America; 6 per cent of the 1927 figure.

I want to frame the following argument in the context of this late 1920s upsurge in production of and interest in the products of the gramophone industry.

What Were Electrical Reproducers?

In its basic form, an electrical reproducer consisted of an electric pick-up, turntable, amplifier, loudspeakers and optional wireless, all housed in a wooden cabinet. The powerful amplifier could, alternatively, be connected by wires from some distance away. The secret of the improvement was that in replay 'a gramophone instead of being played through an ordinary sound box, goes through a special attachment known as an electro-magnetic pick-up and is then passed through wireless valves until it is amplified many times and comes out of loud speakers at a volume much greater than any gramophone could give.'[2] This volume was distortion free, by virtue of 'the power required for the reproduction [being] supplied not from the record but from an independent source, [which] has no limitation, and in practice very great volume of sound free from distortion, can be obtained.'[3]

At a point fairly early in their development, it was realised that electrical reproducers could be used for cinema work. The first use, perhaps inevitably, was in America. An entry in *Variety* in November 1926 under the headline 'Victriola substitutes' informed readers that:

> It is reported from the smaller towns that picture houses are placing ordinary (but improved) phonograph instruments.
>
> Through inability to make use of the muchly publicised 'phone' [in other words Vitaphone] subjects of music, the exhibs have hit upon the canned stuff as substitutes for 'talking pictures'. No reports have been received as to the influence of the substitute at the box-offices. It is presumed they have been installed to meet a demand by the natives for the talking pictures they have read about.[4]

Although the report is vague and refers to 'talking pictures', the use of the brand-name 'Victriola' indicates that the machine in question was a standard-issue, single turntable model, manufactured by the Victor Talking Machine Company. It must only have been used to provide the sound for musical shorts – a ten-inch, 78 rpm disc lasted about four minutes, the average length of an early Vitaphone short. Actual 'talking' pictures would not appear for almost a year, with *The Jazz Singer* in October 1927.

There is some vagueness about the first installation of an electrical reproducer in a British cinema. According to the *Kine Weekly* of 26 April 1928, it happened 'a little over a year ago'[5] in other words, sometime in March or early April 1927, but an earlier entry, on 29 December 1927, notes that a Mr Outwin [of Swan Picture Hall, Westerham]

> advances a substantial claim to being the originator of the fitting of gramophone records to films. He says he first introduced this method partially nearly five years ago, and it proved so successful that for the past two years he has completely superseded his orchestra in favour of the mechanical musical accompaniment.[6]

If this is indeed the case, his first use must have been fairly modest, using pre-electric gramophone records which would have been hard to amplify to any significant volume without an unacceptable level of scratch and surface noise, while the 'serious' use of the past two years could, just, have been with the new electric recordings (they appeared at the end of 1925). If this latter use was, as claimed, for 'the fitting of gramophone records to films' rather than just to provide general music in the auditorium before the screening, then, even if he was only using a single turntable model, Mr Outwin was visionary indeed, seeing the possibility almost a year before exhibitors in America did.

In its cinema version, the single turntable soon became double. Some later models had three or even four.[7] Microphone and wireless connections were added, and there was storage space for a large number of records. While I have not been able to discover the motive behind the development of twin turntables, it is possible that the twin model may have evolved from the practice of using two separate single turntable models side-by-side to give the first exponents greater flexibility. The article cited above continues by reporting that:

> In fitting the film Mr Outwin uses two HMV gramophones, with slight additions introduced by himself . . . Apparently no amplifier is utilised, but Mr Outwin says he finds the volume obtained with the new HMV model, using electrically recorded records, surprising, the tone being particularly clear.[8]

It would be a small move from this use of two reproducers side-by-side to one larger unit housing two turntables.

Various sizes of model were developed to cater for the range of auditorium size, as can be seen in a report on an early Panatrope recital demonstration at the Philharmonic Hall in London: 'The various mechanical items on the programme were played on the "Junior", "Senior", a larger model suitable for small halls, and the "Special", the model designed for use in kinemas, ballrooms and other places of entertainment.'[9] This range of sizes was perfectly suited to smaller theatres and their more cash-strapped exhibitors. It threw emphasis onto musical quality rather than image quality; although image size was variable, print quality was relatively consistent across cinemas, certainly more so than the quality of live musical accompaniment could vary widely from single pianist to full orchestra. Some reproducers, such as the Phonovox, were marketed specifically for these smaller exhibitors.[10]

Between the two turntables was a control panel which allowed the operator to adjust the volume control of either turntable and, by using a toggle control, to either switch between the two during changeovers or, by keeping it in the middle position, to mix the audio from the two turntables together. Thus the operator was offered a range of audio-effect options, and a great deal of ingenuity was required to maximise the impact of the machine.

Musical Interludes

Electrical reproducers, in their single-deck format, were initially intended to be used to provide interval music in British cinemas; to replace the orchestra for economic reasons, or simply to give them a rest from playing incidental music between screenings so they could concentrate on providing quality accompaniment for the film itself:

> When, four or five months ago, the Panatrope was put on the market, it was sold purely and simply as an 'added attraction', something that could be used as an interlude between pictures. Even British-Brunswick, the company that handles the machine, did not look upon it as suitable for accompanying pictures. They were content to put it out as a novelty and leave it at that.[11]

This was partly a consequence of increasingly longer screening days, Sunday showings, and so on, all of which put an additional physical burden upon the live musicians.[12] Part of the 'added attraction' for the audience was that they would be able to listen to the world's leading orchestras, rather than the far more modest local bands, as well as to a far wider range of instruments than any smaller orchestra could hope to offer: 'The exhibitor who has installed an electrical reproduction machine can put before his audience the whole world of music . . . his interludes may now include music which previously would have been beyond the reach of the average picture patron, thanks to the enterprise of the various recording companies.'[13]

But this attraction brought with it certain problems, namely the difficulty of keeping up with popular music tastes. 'Expenditure on operatic, symphonic or effects records should be reasonably low after the first few outlays; single additions to the library need only be made now and again; but the man who wishes to really please his audience must be able to produce good recordings of popular jazz numbers.'[14] Classical music was not a problem; once a library of classical titles had been built, its perpetual appeal made it easy to maintain. Popular music, by its very nature, had a much shorter shelf-life because, although a record could sell in large numbers very quickly, its short-lived appeal meant that, as quickly, the discs became virtually redundant. Moreover, records wore out with repeated playings, making ownership an unattractive option for cinemas. As a result, rental and cheap sales companies grew to cater for the need for rapid turnaround in popular music titles, much in the manner of early film exchanges in the early 1900s.[15]

A more specialised 'pre-screening' use of reproduced music was to provide themed prologue entertainment, again usually replacing the live acts which had previously been responsible for this aspect of the evening's entertainment:

> In a picture such as *The Clown* [William Craft 1927] or *He Who Gets Slapped* [Victor Sjostrom 1924], an excellent prologue is available in *The Prologue to Pagaliacci*. Most of the gramophone companies have made a vocal record of this number, and it is, considering the great number of pictures it can be used with, well worth getting.[16]

A further extension of this idea of the prologue took the form of records of spoken text, which set the scene, or in some way provided a context, for the film to come: 'As an example, at the Tivoli recently the film *Trail of '98* [Clarence Brown 1929] was preceded by a prologue expressing the theme of the picture, the record having previously been made by a well-known elecutionist.'[17]

The high quality of reproduction, made possible by the use of gramophone records revolving at 78 rpm (rather than the Vitaphone's slower 33.3 rpm), was emphasised in all reports:

It says a great deal for the artistic and technical excellence of the music rendered by electrical reproducers that they have been found to be a success in all classes of halls – and even in communities where there might be expected to exist some prejudice against mechanical music, they have been most popular.[18]

This high quality helped set a benchmark for the quality of reproduced sound, against which film systems would have to be compared. Britain was lucky in this sense, because the time lag before Britain began receiving Western Electric (WE) and RCA systems enabled those companies to improve their apparatus to a point where lack of surface noise and wide frequency range had become a feature of the systems.

By late October 1927, adverts for Panatrope operators were regularly appearing in local papers. As *Kine Weekly* noted, 'It is quite a common thing to see advertisements in the Leeds papers asking for expert Panatrope operators. "Panatrope operator" is a new profession which offers a good salary to suitable people.'[19]

The infiltration of electrical reproducers into British cinemas was so successful that they soon became attractions in themselves. Cinemas began opening earlier than the stated screening time, simply to allow their audiences to attend special recitation sessions: 'The musical trade and the Press had an opportunity of hearing a Panatrope recital the other night at the Philharmonic Hall, and, to a certain extent, of gauging the possibilities of the instrument as a solo entertainer.'[20]

> The electrical reproducer can be used as a 'turn' in itself. An effect somewhat of this kind was recently introduced at the Coliseum, and was very successful. There, the song *On With the Motley* (Pagliacci), sung by Caruso, and reproduced by an electrical reproducer, was introduced into the selection by the orchestra, which continued to play the accompaniment to the song. It does not require great ingenuity to imagine variations of this idea, which can be introduced into the programme.[21]

This mixture of the live and the recorded not only created a unique entertainment form, possible only since the advent of electrical recording, but also indicated the creative possibilities of multi-layered, multi-source musical 'mixing': live and non-repeatable in this instance but soon to be absorbed into the industry through the development of electronic mixing equipment. Public interest in the reproducer even furnished idiosyncratic versions such as the 'Phantom Orchestra', in which an electrical reproducer was connected to actual musical instruments:

> Briefly described, the Phantom Orchestra consists of the usual form of electrical reproduction apparatus, amplifiers, etc. but instead of the ordinary loudspeakers, a series of reproduction units are attached to actual instruments, in the case of brass and woodwind the mouthpiece is removed and the unit substituted. For stringed instruments, the unit is located inside the body, the idea being that the gramophone record is reproduced over precisely similar instruments which were used in the making of the records, thereby producing natural characteristics of the instruments themselves.[22]

Such a Heath Robinson set-up, involving a number of individual reproducers all of which required a separate operator, clearly made the Phantom Orchestra impractical as anything other than a novelty act. It did, however, indicate the general interest being generated by reproducers: musical and film exhibition practitioners being continually inspired to find new uses and new adaptations for them as public attractions.

Musical Accompaniment

The use of reproducers to accompany films began in the north of England, specifically in Yorkshire, during the summer of 1927, expanding into Lancashire by January 1928 and down into the south – Welwyn Garden City – by February 1928.[23] There is evidence that Scottish exhibitors were similarly interested in developing their use.[24] In June 1927, *Kine Weekly*'s column, 'The Observation Window' had offered a prediction as to the consequences of the possible use of mechanised music in cinemas:

> Adequate musical accompaniment is not provided merely by selecting a record or records suitable to the theme of the picture, and leaving it to the discretion of an operator to manipulate. Properly prepared records will have to be made, specially fitted to the ever-changing themes of the picture, and run synchronously with the screening of the film. Unless the management can afford to offend the musical sensibilities of his patrons he will be exceedingly foolish to engage upon such a haphazard manner of picture accompaniment. Although I understand the question of specially arranged musical fittings is now being considered by the Panatrope people, until the records are ready it would be well if exhibitors were carefully to consider the question of the substitution of their orchestras.[25]

Significantly, directly beneath this report was a second, regarding the possibility of British exhibitors obtaining Vitaphone equipment from America:

> The announcement of the formation in England of the Vitaphone Company has led some people to imagine that this instrument will shortly be seen and heard on this side. This is not the case, as the American factories are working to full capacity to supply the home demand, and it will be many months before the Vitaphone will reach these shores. The owners of the mechanical patents have registered the name in England to prevent their claim being jumped.[26]

This difficulty in obtaining American equipment, at least in the short term, was to prove a – possibly the – major incentive to the development of electrical reproducers to provide soundtracks for the first sound films appearing from the middle of 1927 onwards. Even by mid-1928, the American systems were almost impossible to obtain:

> The success at the New Gallery of the Movietone, which, by the way, has the sound record photographed on the side of the film, has led many exhibitors to inquire when this system will be available elsewhere. It is understood, however, there is little likelihood of an early general release for Movietone.[27]

Diffusion and take-up of electrical reproducers was rapid, as *Kine Weekly* recorded as it took place:

> It is barely six months ago since mechanised music invaded the kinema, and it would have been a bold man who then would have declared that within a short space of time pictures would have been fitted to gramophone music. This I am assured by Dudley A. Bott is the case. He tells me that over 50 kinemas have actually dispensed with their orchestras, which have been supplanted by the Panatrope.[28] At the very least, there must now be about 1200 kinemas equipped with electrical reproducing apparatus, a remarkable number, considering that it is just over a year ago since the first complete machine of this type was installed in a kinema.[29]

The obvious object of this use of reproducers was, as with their use as musical interludes, to either rest the live orchestra,[30] and, increasingly, to dispense with them entirely, thereby saving on the costs of both orchestras and specialist accompanists.[31] Inevitably, such developments antagonised both British and American music unions, who fought against the erosion of their workforce by mechanical substitutes, seemingly to little effect.[32] In this last respect, the mounting unemployment of British cinema musicians caused by increasing use of reproducers mirrored the impact of Vitaphone or RCA Photophone synchronous sound equipment on the American musicians which was occurring at the same time. For both sets of workers, although resistance was initially quite aggressive, there was a mounting feeling of inevitability as the mechanical sound equipment was installed in ever-increasing numbers of cinemas.

Ironically, having been put out of work, many musicians were then re-employed to operate the reproducers. Indeed, their musical skills were seen as essential to the correct operation of the machines:

> The *Theatre de Luxe* management have realised that unless the machine is intelligently handled, results will be bad and so they have engaged a lady pianist who has had a great deal of experience of playing to pictures, and they have paid her a good salary.[33]

An added advantage of hiring musicians to operate the reproducers was that if for any reason the reproducer failed, the musician could always resort to accompanying the film on a piano.

The shift from live to recorded accompaniment was gradual. In the short term, film accompaniment often involved a mix of live and recorded music; of live orchestra, augmented or supplemented by records: '[u]ndoubtedly the incursion of the human orchestra produced a break from that deadly monotonous tone colour of the robot accompaniment, and what is vastly more important, it lent added realism to the scenes accompanied.'[34]

A final consequence of the move to using the reproducers to accompany the films themselves, and the consequent sacking of in-house orchestras and their musical directors, was the generation of a support industry of specialist companies who offered to take the effort of musical selection away from the cinema managers:

> Handel and Company, a London firm, has been formed with this object. An exhibitor who is playing, let us say, *The Flag Lieutenant* [Maurice Elvey 1926] sends along the musical suggestions to Handel and Co., who then attend to the picking of suitable records and supply a complete set for the film.[35]

Other companies, for example the International Talking Picture Musical Service, offered to arrange the recording of special musical scores for specific films onto gramophone records or any disc system, thus avoiding the potential copyright problems inherent in using famous commercially available recordings.[36] Some film companies, such as Butcher's (manufacturers of the Electrocord reproducer) began, as late as July 1929, to offer the services themselves, in an attempt to maintain control and quality standards over the accompaniment to the films they released:

> In connection with the release of their dramatic picture *Shadowed* [1929], Butcher's Film Service has prepared a special list of musical suggestions for gramophone record synchronisation to be used on Panatrope or similar amplifying apparatus with two or more turntables.
>
> The list follows the usual method of directors' cue sheets, three records having been selected for the three main themes, and others suggested for incidental passages. In certain cases where two melodies are on the same record, both have been employed at various stages in the picture. Special care has also been taken to avoid unnecessary changing of records.
>
> The innovation has received a warm welcome from exhibitors, and numerous letters have already been received expressing hearty appreciation of the idea and asking for similar lists of suggestions for all features booked.[37]

Whether the selection of music was made in-house or by external services, whole pieces of music were seldom used. Rather, specific sections of musical works were identified and combined with numerous others to produce the composite musical accompaniment. This required that the specified sections of records be physically marked up:

> If a few bars of a certain melody are required and the melody happens to occur in the middle of a record, the record is played through at the rehearsal and when the needle comes to the melody required, a chalk mark is made, so that at the evening performance the operator can find the exact spot where the melody begins without any difficulty.[38]

The skill and intensity required to construct such a composite musical soundtrack 'live' at the moment of screening in this account by a prominent operator in his description of the basic operation:

> Anticipating the change-over of records, with my eyes on the screen, left hand on volume controller and right hand on tone arm over record not in use, both records in position and revolving, new needle in. I reduce volume to a whisper, lower tone arm to allow of needle gently

falling on next record and with right hand now freed reverse change-
over switch, directly musical phrase being played is finished.

As soon as [a] new record is playing I gradually increase volume to
the required strength at the same time my right hand lifts the tone arm
from the record just finished. I then immediately take off the used
record and place it on my left. Now I take up a new record on right and
place it in empty plate. I then replace used needle and am ready to
continue above process. It is essential for the operator to make the
above operation a habit, so that his gaze is concentrated on the screen,
and his control of intensity of sound uninterfered with.[39]

The separately controlled twin turntable set-up offered by the reproducers enabled operators to perform very subtle and complex sound
control. It enabled them, for example, to reduce or increase the volume
of the music according to the demands of the scene:

I reduce or amplify sound according to the action on the screen. For
instance, suppose the sequence is of persons fox-trotting, the Panatrope is played at full volume. As lovers leave ballroom for balcony, the
volume reduced *pp*. When they return to ballroom volume *ff*. Now as
to mysterious situations. Note burglars do not wear hobnailed boots.
They creep about in carpet slippers, hence very softly, please. Again,
during situations of gossip and all conversational modes, *pp*., please.
Dramatic climaxes can be intensified by cutting off the music to a dead
silence. The situation should be worked up to *ff*., and then at the
climax of the situation cut off dead. This influences the tense atmosphere peculiarly appropriate to the situation.[40]

This elementary form of soundtrack control obviously has precedents
in the similar level control executed by the conductors and live
orchestras sensitive to the demands of silent screen drama. The
difference lay in the ability to mix separate musical sources, such
that one could overlay the other, whereas with 'live' orchestral
accompaniment, the entire soundscape emanated from the same
source; it could raise or lower its volume level, but could not,
obviously, overlay itself upon itself. In contrast, the primitiveness
of the early American sound systems prevented the construction of
complex multi-layered soundtracks without the degradation of quality
caused by dubbing. It could therefore be said that the soundtracks
created using electrical reproducers were in some ways more sophisticated than the sparser soundtracks accompanying the more 'desirable' American sound films. It might also not be too fanciful to
speculate that the development of complex multi-layered soundtracks

in the mid-1930s have their genesis, conceptually at least, in these early experiments.

The growth in use of reproducers for musically accompanying films prompted a range of advice columns to appear in the British trade press. *The Bioscope* began a monthly feature, designed to operate as a nexus point through which exhibitors might exchange information and ideas as to how best to use reproducers in their cinemas:

> The use of gramophone records for supplying not only musical accompaniments but also sound effects in conjunction with the presentation of pictures is now playing such an important part in the equipment of many cinemas that, as announced in a recent issue, we are instituting a section to deal with the subject. That it is one which will be of interest to a large number of readers there can be little doubt, since the number of instruments for the reproduction and amplification of gramophone records already installed in cinemas must approximate to a thousand (we believe that one type of instrument alone is fitted in over 700 cinemas).
>
> We wish to make this section of value to users of these devices, and its success in this respect must depend very largely upon the support we receive from exhibitors. Let us, and our readers, know how you have installed it, where are placed the loudspeakers, who operates it, what controls are employed, for what purpose it is used, how does it result, what troubles have you had and how have you overcome them, what records do you find useful and suitable.[41]

Similarly, *Kinematograph Weekly* began running a 'Mechanised Music' column from late October 1927, in which the new phenomenon of the cinema reproducer was to be regularly discussed: 'Owing . . . to the ever-spreading use of the Panatrope and similar instruments arrangements have been made for an expert to contribute a series of articles dealing with every phase of this important subject, including criticism, suitable records and the installation and adaptation of apparatus.'[42] As late as April 1929, *Kine Weekly* began a record review column: 'In response to requests from many exhibitors who have installed electrical reproducers, we are giving in this weekly column particulars of records suitable for intermissions or film accompaniment.'[43] For example, the review column on the 4 July 1929 noted that in Rimsky-Korsakov's *Capriccio Espagñol*, 'sections of this number can be effectively used for film fittings', while two modern numbers 'both lend themselves to film adaptation, especially in church interior scenes or any religious episode or tone colour.'[44]

Music and Effects

In the coming year at least, the way forward for sound films – as music-and-effects soundtracks – was figured by the release of *Don Juan* in August 1926. The replication of this format on reproducers might have been seen as a problem – commercial record releases did not cover effects; there was obviously no public demand for them. But such was the widespread importance of reproducers for creating 'live' music-and-effects soundtracks in British cinemas that effects records were produced from very early on. In early December 1927, *Kine Weekly* reported that:

> A new use to which the electrical reproduction is being put is that of effects machine. British-Brunswick is working upon a series of special records which make it possible to reproduce any type kind [sic] of effect. Instead of engaging a crowd to murmur during the mob scenes, it is now only necessary to switch on a special record of a mob. Cheering crowds, trains, aeroplanes, storms, wind, and dozens of other noises can now be reproduced without difficulty . . . As an effects machine the instrument obviously has very great possibilities. Already the Trade has had an opportunity of hearing the effects as the foreground noises in *The Ring* [Alfred Hitchcock 1927] were reproduced by this means.[45]

Columbia also produced a special set of effects discs made in ten-inch or twelve-inch format, which was used for their presentation of *Chang* (Ernest Schoedsack 1927). A report in *Kine Weekly*'s 'Observation Window' of mid-September 1927 noted that:

> An innovation which promises to be the precursor to a new era in film effects was introduced at the Plaza at the premiere of *Chang*, a picture of native pioneers in the Siamese jungle. It is in effect animal cries recorded in [sic] the gramophone and reproduced through an Amplion loud-speaker so that one hears as nearly accurately as possible the noises common to the environment . . .
>
> So far as this interesting experiment went, it was undoubtedly successful, although at the first night showing there was a tendency on the part of the orchestra to overwhelm the 'effects'. This, however, was adjusted subsequently, and when I looked in at the Plaza on Monday night the animal accompaniment proved not the least successful portion of the programme.[46]

Adverts appearing in *Kine Weekly* during February 1928, announced the use of both music and effects discs for the presentation of *Sunrise*

(F. W. Murnau 1927) at Marble Arch Pavilion, London, in which the Panatrope 'supplies the Storm, Bells, Jazz Band, Fair Ground and Organ Effects.'[47] In a further development, the British Phototone Company recorded the entire musical score and effects of *Wings* (William Wellman 1927) on to a set of discs:

> It will be especially interesting to exhibitors to note that the use of synchronised sound with *Wings* is now to be carried a stage further by the decision of the British Phototone Company to record the entire musical score of the picture for the Panatrope. This will mean that in every theatre in the country, including the smaller halls where a large orchestra is not practicable, it will be possible to present *Wings* with the same musical setting and effects as are at present being used for the successful Carleton Theatre run.[48]

The ultimate aim of British Phototone, the company which marketed the Panatrope in Britain, was to make arrangements 'for the recording of complete musical accompaniment to all feature films. On the basis of a six-reel feature the cost of the accompaniment and effects will only work out to about 30 [shillings], for each record, which will cost 5 [shillings], and will synchronise with a reel of film.'[49] In reality, the speed of development of both electrical reproducers and 'official' synchronised systems was such that this aim could not be realised.

The ability of reproducers to build such effective and complex music-and-effects soundtracks lay in their design; specifically in the variable switch controls which allowed the output from each turntable to be played separately or merged together if the switches were positioned in more central positions. As *Kine Weekly* reported in mid-November 1927:

> Novel and effective results where 'effects' records are necessary to screen situation can be got by careful and gentle handling of the change-over switch. On one table a heavy *agitato* movement is playing, an 'effects' record for an exciting fire scene is in readiness on the other table. Drop the tone arm on to this record, then, by gently moving the switch to the *exact* centre position, you have the heavy *agitato* music being played on one table and the bells and whistles and calls from the 'effects' record on the other table *at the same time*.[50]

The *Wings* presentation, 'the first really comprehensive demonstration of sound-synchronised pictures that has been systematically brought to the notice of the Film Trade in every part of the country', resulted in increased sales of reproducers in general and the Panatrope in particular.[51]

Later models of reproducer, employing three or even four turntables, such as The Sonotone and Magnatone, allowed operators to construct even more complex soundtracks, involving a flexible combination of music and effects tracks. As late as August 1929, new versions of reproducers were being put on market. The revamped Ethatrope, for example, which had separate fade-out controls (to avoid clicks as the pick-up was raised from, or lowered on to, the disc), and control of diminuendo and *crescendo* (to further the illusion of a real orchestra), was designed to allow

> The provision of superimposing 'effects', the volume of which is independently controlled, is an asset of value, especially as the MPA [Motion Picture Association of America] themselves are prepared to supply these special records. The success of the Ethatrope is such that demand at present is even greater than the supply, and fully bears out the words I felt compelled to use when I reviewed the first model, viz., 'that the machine was likely to cause a small revolution in the reproducer market'.[52]

Synchronised 'Talkies'

The move from using reproducers to provide music-and-effects soundtracks to providing synchronised music, effects and singing/dialogue soundtracks was gradual and involved several stages. Initially they acted simply as additional amplifying systems for talking pictures appearing from America in the few British cinemas rigged up with RCA or WE systems: 'British-Brunswick, who have made during the last year something like 800 installations of the "Panatrope", which, in addition to its use as an electrical reproducer of gramophone records, constitutes in itself a complete amplifying unit suitable for synchronised sound-pictures.'[53]

From late June 1928, reproducers were being seen as a means of providing some kind of voice-synchronised soundtrack to films. As I have noted above, at first this was for shorts only, to provide the music and singing voice. Certainly, the use of reproducers to provide musical interlude and screening accompaniment in American cinemas remained a reality until at least the end of 1927: 'The Robert Morton Organ Co. has arranged to take over exclusive distribution of the magnolia, a mechanical instrument playing records and designed for theatres. This instrument is primarily intended to furnish musical accompaniment in the smaller picture theatres, although it is adaptable to any size house.'[54] But their use in American cinemas was nowhere near as far reaching or as successful as in Britain, largely because by the time they had become a viable option, the possibility of acquiring the 'real thing' – Vitaphone equipment – was becoming a real enough possibility to persuade exhibitors to hang back and wait; it was simply uneconomical to invest in even a relatively inexpensive electrical reproducer system when it would have to be replaced a couple of months later by an extremely expensive 'legitimate' synch-sound system.

As early as the end of April 1928 – that is, several months before the film opened in Britain – *Kine Weekly* was arguing that commercially available records could be used to provide the voice for the songs in *The Jazz Singer*: 'In *The Jazz Singer*, Al Jolson sings a song called *Mother of Mine, I Still Love You*. This record has been made by Jolson for Brunswick, so that the exhibitors can not only let their patrons see America's leading jazz singer, but they can also hear him.'[55] In February 1929, *Kine Weekly* was reporting that:

> The recent experiment at the New Palladium Cinema, Shepherd's Bush, in which the silent version of *The Jazz Singer* was given, accompanied by Celebritone rendition of the appropriate songs, has been watched by other exhibitors with great interest. The fact of its undoubted success has encouraged another exhibitor, the manager of the Grand Palace Poplar, to give the same performance on his Celebritone installation. It is to be anticipated that other owners of electrical reproducers will follow this lead which has proved so eminently successful![56]

But this use of reproducers to provide manually synched records of the songs from the film had to compete with a fairly common use of live singers to do the same. An entry in *Kine Weekly* of 7 March 1929 reported that:

> The extraordinary publicity which has been given to Al Jolson in recent times assured E. B. Dickenson of the Majestic, Leeds, of heavy demands for seats during the screening of *The Jazz Singer* which was preceded by a splendid vocal presentation, while the orchestral setting was exceedingly well done. S. Ehrlich rendered *Kol Nidre* twice during each screening in an appealing manner, and in singing *Mammy*, Harry Rosebourne, the musical director, demonstrated his versatility. His rendition of the famous Jolson hit came as a pleasant surprise to the audience.[57]

Other accounts described Dennis Allison, 'the well-known Yorkshire baritone', performing a prologue, consisting of a scene from the film, and then singing along to the song sequences in *The Jazz Singer* at Sheffield Picture Palace,[58] and also at Rotherham, where a report ironically entitled 'Jolson at Rotherham' described an event at which live and recorded renditions were combined when a Jolson impersonator took to the streets to drum up interest in the film being shown at the cinema, and then 'manipulated a powerful gramophone at the entrance to the kinema, and every recorded song by Al Jolson was played.'[59]

The framing of the arrival of true 'talkies' (as opposed to music-and-effects films) in terms of American advantage/British disadvantage and the necessity of finding an alternative to the absent American sound systems pinpoints the central usefulness of the use of electrical reproducers in providing such soundtracks. If the British could not have the actual music, effects and singing/talking soundtracks, they would construct their own substitutes.

Interestingly, and perhaps significantly, the voice on the record need not necessarily be that of the artist on screen; a point which, again, the review columns frequently noted: '*The Singing Fool* selection, featured by Debroy Somers' Band, with vocal chorus by George Dewey Washington, contains all the favourite melodies *used in the synchronisation* of this popular film' [emphasis mine].[60] Although not explicitly stating that these records were used on reproducers to simulate the Vitaphone synchronised song sequences, the insinuation that they could be was fairly clear. In an extension of this phenomenon, special recordings were made to allow the real voices of on-screen performers to be replaced by others. A curious experiment took place in early January 1929 at the Theatre de Luxe, Leeds

> by Electrocord [when] one of their artistes, Mary O'Hara, sang *My Blue Heaven* in view of the audience. Then came the sound film. The voice was different, and a moment or two sufficed to identify the record as that of Gracie Fields. Yet to all intents and purposes it was Miss O'Hara singing from the screen.[61]

The lip-synch, while not perfect, was good enough not only to fool the audience for a while before they realised the mismatch, but also to continue being satisfactory once they had done so (one wonders if they would have noticed if they hadn't heard Mary O'Hara's real voice moments before).

Conclusion

Electrical reproducers grew to be a vital part of the early sound exhibition arena in Britain because they were both familiar and multi-tasking. Their familiarity – by the late 1920s, almost everyone had a gramophone player and was used to hearing the sound of mechanically reproduced music and singing – meant that their take-up and employment in cinemas was not perceived to be a radical move; a smoothness partly aided by their cheapness and ubiquity. Their multi-tasking – providing background music in other parts of the cinema, public announcements, interlude music, musical accompaniment to the films themselves, combination music and effects and, finally, fully synchronous sound – gave their owners great economies of usage.

All of this could be accomplished by employing one person in place of the many required to form an orchestra and vocalists, or 'perform' live effects. This use of the same machine for several tasks was a product of the non-linear nature of late-silent and early-sound films. Even once fully synchronised dialogue films had appeared, there was a considerable time-lag until silent films, requiring just musical and effects accompaniment, finally disappeared.

During that time-span, the electrical reproducer was found to be an ideal instrument for catering to various British exhibition needs, capitalising upon an intensified culture of aurality which had been in evidence since the emergence of electrically recorded-music in the mid-1920s. Economic common sense – the distribution of Hollywood sound films on a global scale – dictated that they were inevitably to be superseded by 'official' American synchronous sound equipment. But in that brief two-year hiatus between 1917–29, when those American systems were impossible to procure, the electrical reproducer offered a more than satisfactory substitute.

Electrical reproducers appeared as a specialist outcrop of the gramophone industry, an industry which, after a period of massive economic growth and success in the late 1910s, had fallen on increasingly hard times during the 1920s. An unexpected interest in new gramophone equipment from the film industry was a much-needed fillip to this ailing industry, even if it meant the development of new, hybrid machines with multiple turntables. The symbiosis between the two industries continued to develop, with record companies working alongside film studios to produce special sets of discs to accompany specific films, and support companies appearing to offer advice and a range of selection and organisational services.

The effect of the electrical reproducer on the British cinema exhibition field in the late 1920s was therefore multiple and profound. It changed the presentation of music within cinema auditoria from 'live' to 'recorded'; it introduced audiences to the phenomenon of films accompanied first by recorded music *and* effects and then by synchronised music, singing and even dialogue; and it fostered a wide range of support industries which would continue, albeit in modified form, even with the arrival of American synch-sound equipment. The use of electrical reproducers in this way was, I think, unique to Britain and, as such, provides a significant addition to the history of the coming of sound in this country.

Notes

1. On 15 August [1925], there was a news story in the *Talking Machine World* which said that the Panatrope would be demonstrated to the trade around 15 September. An advertisement on 15 September spoke of the instrument as having 'magnetic' reproduction, although Dr Kellog, who made important contributions to the dynamic speaker, does not think that they ever made extensive commercial use of the magnetic type.

   An advertisement in the 15 October issue of *The Talking Machine World* said that they were getting ready to feature the Panatrope and that the rest of the Brunswick line would be dropped. On 15 November, two weeks after the Orthophonic Victriola had been introduced, they advertised that the Panatrope was the first, and only, purely electric reproducer. On 15 February 1926, their monthly advertisement in *The Talking Machine World* said that more than 1 million people had heard the Panatrope in the past sixty days. On 15 March, they increased the total to 2 million. They also featured 'amazing music' by Brunswick light-ray recording. On 15 April, they announced three new phonographs (evidently reinstated to meet competition with Victor's low priced Orthophonic models).

   The first Brunswick advertisement in the Post did not appear until 11 September, 1926. It was a double-page spread and featured Brunswick Records. On 9 October, 1926, their advertisement in the Post said that the Panatrope had been demonstrated in New York just before Christmas 1925, and had been heard by 4 million (Fagan and Moran 1983: 95).
2. Anon., *Kinematograph Weekly*, 15 September 1927, p. 86.
3. W. H. Sayers, 'Electrical reproducers: Their installation, use and maintenance', *Kinematograph Weekly*, 31 January 1929, p. 23.
4. Anon. *Variety*, 17 November 1926, p. 9.
5. H. Hutchison, 'Electrical reproduction: How the advent of 'mechanised music' has revolutionised film accompaniment in the kinema', *Kinematograph Weekly*, 26 April 1928, p. 31.
6. A. L. Carter, 'The observation window: British kinema', *Kinematograph Weekly*, 29 December 1927, p. 35.

7. For example, the three-table Musikon, marketed as late as May 1929; an unnamed model designed specifically to accompany silent films with music and effects, in July 1929, which had four, and the improved Ethatrope, unveiled in late August 1929, which offered either two or four turntable models.

8. Carter, op.cit., p. 35.

9. Anon., 'Mechanised recitals: reproducers supercede orchestras', *Kinematograph Weekly*, 9 February 1928, p. 85.

10. Anon., 'The phonovox: providing good music for the small theatre', *Kinematograph Weekly*, 1 November 1928, p. 71.

11. Anon., 'Mechanised music: The new picture fitting', *Kinematograph Weekly*, 20 October 1927, p. 66.

12. 'Discussing the subject recently with a musical director of one of the important London kinemas, he said: 'Is it fair to expect any man or even superman to bear the strain imposed upon him by his conditions of work?' The previous week's work had consisted of supervising two orchestras, conducting the larger one and fitting for both.
    Sunday: two films, one for each orchestra, and vocalist to accompany.
    Monday: Two whole programmes, consisting of two star films, comedy, gazette, etc., and vocalist or variety acts to rehearse.
    Thursday: Complete change of programme.
    Saturday: Special matinee, with notice of names of films given late Friday night and no opportunity of viewing same.
    The orchestra on Sunday consists of an entirely different set of musicians.
        Later – seen as not necessarily as cheap as first seemed:
        Then there is the question of electrical reproducers. Their use is increasing, and is certain to affect the smaller halls in the provinces and even in the outer London suburbs; in fact, it *is* doing so now.
        This, in spite of the fact that to get a really first-class machine costs anything from £200 to £300, and the first is not by any means the last cost. The expense of hiring or purchasing suitable records for the complete programme is a very considerable item, and two operators, one an experienced musician to fit the films by the records, as he would have done with the orchestral music, will add very appreciably to the expense.' *Kinematograph Weekly*, 13 December 1928, p. 95.

13. Anon., 'Gramophone records: interesting new issues', *Kinematograph Weekly*, 16 February 1928, p. 81.

14. Anon., 'Up-to-date: records for reproducers', *Kinematograph Weekly*, 22 March 1928, p. 81.

15. Ibid., which describes, for example, the Crystalate Manufacturing Company.

16. Anon., 'Mechanised music: electrical reproducers – novel uses and some suggestions', *Kinematograph Weekly*, 8 December 1927, p. 79.

17. W. H. Sayers, 'Electrical reproducers: their installation, use and maintenance', *Kinematograph Weekly*, 31 January 1929, p. 23.

18. Anon., 'Mechanised recitals: reproducers supercede orchestras', *Kinematograph Weekly*, 9 February 1928, p. 85.

19. Anon., 'Mechanised music: the new picture fitting', *Kinematograph Weekly*, 20 October 1927, p. 66.

20. Anon., 'Mechanised recitals: reproducers supercede orchestras', *Kinematograph Weekly*, 9 February 1928, p. 85.

21. W. H. Sayers, 'Electrical reproducers: their installation, use and maintenance', *Kinematograph Weekly*, 31 January 1929, p. 23.

22. Anon., 'Two electrical reproducers', *Kinematograph Weekly*, 30 May 1929, p. 57.

23. 'It was left to Yorkshire to make the first experiments with the Panatrope as an orchestra. First of all it was tried out as a relief orchestra and so successful was the experiment that it was then used to accompany the whole performance. The Theatre de Luxe, Leeds, has for many months now been accompanying all its pictures to music supplied by the Panatrope only, and as a result of the success of this experiment over twenty-five kinemas in Yorkshire have dispensed with their orchestras in favour of the Panatrope. Yorkshire has turned the machine from a luxury into a necessity.' Anon., 'Mechanised music: the new picture fitting', *Kinematograph Weekly*, 20 October 1927, p. 66.

24. 'One of the latest gramophone recording instruments is "The Magnatone", which in a recent demonstration at the Regent, Glasgow, has proved its undoubted merits for picture theatre work . . . Several installations have been carried out in Scotland and one exhibitor at Baillieston declares it has increased business by 10 per cent.' *Kinematograph Weekly*, 10 November 1927, p. 84.

25. Anon., 'The observation window: mechanised music', *Kinematograph Weekly*, 30 June 1927, p. 77.

26. Ibid.

27. Anon., 'The observation window: service, *Kinematograph Weekly*, 17 May 1928, p. 65.

28. Anon., 'The observation window: prosperity', *Kinematograph Weekly*, 29 September 1927, p. 87.

29. H. Hutchison, 'Electrical reproduction: how the advent of "mechanised music" has revolutionised film accompaniment in the kinema', Supplement to *Kinematograph Weekly*, 26 April 1928, p. 31.

30. A report in *Kinematograph Weekly* as late as May 1929 noted that 'A few weeks ago a feature film at the Theatre Royal, Manchester, was accompanied by Celebritone whilst the orchestra rested, and this was repeated throughout the week. This instrument entirely fulfilled its task, and its rendition met with unstinted praise from musical critics.' *Kinematograph Weekly*, 2 May 1929, p. 19.

31. 'An instance of the great help these machines can be for prologue work can be found in *The Volga Boatman* [Cecil B. DeMille 1926]. Here it was practically essential that a company of male singers be engaged during the showing of the film, but those exhibitors who were fortunate enough to possess an electrical reproducing instrument such as the Panatrope, Reprovox or similar instrument were saved the expense of booking a quartette [sic] and instead simply bought a 4s 6d, gramophone record, which was switched on whenever the boatmen were shown on the screen. Kinematograph Weekly, 6 December 1927, p. 79.

32. '. . . the musicians' unions . . . have launched a drive to eliminate all forms of mechanical music from the theatres. This move is directed against the use of mechanical organs and what is termed 'phonograph' music. While it is possible to sympathise with the musicians displaced, it seems difficult to understand how they hope to prevent the inevitable march of progress.' A. L. Carter, *Kinematograph Weekly*, 14 June 1928.

33. Anon., 'Mechanised music: the new picture fitting', *Kinematograph Weekly*, 20 October 1927, p. 66.

34. A. W. Owen, 'A "Regal" innovation: the talkie and the human orchestra', Kinematograph Weekly, 20 June 1929, p. 65.

35. Anon., 'Mechanised music: the new picture fitting', *Kinematograph Weekly*, 20 October 1927, p. 66.

36. Anon., 'Musical service: synchronising silent films', *Kinematograph Weekly*, 18 July 1929, p. 34.

37. Anon., 'Butcher's service: gramophone record synchronisation', *Kinematograph Weekly*, 25 July 1929, p. 67.
38. Anon., 'Mechanised music: the new picture fitting', *Kinematograph Weekly*, 20 October 1927, p. 66.
39. Reginald Jonson, 'Fitting gramophone records: how the Panatrope accompanies the film', *Kinematograph Weekly*, 10 November 1927, p. 81.
40. Ibid.
41. Anon., 'Mechanised music', *The Bioscope Service Supplement*, 12 January 1928, p. x.
42. Anon., 'Mechanised music: the new picture fitting', *Kinematograph Weekly*, 20 October 1927, p. 66.
43. 'Discus', 'Records reviewed: our reproducer corner', *Kinematograph Weekly*, 11 April 1929, p. 67.
44. 'Discus', 'Records reviewed: suggestions for electrical reproducers', *Kinematograph Weekly*, 4 July 1929, p. 83.
45. Anon., 'Mechanised music: electrical reproducers – novel uses and some suggestions', *Kinematograph Weekly*, 8 December 1927, p. 79.
46. Anon., 'The observation window: celluloid factories', *Kinematograph Weekly*, 15 September 1927, p. 75.
47. *Kinematograph Weekly*, 2 February 1928, p. 66. A review of the presentation in *The Bioscope* was fulsome in its enthusiasm: 'The first real demonstration of the Panatrope as an effects machine is being given at the Marble Arch Pavilion during the run of the Fox Picture *Sunrise*. The Panatrope is introduced during the film as a jazz band, an organ, during the storm, and in the fairground scenes. Few people in the hall would believe that such a variety of sounds could be reproduced from a gramophone record. The storm is most realistic, the howling of the wind and the lashing of waves are almost terrifying in their realism. The organ solo during the wedding scenes is also most effective, and anyone who has attended the Marble Arch Pavilion will be ready to swear that a real organ is being used.

    To reproduce the fairground noises by any means other than the Panatrope would mean an army of men with squeakers, bells, hooters, trumpets, drums, and barrel organs. The Panatrope reproduces all this din from a twelve-inch record.

    The importance of this new Panatrope development cannot be over-estimated. It means that in future the smallest hall in the country can stage its pictures with effects identical to those used at the London presentations.

    Arrangements are being made for a trade show of the new Panatrope Effects Records. *The Bioscope Service Supplement*, 2 February 1928, p. xvi.
48. Anon., '*Wings* realism: To be released as sound film – Paramount's Phonotone tie-in', *Kinematograph Weekly*, 12 July 1928, p. 38. In a strange inversion of public interest in artificially reproduced effect, a performance of *Wings* was broadcast from the Criterion Theatre, New York to eager radio listeners, complete with 'a graphic oral description of the thrilling scenes of air fighting shown on the screen in 'Wings', with which were blended the appropriate noises of planes taking-off, in mid-air, machine guns in action and the eery [sic] mournful note given out by the wires of stricken machines descending in flames.' Here was a case of the music and effects created on the reproducer becoming the sole attraction, rather than simply providing accompaniment for the visuals. *The Bioscope*, 3 May 1928, p. 59.
49. H. A. Johnson, 'British Phototone: new sound-film demonstrated', *Kinematograph Weekly*, 28 June, 1928, p. 75.
50. Reginald Jonson, 'Fitting gramophone records: how the Panatrope accompanies the film', *Kinematograph Weekly*, 10 November 1927, p. 81.

51. 'Since the Trade showing of *Wings* was completed, over three hundred British kinemas have been equipped with the device known as the Panatrope (the actual system employed in the presentation of *Wings*) or similar instruments reproducing sound or musical effects by electrical means.' Anon., '*Wings* realism: to be released as sound film – Paramount's Phonotone tie-in', *Kinematograph Weekly*, 12 July 1928, p. 38.
52. A. W. Owen, 'The Ethatrope', *Kinematograph Weekly*, 22 August 1929, p. 59.
53. Anon., 'British activities: a brief survey of sound-film systems', Kinematograph Weekly, 7 June 1928, p. 33.
54. *Variety*, 28 December 1927, p. 47.
55. H. Hutchison, 'Electrical reproduction: how the advent of "mechanised music" has revolutionised film accompaniment in the kinema', Supplement to *Kinematograph Weekly*, 26 April 1928, p. 33.
56. Anon., 'Celebritone accompaniment', *Kinematograph Weekly*, 21 February 1929, p. 70.
57. Anon., 'Leeds boost for *Jazz Singer*', *Kinematograph Weekly*, 7 March 1929, p. 64.
58. Anon., 'Human "Talkies"', *Kinematograph Weekly*, 25 April 1929, p. 53.
59. Anon., 'Jolson at Rotherham', *Kinematograph Weekly*, 25 April 1929, p. 53.
60. 'Discus', 'Records reviewed', *Kinematograph Weekly*, 22 August 1929, p. 60.
61. Anon., 'More talkies: Electrocord demonstrated', *Kinematograph Weekly*, 17 January 1929, p. 75.

In another example of this 'dubbing' replacement of voices, a short film made using the Filmophone system, telling the story of an Italian singer who is eventually discovered when he is accidentally overheard singing, used a Caruso recording to provide the singer's voice (*Kinematograph Weekly*, 20 December 1928, p. 55). It is a tantalising thought that incidents such as these might have contributed to Hitchcock's solving his audio problem in *Blackmail* – namely that Anny Ondra's heavy Czech accent had to be dubbed 'live' by Joan Barry talking just off camera as Ondra acted out her scenes. This divorce of voice from person, at a time when recording limitations were supposedly heavily welding the two together, indicates an conceptual freedom in early sound cinema which might not be assumed to be an option.

Bibliography

Fagan, Ted and William R. Moran (1983) *The Encyclopaedic Discography of Victor Recordings*. Westport: Greenwood Press.
Gelatt, Roland (1956) *The Fabulous Phonograph: The Story of the Gramophone from Tin Foil to High Fidelity*. London: Cassell.
Low, Rachel (1971) *The History of the British Film, 1918–1929*. London: Allen and Unwin.
Murphy, Robert (1984) 'The coming of sound to the cinema in Britain'. *Historical Journal of Film, Radio and Television*, vol. 4, no. 2, October.
Whitcomb, Ian (1986) *After the Ball: A Chronicle of Pop Music from Ragtime to Rock*. London: Limelight.

Chapter 4

King Kong and Film on Music: Out of the Fog

Peter Franklin

It was disappointing that Lawrence Kramer's liberating 1995 quest for a 'post-modern knowledge' of classical music should venture no further than Ives and actually conclude its formal business with a cautionary word about mass-consumption in pre-First World War Paris. 'Purely imaginary' were its pleasures, he tells us, apparently rehearsing a standard critique of commodified popular entertainment. Even the references to Elvis in his epilogue (Kramer 1995: 229–40) send us back, if with deliberate ambivalence, to another dream: the dream of musical autonomy. Fearful of no contradiction, however, Kramer boldly interprets that dream as an ideological fiction whose job has been to bar access to the 'labyrinth of another voice' (Kramer 1995: 230) – the other voice of music itself. A lesson to be learnt here may be that the very category 'classical music' can bar access, as effectively as the gate in the great wall on Skull Island, to the labyrinth of some hitherto marginalised musical voices: like those that fill the fantasy world of mass consumption and pleasurable imaginings, the world where puppets masquerade as monsters (or is it the other way round?) and whose triumph RKO's *King Kong* helped to celebrate and seal in 1933.

Film music positioned itself from the start as being even further than Italian opera from the once culturally and historically specific category of the musically 'classical', with its instrumental bias and German accent. It did so by insisting on the practice of all that the ideology of autonomy ostensibly disallowed: narrating, 'representing', dispensing manipulative pleasure and so on. To what extent may it be reclaimed by musical scholarship as anything more than a site where jaded musicologists might play? Even Sir Harrison Birtwistle and Russell Hoban, for all their bold operatic allusion to the film,[1] signally distanced themselves from the first Mrs Kong, leaving her to swoon, scream and roll her eyes in the disreputable world of popular entertainment, where she apparently belongs.

But to say that is to stir the cauldron of gender trouble and invoke uncomfortable echoes of the original movie's script, where the threat posed by passionate, weak and yet demonstrative women is registered in lines like: 'This is no place for a girl like you! . . . Women can't help being a bother'. In the second chapter of *Classical Music and Postmodern Knowledge*, Kramer himself noted a strategy of the German musicologist Carl Dahlhaus, who in discussing Beethoven and Rossini, plays the game of historical objectivity only to slip back into the mode of casting Rossini 'as a hysteric, the feminised other of the imperious, manly Beethoven' (Kramer 1995: 47). Knowing what we do about the problems that arise when the discourses of music and gender intertwine (did they ever not?), and accepting post-modern criticism not only of gender-strategies in talk about classical music but also in attitudes towards popular culture and film in the era of high modernism – knowing all this, we might be inclined to turn back to that first Mrs Kong and the music which surrounds her. Could Max Steiner's seminal score have anything to tell us, if not about music in general, then about the specific perception of music inherited by a Viennese-Jewish émigré who had arrived in America in 1914? Might we even reclaim *King Kong* for a revised music history that figuratively spans that mysterious wall on Skull Island, the remnant (as Carl Denham authoritatively assures us in the movie) of an older, higher civilisation and built to keep out 'something they fear'?

It would be all too glib to suggest that that something is music. It is not. But this film, which so boldly and thematically flaunts its own strategy as mass-consumable entertainment, does have a good deal to tell us about music in its way. Writers on film-music such as Christopher Palmer, Kathryn Kalinak and, particularly, Claudia Gorbman have dwelt on the pioneering nature of its score, which Steiner himself and others plundered, both literally and figuratively, for innumerable later movies. The relative immaturity of sound film as a medium in 1933 makes the strategies and assurance of the score, like that of the sound effects and even the script on occasions, seem retrospectively all the more remarkable for their improvised and yet foundational quality. It is not just a matter of technology and techniques. As the film's opening section thematises the practices of a ruthless film-maker in securing his leading lady, rather as he secures his shots of monsters and curiosities in nature (before he 'cans' and ships them back to audiences in America), so the improvised and yet always telling practice of the scoring reveals much about music's meanings as cultural practice,[2] not least in the Vienna of Steiner's youth.

First it is a bravura display of portent and fury to accompany the main titles, presented against a nightmarishly shifting field of intersecting planes that resolve back into the initial, graphically stylised art-deco beam of a great searchlight. Opening rather like an orchestral version of Rachmaninov's famous *Prelude in C-sharp Minor*, it subsequently offers a phantasmagoric succession of ungrounded musical images whose model is the 'orgy' scene of some exotic late nineteenth-century opera or a post-Berliozian witches' sabbath of violently disparate activity and agitation. Finally it sinks into an antithetical, perhaps resolving calm (the opening three-note descent figure now lyrically 'transformed'); we imagine that it may presage the story's ultimate conclusion, like a nineteenth-century opera overture (*Der Freischütz*, *The Flying Dutchman*). It coincides with the fake Arabian proverb of the epigraph and the first images of the film: a tugboat in the foreground moves beneath a New York skyline before we cut to the shadowy quay alongside what is quickly designated 'the film ship'.

Is this perhaps 'autonomous music', in its way, engaged in its own précis-rehearsal of the narrative to come? As with the type of opera overture cited (its brevity actually alludes to Verdi at his most epigrammatic or the Puccini of *La Fanciulla del West*), its images will be explanatorily grounded as the drama unfolds. But first, and most significantly, there is a long silence in which nothing that the music had promised takes place. Appropriately, music is absent from the whole opening section of the film. When it returns, it does so almost furtively, as atmospheric scene-painting, as non-diegetic under-scoring. Hindsight knowledge of Steiner's subsequent devotion to recurring themes and motifs with concrete associations has encouraged interpretative glosses on the titles music which are sanctioned by his apparently clear labelling of the initial descending figure 'King Kong' (Kalinak reproduces the relevant page of the short score [1992: 74]). The audience cannot know that and hardly needs to. It may be expected to know perfectly well what music is doing when later *The Venture* literally sails into it. It comes with the fog; its role in the soundtrack is that of a kind of fog, an absence, a lack of visual and aural signification whose slow and quiet harp ostinato suggests the trope of music as nature, as feminised other. Evoking mysterious

portent, magic, eroticism, perhaps a looming threat, it is then won-
derfully reinterpreted as a *ferne Klang*,[3] a distant sound first interpreted as 'breakers', then, as it grows nearer, beating drums and alien
chanting voices.

Every device and strategy of the cinematic narrative seems geared to
signal that we are entering the film's central pleasure zone: as we enter
the fog, so we enter the realm of music – and of Kong. Responding to
the cartoon-strip hype of the newspaper advertisements, the first
audiences knew they were in for a giant ape, wreaking havoc in
New York, making ordinary people like themselves flee in mortal
terror. One of the advertisements in New York itself showed King
Kong holding a car above his head, its driver plunging to his death
while the close-up faces of two fleeing men and one woman, wide-eyed
with panic, fill the lower foreground. 'King Kong is coming!' the
caption reads, followed in smaller print by

> Strangest story ever conceived!
> . . . Thrilling beyond belief! . . .
> A gigantic monster, rampant,
> raging! . . . a city at his mercy!
> (Reproduced on *King Kong* CD sleeve 1997: 10)

They knew they were going to be 'frightened'; that was the game
freak-show entertainment always played, the game that Carl Denham
is playing in the movie when he fatally transports Kong back to New
York as a literally colossal vaudeville attraction: 'The Eighth Wonder
of the World!' If it works, if it 'really' thrills and frightens, then we
know we have got our money's worth, our rush of adrenalin or, for
the men specifically, our moment or two of vicarious 'feminisation'
that we can compensate for by holding our girlfriend's hand, agreeing
with Jack that 'this is no place for a girl'. Or was it precisely the place
for a girl to be what she was 'supposed' to be: a bother ('made that
way, I guess', Jack had added to Ann)? The equivalent advertisement
for Graumann's 'Chinese' cinema in Hollywood contained only two
visual images: the slavering jaws of Kong, top left, and a tiny, scantily-
clad girl bottom right, kneeling in a balletic, art-deco swoon (head
back, hand above her eyes) (*King Kong* CD sleeve 1997: 19). Here the
elaborate reflexivity of the film and its advertising seems playfully, but
unequivocally, to thematise the gender trouble about such entertainment: the woman as erotic object of the lustful male gaze; the male
gaze thus turned into an unappetising, always potentially violent 'ape',

behind which the movie-makers seem to have been flirting with a real source of fear. The 'old Arabian proverb' at the end of the titles, alluded to at strategic points in the movie by Denham, suggests that it is indeed a male fear of women:

> And lo, the beast looked upon the face of beauty. And it stayed its hand from killing. And from that day it was as one dead.

The cards look as if they should stack up neatly: women, nature, music, dancing savages and primeval beasts versus the rational man-as-conquering-film-maker, commodifying it all for the rich financial returns on imaginary pleasure. Except that the 'imaginary' is where the real is represented, controlled, packaged and at the same time 'let loose'. Is that not the message of the film's closing section, back in America? Is that not also the message of the music of orgiastic 'otherness', violence and (of course) erotic excitement that fills so much of the aural landscape of Skull Island and the thrilling events we see unfolding there? A specific model for this music seems to have been the *Venusberg* ballet music Wagner wrote for the Paris *Tannhäuser*: where chaos, sexuality and moving bodies fill the operatic space while conventional drama is suspended; where voices are silent and the passions reign.

If, as I have implied, the gender cards stacked up neatly here, this would represent a vast extension of Ann's (Fay Wray's) famous screams: the sound of 'hysterical' abandonment that would knowingly mark the spectacle of the Skull Island horrors and adventures as irrational, feminised entertainment. This trope has been isolated by Huyssen and others as central to Modernism's construction of the popular (Huyssen 1986: 44). Most commentators on film music stress its predominant association with the construction of the feminine as signifying women, romance, escapism and pleasure. Usually this association is figured as one crudely defined, in binary terms, by its 'other': the music of masculine energy, violence and heroic power. Latching on to what Steiner himself probably imagined to be a Wagnerian 'leitmotiv' technique of associative themes, they find 'his and her' material everywhere. Christopher Palmer stresses this in connection with a belief in film music's power to 'tell us' about the subjectivity (the 'true feelings') of characters on screen, asserting unreflectingly that 'the Kong theme and the Fay Wray theme (which in its pristine state is a pretty waltz melody)' finally converge, at the film's tragic climax:

Here the music is required, perhaps for the first time in an American
film, to explain to the audience what is actually happening on the
screen, since the camera is unable to articulate Kong's intuitive feelings
of tenderness towards his helpless victim. In these last moments the
music becomes almost operatic as it picks up the speech-rhythm of the
last lines of dialogue: 'Beauty killed the Beast'. (Palmer 1990: 29)

In this reading the Beast is unequivocally killed, therefore, by the
music that reveals the feminised heart within its brutishly caricatured
masculine body.

A similar gender-agenda for film music is more subtly suggested by
Claudia Gorbman with reference to this very film. Having set out a
schematic version of the masculine–feminine dualism I have referred
to, she considers the way in which 'a certain kind of music' will signal,
in its emotional excess, the presence of the 'Woman as romantic Good
Object', going on to cite what she admits is the undoubtedly 'curious'
example of the on-deck love scene in *King Kong* between Ann and
Jack, where music is explicitly and exclusively tied to their location on
deck, while crosscut shots of Denham and Captain Englehorn talking
on the bridge are consistently silent (Gorbman 1987: 80). One might
nevertheless observe that the 'curiosity' of the sequence is com-
pounded by the presence of both Ann and Jack in the 'musical' realm
of romance does it also emblematically signal her (Beauty's) taming of
the Beast within him?

The problem in all this is focused not only by that first encounter
with musical underscoring as *The Venture* approaches Skull Island.
From the start Fay Wray is dissociated from it. Denham had first
encountered her stealing fruit; she was presented as distinguished only
by her youth and tidy clothes from the destitutes waiting in line for the
Woman's Home Mission to open (for a moment the external reality of
the Depression impinges). She is saved by her affecting momentary
swoon, which is the inspiration Denham needed. Another composer
might have emphasised with a halo of music the way in which we
briefly see her through Denham's eyes, in soft focus; but Steiner, who
had a fabled and rarely repeated freedom to do what he liked in *King
Kong*,[4] here withholds music until the fog envelops the ship, only then
mobilising all the tropes of musical 'femininity' and 'otherness' in a
manner that is striking for its progressively emphasised spatial detachment from Ann and the rest of the crew. With them, she sails into and
towards it – to become, if anything, its primary victim.

The implication that Ann Darrow is sailing towards music and femininity together, that both are 'out to get her', is further emphasised in the opening section of the film by her on-deck training session with Denham. The film-maker has arranged for her to put on her 'Beauty and Beast costume' (a flowing, vaguely medieval affair) and to practise her acting in some trial shots – to the discomfort of Jack Driscoll but the delight of the ogling sailors. As she learns her film craft, patently that of silent film (Denham hand-winds his camera, with no sound equipment), she also learns how to be cinematically feminine. She must look up . . . higher . . . show increasing amazement, until he shouts ever more excitedly: 'Try to scream, Ann – *scream for your life!*' As she learns the terror that is Beauty's fate, still without music, she helps tighten the ratchet of our expectation; the convincing scream will soon be for real, we know, as we abandon ourselves to the pleasurable fantasy that involves our own sympathetic fear – and her cruelly prolonged subjection to a nightmare. Not only in opera are women systematically 'undone' (Clément 1988). And not only there does pleasure collude with unthinking misogyny to reveal its phallocentric purpose. This, appropriately, is where Kong comes in.

On one level the effusive presence of music in and around Skull Island is cinematically 'explained' by the already mentioned positioning of the central section of the film as a version of the silent movie Denham has come to make. Silent movies always had their music, of course. That was where the genre learnt so many of its favourite tricks, here recorded in textbook fashion: the various forms of sequential excitement-building used in the prehistoric monster and Kong sections of the great chase through the jungle (for long stretches almost literally a silent movie) capitalised on a whole range of existing suspense and horror techniques – as did the editing and camera-work. The diegetic 'sacrificial dance' similarly reconstructs effects that would have been reproduced nightly in innumerable cinemas, whether from cue-sheet scores or an improvising organist or pianist, including the simple 'mickey-mousing' that marks the step-by-step descent of the native chief towards the cowering film-team. In this sound film, of course, the playful device has another implication. Since its numinous introduction as a 'sound of nature' in the fog sequence, music had no confirmed onscreen source until we, as if peering through the tall grasses with Denham and the others, first glimpsed the dance-ritual at first hand. Even then, the sound technology fails convincingly to move from the non-diegetic into the diegetic space until the native chief halts the music, as he halts the ritual, when he sees them and realises (as it seems) that he is being watched, perhaps that it is being heard by ears for which it was not designed or intended. Music's authentic 'otherness' thus confirmed, and reinforced by its subsequent attendance upon his every step, the first stage of Ann's fatal feminisation (as one might put it) is prepared when the chief's alien threat is converted into a specific desire: to secure 'the golden woman' (as Captain Engelhorn bravely translates) as an alternative bride for the great Kong. The black men in 'savage' ape costumes are represented less as utopian innocents than close relatives of the Beast[5] whose regular sacrificial gift they had been preparing in a crude Hollywood version of *The Rite of Spring*, transposed to a tropical island (in spite of the modernity of his musical language, Steiner avoids alluding to Stravinsky's famous score, opting for something closer to Borodin's *Polovtsian Dances*).

The discursive and narrative connection between the dancing natives and the great ape to whom they had initially been preparing to sacrifice a young black woman, ceremonially decked with flowers, is effectively stressed by the music that accompanies Ann on her forced nocturnal march to and up the steps of the sacrificial altar. The exotic, filmable spectacle is now (from her point of view) altogether 'for real' – and had clearly been so from the moment when the suspenseful music of Skull Island had risen up to engulf her as the natives' head-dresses and painted faces had appeared above her over the rail of *The Venture*, before she is pulled out of her romantic reverie (the love scene on deck with Jack had just passed) and into their boat as a kidnap victim. She then becomes an integral part of the spectacle which the men at first gaze at quizzically from the windows of *The Venture's* bridge, wondering what the torches on the island are all about. The ensuing cut to the island finds Ann the new sacrificial victim, being led through the thronging villagers to the garishly blaring 'jungle dance' with its 'tribal' sequence of descending parallel triads without the third (the closeness of the musical image to that employed for native American Indians in films of the period is instructive).

The colossal *Steigerung*, or 'intensification', makes much use of a rhythmically and sometimes intervallically diminished version of what Christopher Palmer calls 'the Fay Wray theme', reduced to an excitedly reiterated figure:

In practice the effect is less that of a musical cut to a close-up of Ann than a fully integrated element of the barbaric processional – signifying excitement, mimicking the intended 'working-up' of the audience's nervous anticipation. This is one of the key figures that earlier led me to associate this music with nineteenth-century operatic 'orgy' scenes (specifically the key Wagnerian example of the ballet in the Paris *Tannhäuser*). Since this is how we first hear this motif in the preludial titles music, the question arises: Which is the 'original' version of it? Is the 'Ann' theme in reality a derivation of this motif, whose subjective associations and effect are more significant than its specific character-linkage? The integrated complementary relationship of this motif to the 'Kong' theme at the outset of the titles is both glossed and implicitly problematised in the next musical cue, ushered in by double strokes on the gong that surmounts the great gate, far beneath which Ann cowers diminutively, tied to the columns that top the ritual altar. Kong is summoned and is heard to approach with slow, dully measured musical footsteps, accompanied by a lion-like roar. These steps are followed by an explicit statement – now once again numinously non-diegetic – of the descending 'Kong' motif. The monster's appearance through the falling trees triggers both the tumbling motif of quasi-erotic excitement and Fay Wray's famous obbligato screams, which accompany much of the music that follows. This is the role she had learnt back on board ship. The literally fantastic aspect of the whole scene is emphasised by the absence of Denham with his movie camera: we are seeing the film he could only envisage.

We begin the journey into the heart of Kong's realm, literally (with Fay Wray) in the monster's hands; at the same time we find ourselves in the midst of successive spans of sequentially intensified *Steigerung* which had been prefigured in the march-to-the-altar and entrance-of-Kong sequences, in which the music both invites and repels 'motivic' interpretation. Kong's discovery of Ann and removal of her, screaming, from the altar sets up what in one sense is a standard version of how music might reinforce the successive close-ups in a shot/reverse-shot sequence. Cinematically, what we have here is a version of just such a sequence, in which the opposition of male gaze and female reaction is, quite literally, monstrously caricatured in the alternation between Kong's momentarily warmer expression as he looks at her and the captive Fay Wray's understandably 'hysterical' response.

The 'Kong' and 'Ann' motifs do indeed seem to succeed each other here, as if employing the crude code of signification that 'leitmotivic' film-score analysis has often been reduced to and Steiner may have believed himself to be using. The underlying musical, *structural* continuity of the cue – helping classically to smooth the dislocations of the unlikely shot succession (here more unlikely than usual, given the doubly 'special' nature of the effects involved) – also suggests a different code of signification in which the audience's reaction, figured in the excitedly whirring, absent-but-really-present camera of Carl Denham, might be included as a third participant in the economy of aural signification here. As neither Kong nor Ann look into the camera in the shot/reverse-shot process – we watch them looking at each other – so 'Kong–Ann' is replaced by 'Kong–Ann – Author/Audience': where Kong has his motif of masculine strength and portent, where the Author/Audience is mimetically whipped into an excited frenzy by the motif of 'feminine' (and feminising?) erotic excitement – but where Ann, on this reading still denied music, has only her diegetic screams. Perhaps this is a way of saying, rather, that the music is all 'Kong', its very ambivalence about gender articulating more about the author as masculine subject than the violently oppressed female object: the author as a nervously hiding extension, or supposedly 'civilised' back-projection of the Beast who will be undone by Beauty's charm.

In a sense this is to concur with the now-standard feminist critique of such films: that time and again the camera's gaze was implicitly and repressively heterosexual-male in its intentions. We have nevertheless seen that *Kong* emphasises and thematises this in a heightened, but (for the genre) not altogether exceptional performance of its own self-consciousness as cinematic text (Denham's voiced aims as a film-maker; his market-orientated need for 'a girl'; his efforts to teach Fay Wray how to express the appropriate terror and hysteria for the role that awaits her). This performance is underlined by the explicitly gendered business of the film's extended central fantasy-adventure sequence, with its emphasis on visual horrors and wonders whose silent-cinema origins are appropriately accompanied by richly tex-tured, virtually continuous music. And these adventures are very much 'boys' stuff': the men rush through the jungle, threatened and then mostly killed by giant prehistoric monsters whose phallic necks and bullet-heads are no less evident in the beasts that Kong himself battles to the death in his efforts to protect Ann. This structural grouping of all the male characters, with Kong as their 'natural' representative, emphasises not only the critical enormity of Fay Wray's predicament but also the unresolved tension about sexuality and desire that lurks behind the cartoon-strip horrors of the magic-lantern show. The underlying tendency of the musical score, beyond its surface concern for motivic referentiality, to construct a generalised and masculinised subject-position is intriguingly suggested by the ubiquitous descending three-note figure that the commonest of music-analytical operations would take as evidence that all the motifs – 'Kong', 'Ann', the 'jungle dance' – are versions, or varied extensions of the same figure. Even the suggested *Tannhäuser* origin of the (hysterical) 'Ann' motif fits the emerging message that is reinforced by a further hinted reference to that opera. Where Ann's motif suggests the passion of the *Venusberg*, the chromatic descent of Kong's motif appears to echo the sequentially repeated motif that links the main statements of the idealistic male pilgrims' march of the *Tannhäuser* overture.

This musical reference is most pointedly noticeable, intentionally or not, in the elegiacally lyrical version of the Kong motif which concludes the main titles music, prefiguring the narrative conclusion of the whole film, where the terrible Beast lies dead, having been reduced to a victim of unrequitable idealistic love. And it is in the titles sequence that we hear the Kong motif strategically linked, via a fanfare, *to* the hysterical-Ann motif and the jungle dance in an urgent, rhetorically unbroken intensification to the climactic crisis of the emphatic re-peated-note figure (decorating the rhythm of the 'Kong' motif) that will feature in central crisis-points in the film, like the moment when Kong bursts through the great barred gate on Skull Island that had so long held him at bay.

Other musical details subtly mark even the exotic or 'feminine' music of the first main cue, the 'fog' sequence itself, as more than just detached from Ann (as suggested earlier). The oboe, at its very outset, slowly outlines the 'Kong' motif above the harp ostinato, suggesting that the magical danger-zone they are entering is indeed 'Kong' and all he represents. It is hardly surprising that the single clearly identifiable new motif generated in the latter part of this cue, well after the island drums have come to dominate the aural landscape, is a jagged figure – rhythmically articulated as '♫♩' – that seems hereafter to function as a sign of threat, specifically *sexual* threat, that echoes similar motifs in Mahler (some suggesting urgently warning bird calls).[6]

We know from Claudia Gorbman's section on 'Music and representation of Woman' (1987: 80–1) how the binary tropes are supposed to work: Man/ Objectivity/ Reason versus Woman/Subjectivity/ Emotion and so on; we also know that music 'should' be on the side of the latter, however implicitly negative the association. *King Kong* clearly requires that we admit a broader repertoire of cultural and psychological contextualisations for such binary oppositions. The 'Beauty and Beast' metaphor reverses what it appears to suggest when Denham's glosses it: Beauty killed the Beast. The misogynist implications of the formula are emphasised in the ostensibly playful image of Ann coming on deck with a small, tethered pet monkey: a diminutive form of the godlike male animal whose undoing she will prove by the time the narrative has run its course. That the movie fails to clarify whether Beauty's undoing of the Beast is to be read as a good or bad thing only stresses the male anxiety that lurks at its heart.

It is the manner in which the final, New York section of the film elicits our sympathy for Kong as suffering subject, as much as our terror of him as a potentially destructive 'force of nature', that heightens the ambivalence. The music marks it eloquently. At first it is all urban diegetic 'entertainment' music, full of jazzy panache and theatrical *élan* (note the fanfares). Only with Kong's escape from his new role as commodified object of a paying audience's gaze, reduced to a form of cinematic 'feminisation', and as he contradictorily emphasises his masculinity by wreaking his jealous revenge on the rational order, does the underscoring come back into its own, with all the unbridled energy of the Island sequences. It apparently declares its role in cementing the subjective bond between us, the cinema audience, and Kong by finally presenting the 'Ann' motif as an elegiac last expression of his own love for her before he falls to his death from the Empire State Building. In this sense only might one agree with Christopher Palmer's point about music 'telling us what Kong is thinking'.

But there is still more to be said about the way in which the score of *King Kong* contrives to reveal something about music's historical character as cultural practice – something which musicologists would find it all but impossible to formulate until assisted by Susan McClary (1991: 14ff) and others in the early 1990s. We need to return to the moonlit, ship's-deck love scene between Ann and Jack, whose underscoring is itself accompanied by the distant ritual drums on Skull Island. Claudia Gorbman describes this as 'curious' for the reason that the separation between the 'woman's' realm of romantic love music (the 'Ann' motif in its most lyrically relaxed and melodically extended form as a slow waltz) and the unmusical realm of the men on the bridge is so schematically asserted (Gorbman 1987: 80). She does not quite explain what she finds curious about it, however. Perhaps that Jack Driscoll is implicitly drawn into Ann's musical and emotional realm here – is thus romantically 'feminised' (what Denham has called 'goin' sappy')? There is something else decidedly curious about the scene, musically, which she does not comment on. Rather than the crosscut shots interrupting the underscoring (which she seems to imply), the music is written in such a way that integral rests, as caesuras between phrases, give almost the effect that the sequence has been cut to the music. The music plays a little game of cadential closure 'around' the crosscut shots, even emphasising the half-suggested lewd implication of Jack's 'Yes, *sir*!' in response to Denham's shouted question 'Are you on deck?' Where the script falls short of explicit innuendo, the music seems to catch him *in flagrante* after his declaration of love – in music which for all its romantic character, is engaging in a playful but sure-footed exercise of that tonal prerogative of teleological structuring and closure-achievement that Susan McClary has polemically gendered masculine in the cultural politics of music's idealised discourse of autonomy.

What is so fascinating about Steiner's *King Kong* score, however, is not that it simply rehearses the old agendas of the old culture in which its composer had grown up. On one level the music does certainly seem to respond to what gender-theorist Judith Butler, after Luce Irigaray, might call the 'phallogocentric' agenda of the film and its script (Butler 1990: ix) by covertly, but consistently, constructing a Kong-orientated subject-position as the metasubjectivity within which the fantasy operates. It equally, and more disarmingly, reveals itself to be just such a 'site of subversive multiplicity' as Butler identifies 'the feminine' in Luce Irigaray's model of gender discourse, which Irigaray nevertheless expects to be *silenced* by hegemonic masculinity (Butler 1990: 19). The delightful paradox is that Steiner's exercise of a high degree of literal 'autonomy' in his work on the score for *King Kong* fails – curiously indeed – to support the ideology of autonomy as we have come to understand it in the aesthetic discussion about high-art music in Europe. Instead, the score seems consistently to work towards the critical *unmasking* of that ideology – as if simultaneously demonstrating and critically highlighting Irigaray's point (in Butler's words) that 'there is only one sex, the masculine, that elaborates itself in and though the production of the "other" . . . that women can never be understood on the model of a "subject" within the conventional representational systems of Western culture precisely because they constitute the fetish of representation and, hence, the unrepresentable as such' (Butler 1990: 18).

The variously passionate, hysterical and exotic music of *King Kong* (might we even read it as reflecting the very category music?) tends throughout more towards 'irrational' representation than 'rational' structural autonomy. It nevertheless presents a direct articulation of male anxieties and fears as much as it colludes covertly in a repressive construction of the 'feminine'. Indeed, this music appears to be no less a revealing negotiator of the tropes of subjectivity and gender than it is limited and controlled by such tropes. Ann, Denham and Jack Driscoll emerge from the fog into the realm of a music, both monstrous and vulnerable, masculine and feminine, that seems disarmingly ready to 'come out' of the mystique of autonomy and tell us what it has long been about.

Notes

1. In Sir Harrison Birtwistle's 1994 opera *The Second Mrs Kong*, with a libretto by Russell Hoban.
2. The phrase was significantly coined by Lawrence Kramer in his book *Music as Cultural Practice, 1800–1900* (1990).
3. Literally 'distant sound' (the phrase was used as the title of Franz Schreker's seminal 1912 opera *Der ferne Klang*).
4. Steiner's often-quoted account of how he had initially been asked to use cheap 'available tracks' before Merian C. Cooper intervened, promising to pay whatever the original score would cost, is reprinted in Thomas 1979: 77.
5. The racial, as well as sexual, implications of King Kong are explicitly considered by Doane 1991: 214.
6. For example *Symphony No. 1*, fourth-movement 3 bars before rehearsal no. 2 (see also the passage between rehearsal nos. 14 and 15; *Symphony No. 2*, first movement, rehearsal no. 25 (Fl.1)ff).

Bibliography

Butler, Judith (1990) *Gender Trouble. Feminism and the Subversion of Identity.* London: Routledge.

Clément, Catherine (1988) *Opera, or the Undoing of Women* (trans. Betsy Wing). Minneapolis: Minnesota University Press.

Doane, Mary Ann (1991) *Femmes Fatales. Feminism, Film Theory, Psychoanalysis.* London: Routledge.

Gorbman, Claudia (1987) *Unheard Melodies. Narrative Film Music.* London: BFI.

Huyssen, Andreas (1986) *After the Great Divide. Modernism, Mass Culture and Postmodernism.* Basingstoke: Macmillan.

Kalinak, Kathryn (1992) *Settling the Score. Music and the Classical Hollywood Film.* Madison: Wisconsin University Press.

Kramer, Lawrence (1995) *Classical Music and Postmodern Knowledge.* Berkeley: University of California Press.

McClary, Susan (1991) *Feminine Endings: Music, Gender and Sexuality.* Minneapolis: Minnesota University Press.

Palmer, Christopher (1990) *The Composer in Hollywood.* New York: Boyars.

Thomas, Tony (1979) *Film Score. The View from the Podium.* South Brunswick: Yoseloff.

Chapter 5

The *Dies Irae* in *Citizen Kane*: Musical Hermeneutics Applied to Film Music

William H. Rosar

Hermeneutics, originally the science (or art) of interpreting texts, has long been more broadly construed in the humanities to encompass the interpretation of non-verbal forms of expression such as music and the arts. Over thirty years ago, historical musicologist Edward Lippman proposed that the purpose or goal of musical hermeneutics should be to 'make clear the complex of feelings, associations, and ideas that were initially formulated in tone by [a] composer and produced by an adequate performance at the time the work was composed' (Lippman 1966: 307–8). While that sounds simple and straightforward enough, in actual practice it requires a good deal of guesswork and conjecture – even luck – on the part of the interpreter or hermeneut, this in addition to knowing and/or reconstructing the historicocultural context in which a piece of music was written. Critical thinking and a good measure of sceptical rigour are also desirable so as to curtail flights of fancy which may lead the hermeneutic process astray into unfounded speculation.

One source of spurious meaning, no doubt responsible for any number of fanciful interpretations, results from a hermeneut analysing a musical work and finding meaningful coincidences as well as meaningful connections. Once observed, such meaningful coincidences can seem convincingly to reflect authorial intention, whether literary, artistic or musical, but are actually attributable to the phenomenon C. G. Jung (1972) dubbed synchronicity – an 'acausal connecting principle' as he called it – rather than being the result of a causal process, as would be the case with authorial intention. As the intentional meaningful connection and the meaningful coincidence are both meaningful, and can be equally compelling to the hermeneut, it is not always possible to distinguish one from the other. Therefore, except for the relatively rare cases where one possesses direct knowledge of, say, a composer's express intentions, meaningful coincidences are always a potential pitfall in hermeneutics. Since such knowledge is more often than not unavailable, one is commonly obliged to rely on parallel cases, whether in a composer's other works, those of another composer, or other relevant historicocultural context and tradition. Thus from a methodological standpoint, hermeneutics typically involves of necessity what has long been known in philology as the comparative method.[1]

Mindful of these considerations, my purpose here is to discuss musical hermeneutics within the context of music composed for films, and I will attempt to illustrate a few of the typical factors which can contribute both to the content and to the use of music in a film, both of which in turn must be taken into account in the process of hermeneutic exegesis. As with music for the theatre and programme music, film music exemplifies for better or worse, as it were, the marriage of the world of music with the visual world of images. Thus the so-called 'extra-musical associations' which plague historical musicology are in many instances more-or-less actually embodied in the work *per se*, a priori exegesis or hermeneutic interpretation.

As has often enough been stressed, the relationship of the music to a film for which it is composed is directly analogous and therefore comparable to the relationship of incidental music to a play in music for the theatre, or music to a programme in programme music and has for this reason sometimes been called functional music, to distinguish it from so-called 'absolute' or 'pure' music (for example a sonata or a symphony) where there is supposedly no 'extra-musical' context – no imagery, film, play or programme are present – while the music is being heard (Dahlhaus 1989).

As an example of how musical hermeneutics can be applied to music for films, I will turn to what is probably the most discussed and analysed film ever made: *Citizen Kane* (1941). Not only did this film represent the cinematic debut of Orson Welles as an actor, writer and director, but it was also the first film score by New York composer Bernard Herrmann, who had previously composed music for Welles' CBS radio dramas in New York.[2] I shall preface my remarks about *Citizen Kane* by relating a casual observation I made some years ago while listening to a radio broadcast of Rachmaninov's symphonic poem of 1909, *Isle of the Dead* (Op. 29), a work inspired by the popular painting of 1880, *The Island of the Dead* (*Die Toteninsel*) by Swiss artist Arnold Böcklin. I noticed that there was a five-note motif in Rachmaninov's symphonic poem which was strikingly similar to a motif in Herrmann's music for *Citizen Kane*.[3] The motif in *Isle of the Dead* (see Figure 5.1 below) is associated with the island itself, according to the 'programme' of the work – or, perhaps more accurately, according to what commentators have written about it, because unlike most symphonic poems which have a literary basis, the 'programme' in this case is not a story, nor a poem, but a painting, and the music is therefore not so much a symphonic poem as it is a 'painting in sound' (Seroff 1950: 112) or 'tone painting'.[4]

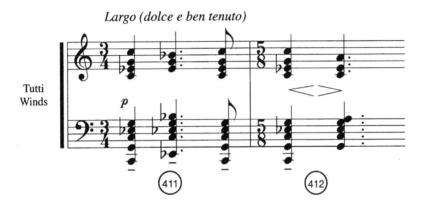

Fig. 5.1: Sergei Rachmaninov, *Isle of the Dead* (1909)
© copyright 1909 by Hawkes and Son Ltd. (London)
(reproduced by permission of Boosey & Hawkes
Music Publishers Ltd.).

Compare now the corresponding motif in *Citizen Kane* (see Fig. 5.2) which is associated with the central character of the film, newspaper mogul Charles Foster Kane (played by Orson Welles). It is a motif which Herrmann himself in discussing the score referred to variously as the 'motif of power', 'motif of destiny', or 'motif of fate'.

Given the obvious similarity between the two motifs, I rather assumed that Herrmann had probably borrowed it from Rachmaninov, and that this was just one of the countless examples of musical borrowing noted and studied by musicologists. It was not until some years later in thinking again about the motifs in *Isle of the Dead* and *Citizen Kane* that I asked myself the question: Why the similarity? Was there perhaps a reason why Herrmann might have borrowed that motif from Rachmaninov, whether consciously or not – that is, if even he did borrow it in the first instance, and it isn't 'just a coincidence' (it is only five notes, after all)? Could it be that Herrmann just happened to like Rachmaninov's motif? Or was it rather, as is so often the case, that Herrmann felt it in some way it also fitted *Citizen Kane*?

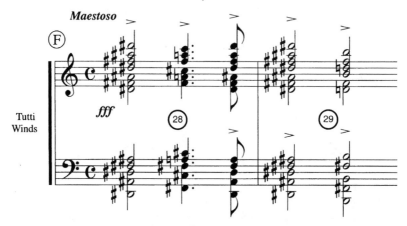

Fig. 5.2: Bernard Herrmann, 'Finale', *Citizen Kane* (1941)

In contemplating the dark, gloomy scene depicted in Böcklin's painting, which was the subject, so to speak, of Rachmaninov's symphonic poem, it spontaneously occurred to me that the settings shown in the two scenes – the island mausoleum in the painting and Kane's hilltop castle 'Xanadu' seen at the beginning of Citizen Kane – are not only similarly dark and gloomy in overall mood, but are also *structurally* similar in gestalt and chiaroscuro. They share a similar visual physiognomy, just as the two motifs share a similar musical physiognomy (Rosar 1994). For that matter, the physical environments of the two scenes have something else in common – a proximity to the sea. Though it is not immediately apparent in the film, the script for *Citizen Kane* which Herrmann read before the film was shot, and before he composed his music, explicitly states that Xanadu is located on the coast of Florida (Kael 1971: 100). There is also a similarity, or at least a connection, between the subject matter of both scenes in that both explicitly have to do with death: the island of the dead is a place of burial, the painting depicting a shrouded figure (sometimes identified as River Styx boatman Charon) in a boat bearing a casket, going towards the island. The beginning of *Citizen Kane* culminates with a death scene inside Xanadu, where Kane on his deathbed utters his immortal last word – 'Rosebud'. Again, one might ask sceptically, 'Mere coincidence?'

It proves instructive to juxtapose Böcklin's painting with Rachmaninov's five-note motif reputedly representing the island, and compare it with the opening imagery of Xanadu in *Citizen Kane* and Herrmann's five-note motif which accompanies the images of Xanadu. It should be noted that the Kane motif actually alternates with another motif which Herrmann fittingly called Rosebud.

We are so accustomed to seeing films with the music composed for them that we may not realise that customarily when a composer first sees a film that he is to score, there is no music accompanying it. On the basis of what the composer and the dialogue heard, he or she will then respond to it, as it were, with musical ideas and material which in some way fits the film. Sometimes the composer may think of another composer's music as a starting point, or they may be lucky and an original musical idea occurs to them spontaneously. Fortuitously, the scoring of the opening scene in *Citizen Kane* was something Herrmann was particularly proud of, and on more than one occasion he used it as an example of his art (or craft) when asked to lecture about film music. He would first show the scene without sound and then again with his music added. When Herrmann was invited to lecture in 1972 at the National Film Theatre in London, and the following year at the International Museum of Photography at the George Eastman House in Rochester, New York, his remarks about scoring the opening scene of *Citizen Kane* were recorded:

> I'm going to do something I don't like to do . . . to reconstruct a moment in my own life where I first saw *Kane*. [T]he first thing I saw of *Kane* . . . is the opening of it, without any sound of any kind . . . this is the way it was shown to me. I had to make up my mind at this point: what approach would I take for the creation of the music to this film? And I decided that I would use the old musical form of leitmotiv, in other words, a theme that is transformed incessantly. So the very first bars I wrote are a series of a few notes that dominate the entire film, no matter what's happening. In my mind it was a sort of variant of the ancient hymn, *Dies Irae*, and seemed to me what the subject of *Kane* was, which is 'all is vanity.'[5] *Kane* is the very first notes – it's associated with him all through the film – and yet Kane through this thing is not a human being, he's a *symbol* [italics added]. (Herrmann in Gilling 1974: 12–13)

Citizen Kane originally had no main title. When it was initially shown, there was no 'RKO' or '*Citizen Kane*' title, just a black screen. The first thing you saw was the pan up to the sign 'No Trespassing'. I remember at the premier that people shouted all over the place 'lights, sound, sound, projection, sound', because they could not accept a film that started in complete silence. Since the studio couldn't put sound in, they unfortunately added a trade mark and a title instead.

Imagine the opening of *Kane* if it were silent, without music. That is the way it was turned over to me. This was the first sequence I scored. If I remember correctly, I didn't have the idea of the 'Rosebud' theme, nor of a 'Destiny' or 'Fate' theme. Both themes sort of automatically presented themselves to me. You don't write music with the top of your mind; you write it from a part you don't know anything about. Anyway, I was very lucky in the first hour of the composition: I hit on two sequences of sound that could bear the weight of this film. The picture opens with a motive [sic] I call 'the Motive of Destiny', of Kane's destiny. (Herrmann in Cameron 1980: 125–6)

On yet another occasion, in an interview with Mischa Donat in February 1973, Herrmann commented that his music for the opening scene was to evoke a 'subterranean, strange heaviness of death and futility' (Smith 1991: 78). Though Herrmann makes no mention of Rachmaninov in his remarks, it is significant that he does mention the *Dies Irae*, as it has long been observed by musical cognoscenti that the five-note motif in *Isle of the Dead* seems also to be a musical quotation of the first four tones of the *Dies Irae* chant. Rachmaninov's biographer, Victor Seroff, noted:

> [In *Isle of the Dead*] Rachmaninoff introduced, for the first time, the medieval choral *Dies Irae*. Two reasons have been advanced for the strong attraction this particular melody held for him which made him return to it again and again in his compositions. Some maintain that Rachmaninoff thought of the *Dies Irae* as a sort of *memento mori* and that despite its ominous foreboding it exacted an extreme activity while yet alive. Others think that Rachmaninoff, in his gloomy preoccupation with the word 'fate,' finally came to the conclusion that Fate can be conquered only by Death. (Seroff 1950: 112)

Did Herrmann know that Rachmaninov may have associated the *Dies Irae* with 'fate' or is it just a meaningful coincidence that one of the words Herrmann associated with his motif in *Citizen Kane* was also 'fate'? It is also significant that Hansjörg Pauli (Pauli 1990), in analysing Herrmann's music for *Citizen Kane*, noted that the motif in question resembled the *Dies Irae*, apparently unaware that Herrmann himself had indeed stated the motif was 'a sort of variant of the ancient hymn.'

An old crony of Herrmann's in New York was record critic Irving Kolodin, and Kolodin might have explained the similarity between Rachmaninov's and Herrmann's motifs in terms of seven 'axioms' he formulated to characterise all the various ways, both direct and indirect, that one musical work can be influenced by another (Kolodin 1969). Kolodin's fourth axiom states that 'The obvious source is not always the true source,' which in turn, leads logically to his fifth axiom, which states that 'Two well-known manifestations of a similar impulse may be related not to each other, but to a common source.' (Kolodin 1969: 43–4). In other words, two works (or motifs as in this case) may resemble each other because each resembles a common source – in other words, each piece was influenced by the same source, hence the similarity. But how can we know which might have been the case with Herrmann and Rachmaninov? Perhaps by comparing the details of each motif, in much the same way as Robin Holloway (1979), for example, demonstrated the influence of Wagner on Debussy by comparing the minutiae of musical passages in their works.

As it turns out, close scrutiny reveals that there are several details which suggest, but do not prove, that Herrmann was probably directly influenced by Rachmaninov (whether consciously or unconsciously) and indirectly by the *Dies Irae* itself, as he implies in his remarks quoted above:

- Herrmann's motif consists of the same number of notes as Rachmaninoff's – five – which, as pointed out, correspond to the first four tones of the chant.
- Both motifs share a distinctive rhythmic feature not in the original chant; in each motif the third tone is repeated in a dotted rhythm, that is a note of short duration followed by one of longer duration (see Fig. 5.2), rendering the chant phrase quite un-Gregorian, and connecting it with the tradition of the funeral march (*marcia funébre*).
- Though Rachmaninov's motif is first stated as a single melodic line, when harmonised, he like Herrmann scored it principally for brass and wind.
- The orchestration for wind combined with the dotted rhythm gives the motifs an annunciatory character, rather like a sombre fanfare that one might expect to hear in a funeral band.[6]
- The first big chordal statement of Rachmaninoff's motif and the first statement of Herrmann's significantly both begin with an E minor

chord-which William Kimmel might have interpreted as being an instance of the 'Phrygian inflection,' as he called certain traditional musical gestures in his study of death symbolism in music (Kimmel 1980).

Fig. 5.3: A comparison of three motifs: musical examples from *Dies Irae*, Rachmaninov and Herrmann.

Overall then, the two motifs sound alike, although there are some distinctive differences, which likely merit further exploration for hermeneutic significance, though space only permits me to mention one of them, namely, how Herrmann's harmonisation differs from Rachmaninov's. Whereas Herrmann utilises exclusively minor chords, Rachmaninov uses both major and minor chords, and not just triads (cf. Figs 5.1 and 5.2). Herrmann also uses exclusively mediant progressions – also known as 'third-related progressions' (*Terzverwandtschaft*) – in his harmonisation. For example, the harmonic relationship of the first two chords of the 'Kane' motif as it is first heard in the opening scene, namely E minor and G sharp minor, constitute a chromatic third-related progression, one that Herrmann likely borrowed from the 'Tarnhelm' motif in Wagner's *Ring* cycle, which utilises the same two chords (see Fig. 5.4). Third-related progressions were a harmonic device which Herrmann was particularly fond of, using them countless times after *Citizen Kane*.

In any case, if Herrmann had been thinking of the original chant line in composing his motif, why didn't he use the actual rhythm of the chant, which consists of equal note values, and why did he use only the same first few notes of it which Rachmaninov also paraphrased? The fact that both Rachmaninov's and Herrmann's motifs have the identical phrase length and share a distinctive rhythm not belonging to the *Dies Irae* makes it hard to dismiss this resemblance as mere coincidence. As a well-schooled composer, we can assume Herrmann knew the chant in its original form. Why then might the motif in Rachmaninov's symphonic poem have been the source of inspiration for Herrmann's motif instead of other well-known works which quote the *Dies Irae*, the most familiar of which being the 'Witches' Sabbath' in Berlioz's *Symphonie Fantastique* and Liszt's *Todentanz* – works which, given Herrmann's encyclopedic musical erudition, he surely knew as well as the Rachmaninov work (Gregory 1953)?

Fig. 5.4: 'Prelude' from *Citizen Kane*
and the Tarnhelm motif from *Das Rheingold*.

Again, one might be tempted to dismiss all of this as mere coincidences and conjecture because, after all, we are only talking about five notes (five chords, to be precise). On the other hand one does not find either the phrase length or the distinctive rhythm in the two other famous quotations of the *Dies Irae* in the Berlioz and Liszt works mentioned.

Making a case for influence like this on the basis of musical details is all in a day's work to historical musicologists in seeking differentia in style analysis, particularly in demonstrating the influence of composers on each other and telling similar styles of contemporaries apart. In this instance, however, it serves an additional purpose as well, and that is understanding the relationship of music to images, whether a painting, as in Rachmaninov's symphonic poem, or a film, as in Herrmann's film score. I therefore advance the hermeneutic hypothesis that Herrmann's motif was inspired by Rachmaninov's in large part because Herrmann was, consciously or unconsciously, reminded of Böcklin's painting when he saw the images of Xanadu at the beginning of *Citizen Kane* (or perhaps even earlier when he read the script), which in turn brought to mind Rachmaninov's symphonic poem. So the reason Herrmann might have thought of Rachmaninov's work rather than Berlioz's or Liszt's, was that the process of association for him was triggered by what he first saw – or *visualised*, if reading the script – in *Citizen Kane*: the foreboding, darkened exterior of Xanadu. The sequence or train of associations I am suggesting that may have occurred in Herrmann's mind were as follows:

The *sight* of Xanadu → Böcklin's painting → Rachmaninov's symphonic poem.[7]

Relating this now to Edward Lippman's concept of musical hermeneutics, the group of associations just discussed would constitute the main elements in the 'complex of feelings, associations, and ideas formulated in tone' by Herrmann in the music he wrote to accompany the opening scene of *Citizen Kane*.

Of course, the question arises as how to explain the absence of any reference by Herrmann himself to Rachmaninov and Böcklin when we know now that Herrmann had occasion to quite consciously recall what was in his mind when composing the music for the opening scene of *Citizen Kane*. In all of Herrmann's reminiscences and interviews which I have read or heard, I cannot ever recall him once saying that something he wrote was influenced by another composer, let alone a specific work by a composer. This is ironic in light of a succinct critical remark made by Jerome Moross, a composer crony of Herrmann's, who had known him since they were teenagers: 'Benny never had a style of his own.'[8] (Others have made similar observations, in other words, that Herrmann's music was noticeably derivative.) Yet another possible factor is what is known in psychology as cryptomnesia or 'hidden memory', a well-documented 'trick' of memory where a writer or composer unconsciously borrows from another work they have forgotten. There is evidence that composers are as prone to this as anyone else, Herrmann being no exception, and may even unwittingly borrow from a work of their own which they have forgotten, or otherwise not realised they have borrowed from.[9]

With film music then, the hermeneutic process must first take into consideration the conditions in which music is composed for a film – that it is a sort of 'musical response' on the part of composers to what they see on the screen which, in turn, tends to place certain constraints on what they write to accompany a film. In psychological terms, composers are making musical associations to the film, or to put it another way, the film triggers certain musical associations in composers' minds which, in turn, affects the music they then compose for the film. Now to show that this is by no means unique to composing music for the movies, here is something Rachmaninov said about his own creative process, when commenting on his *Isle of the Dead* music,

> There must be something definite before my mind to convey a definite impression, or the ideas refuse to appear . . . [and on another occasion he stated] When composing, I find it of great help to have in mind a book just recently read, or a beautiful picture, or a poem. Sometimes a definite story is kept in mind, which I try to convert into tones without disclosing the source of my inspiration. (Bertensson and Leyda 1956: 156)

In light of the preceding discussion, by a curious and meaningful coincidence, four years after RKO released *Citizen Kane*, the same studio produced a horror film starring Boris Karloff which was entitled *Isle of the Dead*! The film's opening credits are superimposed over Böcklin's painting, though the painting is not identified in the credits. Needless to say, this almost uncanny coincidence might not seem so unusual if Böcklin's painting was indeed *not* an indirect influence on Bernard Herrmann's musical thinking. If one did not know the facts of the matter, it might be tempting to imagine some causal connection between *Citizen Kane* and RKO's *Isle of the Dead*. However, Val Lewton, the film's producer, who had the idea of making a film inspired by Böcklin's painting, had known the painting from his youth in Russia (Siegel 1973: 71). Now what's musically interesting here is that Leigh Harline, who composed the music for the film, wrote music for the island which sounds more like what Herrmann wrote for *Citizen Kane* than Rachmaninov's symphonic poem which, given its own popularity, would have been an obvious model for Harline's score, or it could even have been used in the film itself, had RKO so desired (see Fig. 5.5).

Coincidentally, Harline's motif for the island, which is also chordal, consists of five pitches (some repeated), and could similarly be interpreted as a harmonisation of the last five tones of the same phrase in the *Dies Irae*, paraphrased by Rachmaninov and Herrmann (see Fig. 5.3). The first note of Harline's motif corresponds to the third note of Rachmaninov's and Herrmann's (cf. Figs 5.3 and 5.6). Actually, while sounding like Herrmann, particularly its scoring for low woodwinds, Harline's harmony is virtually identical to a progression found in the madrigals of the late Renaissance composer, Carlo Gesualdo.[10] But this then is really a topic for another hermeneutic investigation.

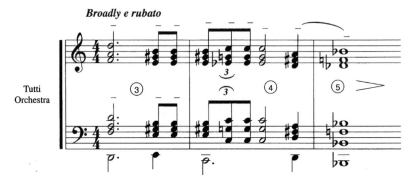

Fig. 5.5: Leigh Harline, 'Main title', *Isle of the Dead* (1945)

Fig. 5.6: The *Dies Irae* and Harline (1945)

Acknowledgements

Based on a paper presented 12 November 1995 on the panel, 'Examples of Applied Hermeneutic Analysis', at the Annual Meeting of the College Music Society, Portland, Oregon. For her patience, encouragement and unflagging support of the author's endeavours, he dedicates this paper to his wife, Leslie.

Notes

1. By an interesting (and meaningful) coincidence, Jung's 'hermeneutic' or 'synthetic/constructive' method of dream analysis, as Jung (Jung 1966: 80–5, 291–4) at one time called his method (Jung 1961: 144–9) so as to contrast it with what he called Freud's 'semiotic' or 'reductive' method, closely parallels in many respects Lippman's approach to musical hermeneutics, though there is no evidence Lippman was influenced by Jung.

2. Herrmann's holograph score for *Citizen Kane* is preserved in the Music Division of the Library of Congress, Washington DC.
3. References to Rachmaninov's *Isle of the Dead* are to the Boosey and Hawkes edition of the score.
4. The German musicologist-psychologist Albert Wellek pointed out that 'programme music' and 'tone painting' are by no means one and the same: 'Tone painting is a technique of art, programme music is a genre or, ironically, the *programme for* a genre' (Wellek 1970: 150).
5. From Proverbs in the Book of Ecclesiastes 1:2–5:
   Vanity of vanities, saith the Preacher, vanity of vanities; *all is vanity.* [italics added]
   What profit hath a man of all his labor which he taketh under the sun?
   One generation passeth away, and another generation cometh: but the earth abideth for ever.
   The Sun also ariseth.
6. Cf. John Jay Hilfiger (1992) for a discussion of some of the characteristic attributes of funeral band music: the low brass and woodwinds, muffled drums, tolling bells, the dotted rhythms – all of which have been imitated by composers wanting to evoke the 'sound' of the funeral band when writing for other instruments (piano) or ensembles (chamber and symphony orchestras), and which can be discerned in Herrmann's 'Prelude' to *Citizen Kane*.
7. Knowing something as we do of Herrmann's love of painting and his taste for Victorian Gothic literature (Smith 1991), it seems very likely that he knew both Böcklin's painting and the Rachmaninov music intimately, and he may even have conducted the symphonic poem on his weekly radio programme 'Invitation to Music' during his days at CBS in New York.
8. Jerome Moross, unpublished interview by Mike Reardon, New York, 1979.
9. When Leslie Zador once called Herrmann's attention to the fact that he had borrowed from himself in writing his opera *Wuthering Heights*, which contains whole passages taken literally note-for-note from his film scores for *Jane Eyre* and *The Ghost and Mrs Muir*, Herrmann became irate, strenuously denying he had done any such thing, and that the reason for the similarity was simply that his opera and the two film scores sounded alike because they were in the same *style*, and that they were in the same style because he had composed them! (Zador and Rose 1989).
10. See the analysis by Dahlhaus (1967: 8) of a few characteristic cadential patterns found in Gesualdo's madrigals (especially musical example 'a') which are correlative to third-related progressions used by composers two and three centuries later, during and after the Romantic era (for example Schumann, Liszt, Wagner, Richard Strauss, Debussy, Vaughan Williams and others).

Bibliography

Bertensson, Sergei and Jay Leyda (1956) *Sergei Rachmaninoff: A Lifetime in Music.* New York: New York University Press.
Cameron, Evan William (ed.) (1980) *Sound and the Cinema.* New York: Redgrave Co.
Dahlhaus, Carl (1967) Zur chromatischen Technik Carlo Gesualdos. *Analecta Musicologica*, vol. 4.
Dahlhaus, Carl (1989) *The Idea of Absolute Music.* (trans. Roger Lustig) Chicago: University of Chicago Press.

Gilling, Ted (1974) Bernard Herrmann: A John Player Lecture (11 June 1972). *Pro Musica Sana*, vol. 3.

Gregory, Robin (1953) 'Dies Irae'. *Music and Letters*, vol. 34.

Hilfiger, John Jay (1992) Funeral marches, dirges, and wind bands in the nineteenth century. *Journal of Band Research*, vol. 28.

Holloway, Robin (1979) *Debussy and Wagner*. London: Eulenburg Books.

Jung, C. G. (1961) *The Collected Works of C. G. Jung, vol. 4: Freud and Psychoanalysis*. Princeton: Princeton University Press.

Jung, C. G. (1966) *The Collected Works of C. G. Jung, vol. 7: Two Essays on Analytical Psychology*. Princeton: Princeton University Press.

Jung, C. G. (1971) *The Collected Works of C. G. Jung, vol. 8: The Structure and Dynamics of the Psyche*. Princeton: Princeton University Press.

Kael, Pauline (1971) *The Citizen Kane Book*. Boston: Little, Brown and Company.

Kimmel, William (1980) The Phrygian inflection and the appearance of death in Music. *College Music Symposium*, vol. 20.

Kolodin, Irving (1969) *The Continuity of Music: A History of Influence*. New York: Alfred A. Knopf.

Lippman, E. (1966) 'The problem of musical hermeneutics: A protest and analysis' in S. Hook (ed.) *Art and Philosophy: A Symposium*. New York: New York University Press.

Pauli, Hansjörg (1990) 'Bernard Herrmanns Musik zu *Citizen Kane*'. *Dissonanz*, vols. 23–6.

Rosar, William H. (1994) 'Film music and Heinz Werner's theory of physiognomic perception'. *Psychomusicology*, vol. 13.

Seroff, Victor I. (1950) *Rachmaninoff*. New York: Simon and Schuster.

Siegel, Joel E. (1973) *Val Lewton: the Reality of Terror*. New York: Viking.

Smith, Steven C. (1991) *A Heart at Fire's Center*. Berkeley: University of California Press.

Wellek, A. (1962) The relationship between music and poetry. *Journal of Aesthetics and Art Criticism*, vol. 21.

Zador, Leslie T. and Greg Rose (1989) 'A conversation with Bernard Herrmann' in McCarty, Clifford (ed.) *Film Music 1*. New York: Garland.

Chapter 6

The Documentary Film Scores of Gail Kubik

Alfred W. Cochran

Gail Kubik (1914–84) was one of the most interesting and talented American composers of his generation. He succeeded, as few individuals have, in writing both outstanding functional scores, as well as music of distinction for the concert hall. Moreover, Kubik's concert music was often based upon ideas gleaned from his cinema, radio and television scores. *Symphonie Concertante* (1951), for example, earned the Pulitzer Prize in Music, and was derived from his highly acclaimed film score, *C-Man* (1949). One of the main reasons for Kubik's success in both the functional and concert areas was an unflagging commitment to giving his media scores the same attention and quality that he devoted to his concert music. He felt that a composer's principal obligation was to express, through music, the myriad aspects of contemporary life.

Not surprisingly, Kubik was quite outspoken in his opinions, as expressed musically or with the literary pen. In a 1946 article, he wrote:

> To know contemporary music, . . . to have assimilated the creative music of our time and to hear in those sounds the life, the tensions of our time – to experience these things is to be, emotionally, fully alive. More than that, to know what our modern composers are saying is to give evidence not only of an emotional maturity without which no adult can claim to be living in complete awareness of his own time. To understand this fact is to help the adult listener into an eventual enjoyment of the sounds made by the men whose special talent is to interpret for us in tone the life we lead today. I cannot believe that film music, as a phenomenon of the twentieth century, poses special problems which make it desirable that it should mirror, not our time, but that of three, four or five generations ago. No other art is so

contemporaneous as motion pictures. No art has ever in the long history of recorded civilisation achieved such wide-spread, democratic support. But why most film music has to reflect not this mass audience support and contemporaneousness, but, rather the days of hoop skirts and the bustle, is more than I can figure out. Could it be that the film public knows its musical 'facts of life,' but the film makers don't? (Kubik 1946)

These comments were preceded the year before by an article he wrote about composing for radio. He said,

In the concert hall there is both good and bad music. But almost all incidental music aired today is bad: very bad; unoriginal, synthetic, derivative; second- , third- , fourth- , and fifth-rate; stylistically and aesthetically bad . . . just so much drivel.

In their relationship to the mass audience the serious composers – at least the men thirty-five and under – have been the victims of some factors over which they have had little control. Any composer knows only too well that the interest in new music, so much talked about, is often akin to that given to the cow with two heads. The world simply wonders – and at a safe distance, too – how music got that way! . . . And no matter what Virgil Thomson says, audiences are not just dying to hear new music.

Guts and talent are the qualities needed most. We assume the talent . . . The big question, however, is not one of talent, but of determination to get on. More than anything else, remember: write your own style . . . If you alter it stylistically to conform to someone else's taste, you are no better than the men you are trying to replace, and your composer prerogatives will dwindle with every score.

Writing for the mass audience of radio is today a social obligation which has been poorly fulfilled by composers whose story is one of professional procrastination on a large scale.

Let the serious composers accept these challenges. Let them use at least a part of their energies to bring creative music to the ears of this enormous new audience. (Kubik 1945)

Kubik's functional music reflects these thoughts consistently. They combine to form a fundamental aspect of his musical persona and provide a valuable insight into what many of his friends and enemies considered to be a complex, and often difficult to get along with, personality. How then did Kubik become involved in writing for the media?

Gail Kubik was extraordinarily precocious. He spent his youth in Coffeyville, Kansas, and at fifteen was granted a full scholarship to the

Eastman School of Music, even though he had not yet finished high school. At the time, he was the youngest person to garner such an honour. He graduated from the Eastman School in 1934, and at age nineteen, Kubik began teaching at college. He went on to teach at two other universities, including Teachers College, Columbia University, became a fellow of the MacDowell Colony, and began doctoral study at Harvard – the youngest person in music to do so, before joining the NBC radio network in 1940. His desire to write media scores was so strong that he agreed to work without pay for seventeen weeks, before being named a staff composer. His success at NBC was immediate, and he particularly enjoyed working with the celebrated NBC Symphony Orchestra, who also performed his music. His work also caught the attention of Aaron Copland, who praised his radio scores to Mina Lederman – prompting her to request an article for the periodical *Modern Music* from Kubik about composing for the radio.[1] Copland shared Kubik's commitment to writing quality music for the media. Indeed, Copland and Virgil Thomson were major influences in shaping Kubik's compositional philosophy, and he was well acquainted with their recent documentary film scores. Through the influence of his boss at NBC, Ernest LaPrade, Kubik received his first film scoring assignment – George Gercke's *Men and Ships* (1940).

The decade of the 1930s was politically, tumultuous and much of the world was poised on the brink of war by 1940, if not already engaged in actual conflict. Newspapers reported daily the ominous news of Germany and Italy flexing their military muscles in Europe, while Japan pursued its own imperialistic ambitions in Asia. Spain and China reeled under the brutal assaults of the Axis powers, and documentary films began to appear, chronicling the unfolding events. These included *The Spanish Earth* (1937), for which Marc Blitzstein and Virgil Thomson assembled music, and George Gercke's *Men and Ships*. Gercke's film told the story of the efforts of the American government and the US Maritime Commission to prepare for the anticipated military conflagration. Its prologue proclaimed:

> Today all the vast resources of America are dedicated to the needs of national unity and national security. Pledged to the renewal of a great tradition, we are rebuilding the American Merchant Marine . . . The Merchant Marine must play a vital part in the national plan of preparedness and no factor in national security can be neglected.

Men and Ships is a quality production and it was made by experienced professionals. Luckily, Gercke had been Pare Lorenz's assistant on several documentary films and he expected a musical score of high quality. Gercke shared these thoughts with Kubik, who was thoroughly delighted, and the composer met the challenge admirably. The score was composed in November and December 1940, as finishing touches were put to the film, which opened in New York City in June 1941 to excellent reviews. Once again, Kubik's music was singled out for special praise, and he received an invitation to conduct the score in a live network broadcast with the NBC Symphony Orchestra. The score accompanies virtually all of the twenty-minute film and provides an effective, and interesting, musical accompaniment. Its moods range from bold and commanding, quiet and introspective, to jazz-influenced, Latin dance music – this section was later refashioned and published for orchestra as *Bachata* (*Cuban Dance Piece*) (1954). Of particular interest are Kubik's non-literal quotations and manipulations of the American folk tune *Shenandoah*. This presages Kubik's predilection for using folk tunes in ingenious ways as portions of larger scale works for the concert hall or as freestanding pieces. In short, Kubik's music for *Men and Ships* succeeds in capturing the essence of the film, amplifying its meaning and intensifying the screen action and narration. He found, to his surprise and delight, that he was adept at writing functional music, and he truly enjoyed the challenges and rewards that accompanied composing for the media.

With the bombing of Pearl Harbor in December 1941, America was suddenly thrust into the Second World War. To justify and support America's position in the conflict, the Office of War Information put together a forty-six-minute film, *The World at War* (1942), which was made up of American and captured enemy documentary footage. The opening states: 'This film represents an attempt to represent history in the making. The editors are Americans, and therefore partisan, but every effort has been made to let the facts speak for themselves.' The film's unique nature, its real-life images and gripping narration, made for a compelling movie, and it was the first-ever released under the imprimatur of the United States government. Because of Kubik's success with *Men and Ships*, he was offered the film scoring assignment, and he accepted it enthusiastically. The film was released in September 1942, and it garnered excellent reviews, many of which singled out the music for special praise – something rather unusual. *The New York Times* set the tone, calling the score 'eloquent'

(Crowther 1942), and this sentiment was reflected uniformly through-out the New York, and national, press. Never before had Kubik received this degree of public attention, and he enjoyed it. His feelings of elation were mitigated, however, by an unfortunate incident with the film's director, Sam Spewak, over cuts to his score and the low level at which the music was mixed in the soundtrack for the film. Kubik recalled, 'In the dubbing session . . . I lost a lot of the music, as they say, on the cutting room floor. I was so upset that I went to a lawyer and tried to buy back the score.'[2]

Kubik was unsuccessful in doing so, however, and the events strained the relationship between director and composer. In truth, Spewak was justified in reducing the amount of music Kubik wrote for the film. Kubik scored virtually the entire film, just as he had done with *Men and Ships*. This was simply too much music, owing to the particular nature of the film, and Spewak reduced the score by roughly half. This infuriated Kubik. Moreover, the music that remains is mixed at levels that are often too low for maximum effect. The naturally suspicious Kubik interpreted Spewak's actions as a personal attack. He was convinced that the director was jealous of him and was intentionally trying to keep the music from being heard. Whether true or not, the incident reveals that the two men did not communicate effectively with one another during the initial spotting of the film, when music allocation decisions are normally made. Despite these problems, Kubik's score provides a powerful reinforcement of the visual images, narration and story line. The film's beginning is particularly effective, as it consists of music and images only, without narration. Here, Kubik is allowed to set the mood for the film, which, despite the extensive cuts to the score, is retained throughout its duration.

Because of his superlative work on *The World at War*, Kubik was put in charge of music for all the Office of War Information films. He planned to score some of these himself, to engage 'serious' composers to provide music for others and to assemble a library of recorded music, in Hollywood, for use with yet other titles. Even as *The World at War* was released, Kubik set to work on another OWI film, *Paratroops*, which he followed with *Manpower*, *Colleges at War* and a series of *Victory* shorts. These films were each under ten minutes in length, with *Paratroops* having the most sophisticated score. Kubik later presented the music from this film as a concert suite for orchestra, consisting of a march followed by a theme and variations. But most of

Kubik's composing time in late 1942 and early 1943 was devoted to another OWI film project *Dover* – referred to as 'Twenty-One Miles' on the manuscript score. This was a production of the British Ministry of Information, and it was released in 1943 by the OWI. With a narration by Edward R. Murrow, Dover is a compelling and dramatic documentary film; its working title, 'Twenty-One Miles', refers to the narrow distance across the English Channel separating England from Nazi-occupied France. The film was shot earlier in the war, when things looked bleaker for Great Britain, and it follows up an earlier Murrow report from the same part of England. Kubik's music is well crafted, but the score is barely audible in some places. While this is aesthetically justifiable in a general sense, the low music levels render portions of the score ineffectual and others distracting. *Dover* was Kubik's last OWI film; he was not exempt him from military service, and would soon be drafted unless on his own initiative he found a position with a military unit and enlisted. Kubik was indefatigable in his efforts to land a job composing for the military, and eventually he succeeded. With the assistance of the Pentagon's Lieutenant Colonel W. J. Keighly and Tom Prideaux of the War Department, Kubik secured a position with the Army Air Force's First Motion Picture Unit, in Culver City, California. The unit was truly unique in military history, for it was located at what had been, before the war, the Hal Roach Studios, and it numbered among its ranks many Hollywood luminaries including Arthur Kennedy, Clark Gable, George Montgomery and Ronald Reagan. Kubik joined a staff of composers at 'Fort Roach' that included David Rose and former *Prix de Rome* winner, Alex Steinert, who was his supervisor. Almost at once, they developed a dislike for one another – Kubik disdained Steinert for 'selling out to Hollywood', while Steinert mistrusted Kubik as an arrogant, League of Composers snob from New York City. Kubik sought to leave the unit but was unable to secure a transfer. Meanwhile, Steinert prevented him from scoring any films by withholding assignments. Eventually, however, Kubik was given Jerry Chodorov's *Earthquakers*, a movie about the 12th Bomber Group of the Ninth Air Force, which was based in North Africa. In a serendipitous turn of events, Kubik's musical score attracted the favourable attention of virtually everyone on post, including the commanding officer, and, in Kubik's words, 'Overnight, in a matter of minutes, I just became the genius on the post'.[3]

Compositionally, the *Earthquakers* score is quite representative of

Kubik's style in 1943 – rhythmically vital and active, harmonically dissonant, with distinctive, and rather angular, melodic lines. And, just as he did with the folk tune *Shenandoah* in *Men and Ships*, Kubik's *Earthquakers* score uses quotes and thematic manipulations of a variety of familiar tunes to excellent advantage; these include *Yankee Doodle*, *British Grenadiers* and *Giovenezza*. Moreover, Kubik's evocative score effectively captures a sense of time and place for the exotic North African setting, and does so in a tightly knit, and carefully thought out, manner. Scoring virtually all of the film's twenty-minute duration, he was able to imbue the music with a surprising degree of musical logic and long-range organisation, elements absent in many film composers' work. The amazing success of this film score secured Kubik an invitation to participate in the 1943 Writers' Congress, which was sponsored jointly by the University of California and the Hollywood Writers' Mobilization. He was assigned to a seminar session entitled 'Music and the War', which included the well-known composers Hanns Eisler, Darius Milhaud, William Grant Still, Adolph Deutsch and David Raksin, among others. Kubik contributed a paper, 'Music in the Documentary Film', which challenged composers to write quality music and to uphold high artistic standards. He wrote:

> Few composers here on the West Coast have been allowed the artistic freedom that is present in the music which Virgil Thomson wrote for *The Plow That Broke the Plains* and *The River*; or Aaron Copland for *The City*; or Louis Gruenberg for *The Fight for Life* . . . This insistence on the use of creative film music is based upon the one premise that creative music, like creative writing, has an ability to 'move' people that is lacking in a stereotyped synthetic style . . . It is only when a composer is allowed to react to the screen with complete sincerity and conviction that you can hope to get from him music that will reflect the particular drama and emotional values peculiar to that particular film.
>
> The real problem, however, which confronts the composer for documentary films is this: can he discover the form which the film itself takes, and . . . can he then translate his reactions to the film's structure into terms that are both musically satisfactory and convincing and yet which also supplement the dramatic impact of the film itself? (Kubik 1944)

Kubik's *Earthquakers* score garnered him yet another exciting opportunity. The noted director William Wyler had shot an extraordinary documentary film, *The Memphis Belle*, about the men who maintained and flew the B-17 bombers of the US Eighth Air Force, which was stationed in England. Wyler approached Kubik's commanding officer, Colonel Owen Crump, who immediately recommended Kubik for the job. Once again, Kubik rose to meet the challenge, and delivered a superlative score for what many have called the finest documentary film of the war. The assignment also served as the impetus for Kubik to forge a friendship with composer David Raksin, who responded to his urgent call for assistance in orchestrating the score. Raksin observed, 'I admired his music and we became friends. It isn't always that orchestrators come away admiring the music of composers; too often, you see the seamy side of a composer's work'.[4] Kubik also spent ninety days in London working on the score; there he got a real taste of the war, when his studio was bombed in late February 1944.

Scoring *The Memphis Belle* was a great opportunity for Kubik, as the film was distributed by Paramount and seen by millions of people all over the world. Moreover, it afforded Kubik the opportunity to work with William Wyler, one of the most widely revered directors of the day. In fact, *The Memphis Belle* served as the springboard for Kubik scoring another Wyler film after the war. That movie was *The Desperate Hours* (1955), a taut drama starring Fredric March and Humphrey Bogart; it was Bogart's last film before his death. Stylistically, Kubik's music for *The Memphis Belle* is quite similar to that which he composed for *Earthquakers*. Indeed, he even substituted the main title music from the earlier film for the new one. The score has a sense of logical unfolding, what Nadia Boulanger called *la grande ligne* – that is, the 'long line of inevitability'. The music succeeds in heightening the dramatic aspects of the film and, in short, provides an apt and sophisticated musical accompaniment for the film. The excellence of the score was recognised at once, and upon Kubik's return from England, *Film Music Notebook* said of him, 'His reputation as the ideal composer of music for war films is now permanently established' (Spaeth 1944).

Back at his unit in Culver City, Kubik was assigned another film to score – Frank Lloyd's *Air Pattern Pacific* (1944). The movie was shot at great personal cost; one officer was reported missing in action, another was wounded, and fully a third of the men were hospitalised for malaria. During the filming, Lloyd participated in five aerial flights, won the Air Medal, and upon returning to the United States, was awarded the Legion of Merit (Wagner 1944: 18–19). The film contains amazing scenes of combat and is quite effective. Kubik enjoyed a good working relationship with Lloyd, and both men were pleased with the score that resulted. To accompany the horrific images of combat and its aftermath, Kubik crafted a score that is super-charged with dissonance, stridency and rhythmic energy. But it is not one-dimensional; there are also moments of quiet reflection and poignancy, and some of these are among Kubik's favourites. Indeed, portions of this score later found their way into his *Symphony No. 3* (1957), which was commissioned by Dmitri Mitropoulos and the New York Philharmonic. Interestingly, that symphony also incorporated music from two more of Kubik's documentaries, *Dover* and *The World at War*. While *Air Pattern Pacific* is a commendable docu-mentary with a very good score, an overly dramatic narration and a blatantly racist attitude mar the film. Still, it provides a seemingly realistic and disturbing view of military action in the Pacific theatre.

By 1945 the war was nearing its end, and Kubik was eager to leave military service. So when Lester Koenig asked him to score another William Wyler documentary, Kubik was reluctant to commit himself to the project. Eventually, he did so, however, and in July, he began work on *Thunderbolt*, a story about the Republic P-47 aircraft, and their crews, assigned to the 57th Fighter Group of the US 12th Air Force, which was stationed in Corsica. Logistically, the film posed daunting problems for the film-makers. Since the aircraft were single-seat planes, it was not possible for photographers to go along on missions, as was the case when Wyler filmed *The Memphis Belle*. This forced Wyler to use his ingenuity to discover ways to get the shots he wanted. Obviously, film exposed in the heat of battle provided much more dramatic footage, but he found that pilots engaged in life and death missions often forgot to turn on the cameras at those times. He overcame this obstacle eventually, but then found himself at the tail end of the war, when there was little interest in putting finishing touches to the project; because of this, the editing of the film moved slowly, prompting Koenig to tell Kubik that the film needed special help from the musical score. By the time the movie was ready to be released, the war was over. This was frustrating for Wyler, who exclaimed: 'The damn war stopped on us' (Madsen 1973: 259). Kubik's score provided a needed unifying element to the film, and it did so in ways both obvious and subtle. As he was wont to do in earlier documentary film scores, Kubik included quotations from a number of popular tunes in the film score, and he handled them masterfully. Some of them include *Santa Lucia*, *O Sole Mio*, *March of the Toreadors* and *Yankee Doodle*. Stylistically, the score is quite similar to his other wartime documentaries – a similar harmonic language, imbued with prominent dissonance, angular melodic lines, rhythmic vitality and sensitive introspection, where called for. Moreover, he again showed his tendency to provide the score with a long-range plan of tonal organisation. Kubik made a concert overture for orchestra from the score (*Thunderbolt Overture*), as well as *Fanfare and March* for concert band, which he dedicated to Major George S. Howard and the Army Air Forces Band. The film was released after the war ended, in 1947, with an introduction appended by General Jimmy Stewart. *Thunderbolt* was Kubik's last documentary score for the military, and the last documentary music he composed for over a decade.

In January 1958, Kubik accepted an offer from CBS Television to score an episode of their series, *The Twentieth Century*. This marked his first offer to write for that medium, and he accepted it with enthusiasm. The programme he was to score was entitled *Hiroshima*, and it recounted the dropping of the atomic bomb on that city by American forces on 5 August 1945. Kubik worked hard on the score for a period of two weeks, completing it less than twelve hours before the recording session was to commence. What he delivered was quite extraordinary – a powerful and forward-looking score that admirably suited the profoundly moving visual images and story line. Portions of the music are incessantly repetitious, and for some of the cues, he used only non-melodic percussion instruments. The score was recorded on 1 February 1958, and producer Burton Benjamin was pleased. Kubik's first television score was hailed a stunning success, and he enjoyed the return to documentary work.

Almost exactly a year later, Kubik did a second score for *The Twentieth Century*, an episode entitled *The Silent Sentinel*, which was devoted to the history and use of radar. The topic initially posed some initially, for the composer, as was related in a CBS press release. It read, 'One of the trickiest and most challenging assignments Pulitzer Prize-winning composer Gail Kubik ever undertook was the original music score for *The Silent Sentinel* . . . How, Kubik asked himself, do you symbolize with music a completely noiseless subject, an object which makes no beeps, squeaks, hums or rattles?'[5] What he came up with was ingenious – a recurring musical theme that appears in most of the cues and which provides unity in the score. Reaction to the music heard in the broadcast on 22 March 1959 was immediate and uniformly positive, from the congratulatory notes of friends to an article in the *New York Times* (Briggs 1959).

Although Kubik did an animated industrial film about spacecraft re-entry in 1959, and scored one more commercial movie, he composed no more documentary scores during the remainder of his career. Spanning nineteen years, from *Men and Ships* (1940) to *The Silent Sentinel* (1959), Kubik's several scores in this genre reveal innovative thought, high standards and quality workmanship. He brought a forward-looking approach to these functional scores, as well as an enthusiastic zest for each project, which comes across the screen clearly. His music served as a standard of excellence for other film composers, and his commitment to artistic integrity, through his music, articles and spoken word, helped to lend credence to an art form that, theretofore, had often been the subject of criticism, much of it well deserved. Moreover, as has been seen, Kubik used musical ideas from these films as seminal material in a number of his compositions for the concert hall. Without question, Kubik's documentary scores contain some of his best, and most inspired, work. They are thus worthy of our study and attention.

Footnotes

1. Kubik refused the offer, though he was later to write an excellent article on the subject, 'The Composer's Place in Radio' in *Hollywood Quarterly*, vol. 1, no. 1, October 1945, pp. 60–8.
2. Gail Kubik, 'Functional Music,' interview with Ralph Titus, Manhattan, Kansas, 1979.
3. Ibid.
4. David Raksin, interview with the author, Los Angeles, California, 16 June 1989.
5. Unsigned press release, CBS Television Network, 485 Madison Avenue, New York, NY, 16 March 1959.

Bibliography

Briggs, John (1959) Aiding the composer: original musical scores are obtained for twentieth century series. *New York Times*, 12 April.
Crowther, Bosley (1942) The screen. *New York Times*, 4 September.
Kubik, Gail (1944) 'Music in the documentary film' in *Writers' Congress: The Proceedings of the Conference* (held in October 1943 under the sponsorship of the Hollywood Writers' Mobilization and the University of California). Berkeley: University of California Press. (Reprinted as Music in documentary films. *Music Publishers Journal*, September–October 1945.)
Kubik, Gail (1945) The Composers Place in Radio. *Hollywood Quarterly*, vol. 1, no. 1.

Kubik, Gail (1946) Movie audiences: musically mature or adolescent? *Film Music Notes*, April.

Madsen, Alex (1973) *William Wyler*. New York: Crowell.

Spaeth, Sigmund (1944) Afterthoughts. *Film Music Notebook*, vol. 3, no. 9.

Wagner, Florence (1944) Artists in Khaki. *Rob Wagner's Script*, 24 June.

Chapter 7

Embracing Kitsch: Werner Schroeter, Music and *The Bomber Pilot*

Caryl Flinn

The New German Cinema's relationship to Western art music and opera in particular is as rich as it is varied: there is Straub/Huillet's deconstructive rendering of Schoenberg's *Moses and Aaron* (1974), Syberberg's *Parsifal* (1982), his nostalgic presentation of Wagner in *Our Hitler* (1977) and Kluge's slicing and dicing of opera in *The Power of Emotions* (1983). But nowhere is the connection more elaborate and elaborated upon than with Werner Schroeter, whose stylistic and thematic association with opera spans over thirty years of working in theatre and film. Where Schroeter differs from his better known colleagues, however, is in his focus on opera's kitschy elements. As Gary Indiana notes:

> Schroeter's use of opera is metaphoric and comically grandiose. He extracts scenes from overworked masterpieces as media for a richly allusive mental theatre, runs bits and pieces together, jumbles the sublime with the ridiculous to the point of indissolubility, with the result that classical opera regains a bizarre vitality in this shredded, irreverent form. As it appears in Schroeter's first feature films, opera evokes not only a canon of musical works but also the modern perception of the operatic mentality as a species of camp. (Indiana 1982: 47)

Not for nothing does Indiana use camp in conjunction with the director's 'operatic radiant spectacles', to borrow some of Timothy Corrigan's influential formulations (Corrigan 1981; 1984). Schroeter's films are filled with the sort of heavy-handed artifice, staginess, recontextualised objects and quotations typical of camp – and, as will be the focus here, kitsch. And while most critics brand kitsch as an asocial, parasitic, emotionally and even morally bankrupt aesthetic condition – an undesirable other – Schroeter passes no judgement. If anything, his is a tender, critical embrace of its emotional intensity, however unfavourably presented.

This essay then pursues the means by which that 'embrace' is engaged. The focus will fall on *The Bomber Pilot* (*Der Bomberpilot*, 1970) one of his few films set both in Nazi and Adenauerian Germany. Not a favourite of the director, *The Bomber Pilot* avails us with a bit of kitschy undesirability and otherness from the start. In other ways, it is in full keeping with the heavily stylised, experimental form associated with Schroeter, and its emotional, operatic states are conveyed with familiar stagy intensity. *The Bomber Pilot*'s achievement lies in overturning prevailing understandings of kitsch as a rejected externality by bringing discarded, distasteful elements of what Schroeter calls German *Kulturscheisse* – be it Viennese operetta or kitsched up *Sieg Heils* – into productive play with contemporary German identities and their ongoing efforts to engage with the past and with alterity. Schroeter's musical kitsch introjects (incorporates subconsciously), rather than rejects, the less desirable artefacts of Germany's past, at the same time supporting the often ineffable desires and emotions involved. Before this, a few words on kitsch.

The Outsider: Trash, Nineteenth-century Romanticism, and Camp

The etymological roots of kitsch are widely contested, but Ludwig Giesz, as Gillo Dorfles summarises, 'attributes it to *kitschen*, meaning *den Strassenschlamm zusammenscharren*, literally "to collect rubbish from the street" . . . origin is in "street picking"'' (Dorfles 1969b: 4). The gathering and dealing in trash, the collecting up of debris, is absolutely indispensable to kitsch. Trading in rejects and the rejected, kitsch itself, as concept, is not quite allowed to enter into the domain of 'pure' aesthetics (the relative dearth of criticism on kitsch remains stunning); tasteful people don't want a velvet painting of pouting puppy dogs hanging on their living room wall; tasteful people don't buy into – or, rather, publicly admit buying into – the hamfisted pining of Rudolfo for Mimi in *La Bohéme*.

One often hears that kitsch occupies a position of art for art's sake, another way of constructing its otherness to historical and cultural context. Moreover, such aesthetic autonomy is bereft of the treasured functionlessness of Kantian art, and of the critical potential of Adorno's brand of autonomous art (though to my mind remaining stubbornly suggestive of both). For most critics, it nearly constitutes a category unto itself, so beyond the pale of aesthetic value, moral and ethical respectability is it. For instance, in the recent *Kitsch and Art*, Tomas Kulka (1996) argues that kitsch cannot even be considered bad art, since the latter reflects poor ability rather than an out-and-out breach of aesthetic value. Kulka's position is heavily influenced by novelist Herrman Broch's work on kitsch: he famously quipped, for instance, that kitsch aims to do something pretty, not to do it well. Using a provocative somatic metaphor, he writes: 'Kitsch is certainly not "bad art"; it forms its own closed system, which is *lodged like a foreign body in the overall system of art*, or which, if you prefer, appears alongside it' (Broch 1969: 62 [my emphasis]). Kitsch thus threatens to exist both inside and out. The 'preference' Broch proposes is a necessary tool for keeping it at bay, externalised not 'lodged' in the body of the aesthetic system. Its outsider status is therefore social, aesthetic, even somatic. It is also historical.

There is a certain consensus that kitsch – and its only slightly better-off cousin, camp – has its origins in mid- to late nineteenth-century Western European culture, when mass-produced commodity clutter and display were on the rise, when Europe was enthralled by deeds both political and aesthetic by the colonial 'other', when opera became a widespread form that staged some of these fantasies, when rising tourism allowed the illusion of interaction, or at least, contact with the other. Indeed, kitsch may well be viewed as a domesticated form of exoticism – a way of managing alterity.[1] But for several critics, its connections with late Romanticism are particularly noteworthy. Matei Calinescu calls kitsch a 'hackneyed form of Romanticism' (1977: 240); Saul Friedlander states 'Kitsch emotion represents a certain kind of simplified, degraded, insipid, but all the more insinuating Romanticism' (1993: 39). Generally careful to avoid claiming that Romanticism *is* kitsch – it is often delicately phrased as giving birth to kitsch – critics are on to something in linking the two: consider Romanticism's investment in precepts such as universalism and timelessness; its frequent returns to classical art do, I think, anticipate the contemporary kitsch of Michelangelo's *David* hawking wristwatches. Romanticism, also like kitsch in this regard, exalted extreme, diametrically opposed states (sublime transcendence on the one hand, abject suffering on the other), as well as intense emotional experience in general.

Kitsch and Camp

This is not the proper context for a full elaboration on the distinctions between kitsch and camp, but they share a number of features. Both have historical roots in nineteenth-century consumer culture, and both have proved to be important aesthetic strategies for lesbian, gay and queer cultures. Camp and kitsch are generally constituted through pejorative notions of worthlessness, cheapness, deception and manipulation. Perhaps out of this very sense of devaluation, lesbian, gay and queer critics and artists have sought a sort of representational refuge (I use the term reservedly) in historically denigrated notions of 'art' and 'beauty'; aesthetic schools sealed off from social and cultural responsibilities, duties, functions and engagement (that a particularly iconic example like *Au rebours* came at the end of the nineteenth century is not incidental). Embracing a disreputable form like camp or kitsch has the potential for refusing the normalising responsibilities and fictions that are imbricated in conventional notions of art and aesthetic function.

The central target and concerns of camp practices tend to revolve around the organisation and maintenance of psychic, sexual and social identity (for example, its send-up of conventional family structures). Kitsch, in contrast, tends to function as a consequence of social and economic structures, structures without which aesthetic 'taste' and 'tastelessness' could not exist. Kitsch is charged with dealing with sentimentality and in evincing predictable, formulaic 'stock emotions' (Kulka 1996: 26).[2] Camp is childish; kitsch, on the other hand, is an irresponsible adult. It should 'know better' and so is tied to a sense of inappropriateness beyond matters of taste or decorum, trespassing proper moral and ethical terrain. As we will see in a moment, nowhere is this made more apparent than in debates on representing the Holocaust. By falling outside the parameters of quality, success and productivity kitsch, unlike camp, remains a deeply denigrated term.

Indeed, kitsch is rarely valued in anyone's scheme. For many, it is the devalued, loveless other to camp's 'affectionate' send-ups (Susan Sontag called camp 'a form of love' (1999: 65). A recent reader wrote to *GQ* magazine that 'Straights don't have camp. They have kitsch'. As the latter makes clear, even queer commentators are happy to keep kitsch at a distance, as if its proximity endangered or tainted the precarious status of camp, or of gay and lesbian cultures *tout court*.

That tendency is especially interesting given the extent to which Schroeter's queer contemporaries, such as Monika Treut, Rosa von Praunheim and the early work of Ulrike Ottinger, have consciously embraced kitschiness, as did Fassbinder, particularly in the gay- and lesbian-themed *The Bitter Tears of Petra von Kant* (1972), *Satan's Brew* (1976), and *Querelle* (1982). This is not to imply that kitsch *is* queer, but the ostensible status of both as outsiders is worth noting given the tendency of the socially and ideologically empowered to project negative features onto 'others'. It is also worth acknowledging camp and kitsch's considerable historic importance to gay, lesbian and queer aesthetic production. Schroeter, for his part, explicitly refuses to buy into kitsch's averred 'lovelessness': for him, the overwrought performative, visual and acoustic presentation of his films is key to capture what Thomas Elsaesser (1989) has called the authenticity of feeling, a feeling that may not be specified except through or as intensity; an emotion or desire without source or goal.

Kitsch and Fascism

It goes without saying that, Schroeter aside, kitsch is not always historically instructive, nor is it of constant significance to queer and gay cultures. It serves many different ends, as two cinematic examples dramatise. One of mainstream cinema's most delightful kitsch sequences is Charlie Chaplin's balletic dance with the air-filled globe in *The Great Dictator* (1940). The sequence is famous for its total absence of dialogue; we hear nothing but Wagner's *Lohengrin*.[3] It renders the 'blood and soil' nobility that Wagner's work exemplified for Hitler ridiculous and light, though still diabolical. The film scene succeeds not for any post-war, retrospective 'camping' of the composer (as is easily done), but for demonstrating the vicious kitschiness of Nazism's Wagner-fetish in the first place.

On a recent *Rosie O'Donnell Show*, O'Donnell gave her guest, Italian director Roberto Benigni, a gift, as is her tradition. It was a hat once warn by Chaplin – she knew Benigni was 'a big fan'. Moved, he said he didn't deserve it. This may be true, if one compares Chaplin's depiction of fascism in *The Great Dictator* with Benigni's *Life is Beautiful* (1998), the Oscar-gilded film which, as the title presses us into belief, is a 'beautiful' film (as opposed, say, to an historical one), a soft, humanist celebration of the human spirit. Kitsch cannot be far off. In his own insightful critique, Jim Hoberman discusses *Life is*

Beautiful's self-proclaimed status as 'fable'.[4] With the precedent set by *Schindler's List* (1993), he notes that the

> Holocaust is now ancient history – the stuff of myth. Imagine a 'simple fable' of paternal self-sacrifice set in a Serbian concentration camp or in the killing fields of Rwanda. Had Benigni done so, he would have had a more difficult time calling his comedy *Life is Beautiful* – let alone getting audiences to sit for it. (Hoberman 1999: 23)

Saul Friedlander has also challenged the transformation of modernity's most brutal era into the realm of myth. His 1982 *Reflections on Nazism* was written in response to the Nazi-retro films popular in Europe at the time, among them German films like *Our Hitler* and *Lili Marlene* (1980) which, together with literary examples, constitute what he called the 'new discourse' of Nazism. In them Friedlander locates strategies of disavowal which mask the atrocities of the Nazi past precisely as that past is depicted and staged. They achieve this, he maintains, by encouraging a 'fascinating fascism' either through eroticism (*The Night Porter* [Cavani 1973]) or banality (the sequences of *Our Hitler* painstakingly detailing Hitler's daily life, producing a sense of his 'ordinariness').

Even the well-intentioned films which might, for example, stress the endurability of fascism in contemporary Europe (for example, *The Spider's Stratagem* [Bertolucci 1970]), Friedlander argues that their spectacularisation (or inversely, their banalisation) of fascism mirrors fascism's own brand of kitsch, a kitsch Friedlander ultimately links to death. In other words, and in contrast to critics who regard it as simply functionless or cheap failure, Friedlander stresses its very costly dangers when the stakes are as high as in representing something as immense as the Shoah. In this scheme, kitsch's tastelessness and inappropriateness resides in its inability to separate the heinous facts of the regime's atrocities, the material horrors of death, from their banalisation, sentimentalisation or glorification. The process eroticises, spectacularises, honours and mythologises. In a word, Nazism's kitschy relationship to death is aestheticised (and anestheticised, to be sure), recalling Benjamin's famous warning about the aestheticisation of politics at the end of 'The Work of Art in the Age of Mechanical Reproduction' (Benjamin 1992). Friedlander puts the matter quite simply: 'Kitsch death is a means to digest the past' (Friedlander 1993: 40). For Schroeter, by contrast, kitsch's introjection of the past does not devour or kill it, but retains it and moves it forward into the present.

Schroeter's Kitschy Bomber pilot

The Bomber Pilot features three women, Carla (Carla Aulaulu), Mascha (Mascha Elm-Rabben), and Magdelana Munn (Magdalena Montezuma). The trio perform as *Cabaret*-type singers during the Nazi era, forced to disband when Carla takes a job with a Viennese theatre and Mascha has a nervous breakdown (the latter is staged within the first minutes of the film). *Pilot* absent-mindedly follows their individual activities, depicting scenes of Carla's 'show', most of them of her singing in a Viennese pastry shop;[5] Magdelana's attempts to find work for the still-fragile Mascha by posing as her aunt and appealing to a Nazi official; Mascha's later rescue of Magdelana from drowning herself – and the two, we hear, eventually land jobs as secretaries. The trio meet again after the war, we are told, at a Bruckner performance, where they discuss regrouping to go to the US, as reformers rather than performers, eager to teach integrationism (apparently we are now in the late 1960s, the time of the film's production). Carla, nostalgic for their previous Nazi stage career, is hard to convince, but the three go to the US. Their downfall as 'teachers' there results from a published photograph of them in a Nazi-era photo; added to this is the controversy of Mascha's un-depicted liaison with an American bomber pilot. We are told there is a trial (also undepicted) and the three go back to cabaret performances in Germany for US troops. Carla has a miscarriage from 'Mascha's' bomber pilot, and suffers badly. The final image of the film shows her, supported by Magdelena, weakly walking around in front of what looks to be the same officious building that appears in the film's first shot. Mascha chews up a Wagner song: 'Does only death bring life? Does suffering create only wounds? Please let me suffer like that, O Nature.'

Bomberkitsch and Cinematic Form

The Bomber Pilot's kitsch elements are simple to identify. It disregards verisimilitude at every turn. Spatial and temporal contexts barely enter the representational field; instead we get metonymic pieces of history and place – swastika banners here, black Americans in late 1960s dress there. Sounds and images are stagy, pre-digested, like the bad recordings of Liszt, or Elvis doing Neapolitan songs. Nothing is shot using synch sound. Props, sets and situations are conspicuously 'cheap' (the scenes in America are clearly shot at a US military base in Germany; baby-dolls, garters and corsets slide continuously off characters' shoulders and breasts), and the film does nothing to hide its low budget. Inappropriate, absurd behaviour rules the day: Mascha informs the Nazi official that she wants to work at a hospice for dogs. Characters are so far removed from the realm of individualised, 'real' feelings that their names are taken from those of the actresses who portray them, blurring boundaries of fiction and production. Their actions are often intertwined to the point of interchangeability – Carla and Mascha share the same lover, and at least once wear the same dress; Mascha and Magdalena each mother the other during breakdowns. The film makes no attempt to convey authenticity or a credible, coherent diegetic world; the acting style is histrionic and over the top, and cameras capture characters straight on. Scenes ostensibly depicting Carla's play are shot no differently than those that follow the story of the women more generally; a sequence at the graveyard of her stage character's lover (?) is shown out of doors, for instance, with no more 'staginess' than most of the other scenes, which are shot as if they were theatre pieces, for example Mascha's breakdown at the beginning. We do not learn what causes Mascha's breakdown; nor do we never see for certain the bomber pilot who sleeps with Mascha and Carla (a photo of Mascha standing next to one of several American military men is all that we get).

Bomber Pilot: Music and *Kulturscheisse*

The music in *The Bomber Pilot* is a grab bag of selections from all over: Verdi, Sibelius, Wagner, Strauss, *Carmen Jones* (1954), *West Side Story* (1961), Elvis and different US and German pop tunes. Its simultaneously kitschy and critical functions are in evidence from the film's opening shot, in which the three garter- and girdled-women *Sieg Heil* in front of a Nazi flag as we hear the final, triumphant section of Liszt's Wagnerian-style *Symphonic Poem No.1, Les Préludes*. Historically, it is an important choice. Key figures in the New German School, both Liszt and Wagner stressed music's dramatic and poetic potential, as in Wagner's well-known concept of the *Gesamtkunstwerk*, which would unify all of the arts; this was fulfilled for him by opera (namely, his own 'music drama'). Thus as Wagnerian and bombastic as the film's opening music is, and with the Nazi kitsch it immediately calls forth, its irony is already fierce, since Wagner's interest in unifying aesthetic elements is, to say the least, not applicable to this film nor to is use of opera. Moreover, the quality of Liszt recordings is deliberately awful. The kitsch continues: just after the brief bit of Liszt, we hear a traditional rendering of Johann Strauss II's waltz, *On the Beautiful Blue Danube*, whose glittery image of rivers and *fin-de-siécle* Vienna and whose sprightly, soprano delivery are kitschily inappropriate to *The Bomber Pilot*'s diegetic world, such as it is.

These initial examples of kitsched-up German and Austrian musical relics recall kitsch's trash-collecting aspect. But unlike the decidedly untrashy compilation works of colleague Alexander Kluge, or the cluttered *mise-en-scène* of Syberberg – directors whose work in the 1970s and early 1980s was interested in *German* identity – *German* history, *German* culture, *The Bomber Pilot* makes clear that identity and desire cannot be patched together from the wreckage of a singularly conceived national culture. The matter is driven home in a key post-war scene, when we are told in voice over that the women meet 'at a Bruckner concert in the Municipal Theatre'. One by one, each woman enters the foyer. The concert has already started, no one else is present and the voiceover tells us that the three do not actually meet until after the long first movement. Obviously, we expect to hear something by Bruckner, a composer whose favoured status under the Reich is well known. (His work was even conducted differently during the war.) We wonder if Schroeter will provide a Nazi sanctioned version, or another. Yet in the end, we get neither: we hear not Bruckner, but part of the overture to Verdi's *Nabucco*.

The selection clearly dramatises the unreliable nature of image and sound. By falsely announcing a Bruckner performance, the soundtrack exposes its own deceptiveness, making that split emerge from within and not from the imagetrack, to which sound is often opposed – or exposed. In one way, the absence of Bruckner mimics the post-Nazi censorship of him, a way of 'refusing to come to terms' with one of the Reich's favoured composers. But why Verdi? To this day, Verdi remains one of Italy's biggest national treasures, a composer who worked out of an entirely different tradition from Bruckner, who was roughly his contemporary. (Like Wagner, Bruckner preferred a slow, developmental, large-scale style of composition, whereas Verdi worked in more episodic musical structures – not unlike the tableaux-like form of *Bomber Pilot* itself.)[6] Verdi, however, does not escape 'German-ness'; in fact he is constitutive of it. First of all, *Nabucco* is an openly political opera about the oppression of the Jewish nation. How can this be anything other than a spur the side of Aryan purity in this context?[7] Schroeter takes the Nazi German-ness Bruckner 'represents' and formally equates it with – replaces it with – the very Jewish community it worked to deny and eradicate. It is that latter voice that must be heard and, in its displaced fashion, it is.[8] But that 'Jewish voice' is, of course, encrypted within another level of non-German foreignness. Verdi, a nationalist composer so identified with Italy as to be labelled the composer of the *Risorgimento,* represents another (less vilified) other, a foreign, externalised term. Lastly, the acoustic presence of Verdi in the scene, like that of Italian opera throughout the film, acknowledges Germany's fascination with Latin cultures like Italy and Spain, a fantasy as economically real (tourism) as it is phantasmatically potent. Although Schroeter does not buy into them, the binarisms that enable such an ethnic 'othering' are, of course, both obvious and obnoxious.[9] Verdi's opera, by assuming the acoustic space that was to have been Bruckner's, in this way elaborates the necessity of (ethnic) difference and alterity in establishing German-ness itself – much like kitsch is required to be traditional art's degraded other.

The German-ness that Verdi censors and constitutes is influenced by other music as well, and establishes German-ness through repeated border crossings. We hear a short bridge from *West Side Story,* whose combined presence of Stephen Sondheim and especially Leonard Bernstein intermingles the musical's usual 'popular' status with higher 'artistic' forms; Elvis sings the traditional Neapolitan song *Santa Lucia* in an especially bizarre regional cross-pollination. American pieces like these might be said to infiltrate the film the same way that the American bomber pilot infiltrates the German bodies of Carla and, to a lesser degree, Mascha.

An especially interesting pop musical example is *Beat out Dat Rhythm on a Drum,* from *Carmen Jones,* the (and to some, already kitschy) film adaptation of Georges Bizet's *Carmen* (*Beat out Dat Rhythm on a Drum* is based on a portion of what was originally the *Gypsy Dance*). *Carmen,* of course, is a particularly striking example of nineteenth-century Europe's colonialist impulses: fetishising, eroticising, yet degrading the ethnic/national/regional/sexual other; curiously, it was almost the only piece of French music not banned by the Nazis during the war before France fell.[10] Its cinematic adaptation is well known as being one of few all-black mainstream Hollywood produc-

tions of the late classical era. Released at roughly the same time that
the women of *Bomber Pilot* consider bringing their integrationist
message to the US, it is worth noting that the director Otto Preminger
– another German who came to American – had an especially intense
interest in the racial 'other', maintaining a relatively long-term affair
with Dorothy Dandridge. (Interestingly, he kept it closeted.)[11]
Rhythm on a Drum appears in *Bomber Pilot* several times, usually
in stagy, repetitive scenes of Mascha, Magdalena and Carla 'smoking
a marijuana cigarette at the breakfast table', perhaps in punning
reference to Carmen's job in a cigar factory in the Bizet opera.
Motionlessly the women prepare their message, collectively and
kitschily jumping slightly out of their seats several seconds after a
voiceover, seemingly influenced by the song's lyrics that say 'our
hearts took a leap'.

It is worth returning to the *Vienna Blood Waltz* that Carla sings to
observe how this clichéd cultural icon functions as an acoustic builder
of national and subjective identities. To most auditors, Johann Strauss
II's tune is already familiar to the point of kitsch, and Carla's frequent
and deliberately awful renderings do nothing to dispel that. The piece
intially was written without lyrics: Strauss later incorporated it into an
1899 operetta of the same title, and another rendering, by Willi Forst
(1942), would prove enormously popular with Nazi officials. The
following are the lyrics from the original operetta.[12] Note their
emphasis on the body as carrier of regional and national identity:

> *Wiener Blut!*
> *Wiener Blut!*
> *Eig'ner Saft,*
> *Voller Kraft,*
> *Voller Glut!*
> *Wiener Blut,*
> *Selt'nes Gut!*
> *Du erhebst*
> *Und belebst*
> *Unsern Mut!*
> *Wiener Blut!*
> *Wiener Blut!*
> *Was die Stadt*
> *Schoenes hat,*
> *In dir ruht!*
> *Wiener Blut!*

Heisse Flut!
Allerort
Gilt das Wort:
Wiener Blut!

(Vienna blood,
Vienna blood,
Makes you fly
Like a song
To the sky.
Makes your heart
Ever gleam,
Gives a wing
To your dream!
Vienna blood,
Vienna blood!
Makes you see
Paradise
In the smile
Of two eyes.
Makes you laugh,
Makes you cry,
Really live
Till you die!)[13]

With this repeated song in mind – and whose adjusted lyrics I am deliberately withholding for the moment – it is worth turning to Saul Friedlander, who has written unfavourably about another popular German song, *Lili Marlene*, as it appears in Fassbinder's eponymous film. Kitsch, he maintains, is produced through deliberate, predictable and formulaic repetition, just as a kitsch artefact is supposed to engender predictable, formulaic emotions. According to him, the constantly repeated, sentimental song functions in just this way. (Interestingly, he shares Goebbels' well-known disdain for the piece – 'A melodramatic song on top of a macabre dance' – quoted in Friedlander [1993: 40], and extends that judgement to Fassbinder's film at large.) Without going into too much detail, it seems to me that Friedlander underestimates how films like Schroeter's or Fassbinder's do indeed acknowledge the 'macabre dance' of Nazism. Gary Indiana has argued along the same lines, noting that *The Bomber Pilot* 'reduce[s] several turgid clichés about Nazi Germany to their actual size', and about the director's work more generally: 'Schroeter's flaunting use of Wagnerian bombast and the species of kitsch most readily identified as fascist food has the peculiar virtue of tapping a tradition that is, in Germany, simultaneously sacrosanct and shameful. In Germany (and even elsewhere), every Schroeter film is a fresh provocation' (Indiana 1982: 48, 46). He uses kitsch against itself, taking aim not just at the overblown expressivity of German Romanticism, but, as Indiana maintains, Nazi kitsch, in all its deadliness.

Schroeter's Homeopathic Embrace

I want to reformulate what I initially presented as Schroeter's 'embrace' of kitsch in terms of the medical concept of homeopathy, whose relevance to post-war Germany was made evident in Eric Santner's 1990 study of the New German Cinema, *Stranded Objects*. Homeopathy is a naturopathic medical treatment in which small, controlled doses of a harmful element (for example illness, allergy or poison) are administered into an afflicted body, enabling it to heal. Science is not sure how it works – and indeed, homeopathy itself functions as a stubborn, indigestible and potentially upsetting 'other' to the medical establishment, just as kitsch does to traditional aesthetics.[14] Homeopathic principals describe equally the kitsch process as well, since both absorb (literally in homeopathy, whose small pills are absorbed sublingually) and encrypt undesirable 'poisonous' elements.

Psychoanalytically applied, homeopathy can describe, for example, the encrypted losses and attachments Abraham and Torok discuss in their work on formation of the ego-body. For Santner, standard psychic development is a kind of homeopathic process, beginning with the *fort/da* game, in which the child stages and controls the disappearance of its mother through transitional objects that function as substitutes (toys, and so on). '[T]hanks to this procedure, he [sic] is able to administer in controlled doses the absence he is mourning' (Santner 1990: 20). The *fort/da* game, the dosing out of negative elements, may give the child a sense of 'mastering' its initial traumas, it must be remembered that that mastery is illusory since with it the child homeopathically 'integrate[s] the loss of its narcissistic fantasies of centrality and omnipotence' (Santner 1990: 21). As Santner goes on to say, the self-administration of negativity, absence and death recurs more forcefully in the Oedipal phase of psychic development since castration, an inferior relation to the father's phallus, is inscribed on developing ego-bodies. Again, such 'integration' of loss, 'empowers the child to have a future of his [sic] own' (Santner 1990: 22). So while necessary for survival, the homeopathic process cannot be confused with conquest, or moving past a painful loss or trauma. Nor is it a form of recovery to reclaim imagined lost 'states'.

One always takes a certain methodological leap when moving from medical or psychoanalytic processes to cinematic texts and even more so, to national bodies at large. Yet Santner compellingly argues how homeopathic principles are relevant to the New German Cinema, emerging from a 'wound culture', and whose films are filled with fragments, reworked icons, music and histories in its well-known efforts to 'come to terms with the past'. In the hands of Schroeter, German *Kulturscheisse* offers a means of accepting the most unwanted elements of aesthetics, subjectivity and history. Such objects that connect us to the past – at conscious and unconscious levels – help us establish an active relationship to it, even when it seems at considerable remove to our own cultural, historical and subjective position. Ours is thus less a control over undesirable aspects of the past but an encryptment of its losses, a homeopathic embrace, a bringing *into relationship with* present identity, at sociopolitical and psychological levels.

Viennese Poison

The acoustic haunting of Carla by Johann Strauss II's *Vienna Blood Waltz* gives the most conspicuous example of potential homeopathic introjection in *The Bomber Pilot*. The piece may be said to haunt the body of the film as well, so obsessively is it played, along with other Strauss compositions. The stranded object of a lost time, the familiar tune is frozen into acoustic iconicity, a kitschy emblem of *fin-de-siécle* Viennese culture – with its waltzes, twinkling rivers, lavish pastry and coffee shops – impossibly interwoven and idealised. As the original libretto reveals, that fantasy extends into the body itself, intertwining geographic and somatic elements into a rigid fiction of regional identity: Vienna literally runs through your veins. In other words, so fully at one are Viennese subjects with their surroundings as to be physically indistinguishable from them – blood, rivers, all flow together, the very sources of this propped up identity. From a post-Holocaust perspective, and in an era of continuing nationalist bloodshed, the notion is hardly reassuring, being so conspicuously close to Nazism's ideology of establishing national and racial identity through bloodlines (in these terms the Jews, of course, with no homeland, could boast no such purity).[15] Blood and soil, indeed.

Schroeter kitschy exaggerates the pernicious element of the original *Wienerblut* through Carla's modified lyrics, which are loosely translated here:

> Vienna blood,
> Vienna blood,
> Full of movement,
> Full of life,
> Full of Spite.
>
> Vienna blood,
> Vienna blood,
> Full of movement,
> Full of life,
> Full of Spite.
>
> You have conquered
> our hearts and our souls
> All of Vienna
> Runs in our veins
> With its floral bouquets of melodies.
> Only Vienna blood
> Completely understands us,
> The real Viennese.
>
> People who're always nervous
> Who argue
> And get angry
> Throughout the year
> Vienna's best
> Return quickly to good feelings.
> And who's to blame?
> Only Vienna blood!
>
> When our hearts are nearly broken
> We never complain
> Because what's done is done
> The past is past
> What good is it to discuss?
> You have to hold hands.

Vienna blood,
Vienna blood,
Full of movement,
Full of life,
Full of Spite.

You have conquered
our hearts and our souls
All of Vienna
Runs in our veins
With its floral bouquets of melodies.
Only Vienna blood
Completely understands us,
The real Viennese.

With his new lyrics Schroeter reveals some of the non-homeopathic choices postwar German subjects might take: 'what's done is done/ the past is past/ what good is it to discuss?' Instead of integrating the Nazi past into the present, it is cast out like bad blood, its negative aspects projected on to others for fear of contaminating the lively Viennese strain, which alone is believed to veil over (as opposed to working through) irritability, bad moods or, one imagines, an unpleasant little experience like Nazism. Yet Carla holds on to the poisonous song, unable to release the past pleasures it represents for her – namely, the fulfilment and accomplishment 'she' experienced in the Nazi era.[16] Singing it over and over again, she is oblivious to its potential as a homeopathic object that might enable her to move forward. She is equally unaware of its deadliness. Not accidentally, she learns about the death of her real or theatrical lover (played by Schroeter) immediately after first performing it. Nor is it incidental that she is actively harmed by the 'angry', 'spiteful' blood on which the lyrics insist, and it is she who loses blood during the miscarriage of the bomber pilot's fetus. It would seem that the introjection of American otherness cannot be sustained by her 'real Viennese' body, and she is left barely able to walk. It is utterly plausible that Carla be associated with the piece, since of the three, she is the most enticed by theatrical exhibitionism, performing for the other, and receiving its approving gaze and ears. That approval, of course, was lost after the war. Subsequently, her body-ego was particularly susceptible to all sorts of poisonous introjections, be they that of her beloved but spiteful Viennese blood, or the damaging sperm of the US military pilot.

The other two women, on the other hand, while equally performative, seem unconcerned about the approval of Viennese, Nazi or US military audiences (although I hesitate to psychologise the characters this way, see note 14). Even the choice of music they perform individually for US troops in German at the end of the film reveals a disregard for what might have pleased the audience. Mascha, clad in mink, offers an off-key rendition of *Schmerzen* (The Bliss of Sorrow) from a Wagner song cycle to virulent hisses, Magdelana performs her equally inappropriate Diamanda Galas-like *Snake Dance*. Carla, by contrast, perfectly at home, sings a well-received *Habanera* (kitsch and exoticism again) called *Abschied am Meer* – apparently still unable to leave water imagery behind. The intensity of Mascha's and Magdalena's performances is important as expressions of undefined emotion – quite unlike the predictably, saccharine feelings with which kitsch is usually associated.

Despite these and other efforts, most conspicuously their efforts to promote racial integration to American audiences,[17] it would appear difficult that the women do not succeed in homeopathically working through their past, especially given that the film militates against psychological readings of its figures. But if *The Bomber Pilot* does not offer a successful homeopathic cure to these fictional figures, it does reveal the way the process works, in large part through its use of music.

It is worth returning here to Hermann Broch, cited earlier. The full quote reveals how the attempt to ostracise kitsch, which he certainly wanted to do, is actually impossible. Kitsch is like an unwanted body part, for him a transplant organ that the body cannot reject:

> Kitsch is certainly not 'bad art'; it forms its own closed system, which is lodged like a foreign body in the overall system of art, or which, if you prefer, appears alongside it. Its relationship to art can be compared – and this is more than a mere metaphor – to the relationship between the system of the Anti-Christ and the system of Christ. Every system of values, if attacked from the outside in its autonomy, can become distorted and corrupt: a form of Christianity that forces priests to bless cannons and tanks is as close to kitsch as any literature that exalts the well-loved ruling house or the well-loved leader, or the well-loved field marshal or the well-loved president. The enemy within, however, is more dangerous than these attacks from outside: every system is dialectically capable of developing its own anti-system

and is indeed compelled to do so. The danger is all the greater when at first glance the system and the anti-system appear to be identical and it is hard to see that the former is open and the latter closed. (Broch 1969: 62–3)

Why do the homeopathic doses of the poisonous past fail in *The Bomber Pilot*? At one level, it might be explained by the Adenauerian historical context in which the characters find themselves. Given its amnesiac, forward-driven agenda and its preoccupation with the 'German miracle', the period could hardly have offered the supportive context Santner notes is crucial to the homeopathic process in psycho-analytic terms. Nor would the American occupiers, who were also eager to purge the country of traces of Nazism, offer anything better. But *The Bomber Pilot* nonetheless reveals possibilities of socially supportive spaces through formal and stylistic means. Key to that socially supportive space, as Santner contends, is the 'presence of an empathetic witness' – think of Holocaust testimony (Santner 1990: 24–5). Homeopathy thus not only involves the introjection of a 'poisonous', external substance, but the alterity implied by this ex-ternality more generally. Its difference is accepted and acceptable to the body-ego: the poison becomes so non-poisonous as to be bene-ficial.

The Bomber Pilot shows how such appeals to the other are made. With Mascha's breakdown at the beginning of the film, for example, the temporal and physical separation of sound and image, of voice and body, discourages psychologisation of the character – and indeed, the film militates against identifying with them in any conventional sense of the term. Yet the distance is not the unemotional one critics (somewhat simplistically) have attributed to Brecht. Nor is it ironic and critical. Instead, the space is charged with the signs of emotional expressivity. Without having a clue as to how to situate ourselves in terms of understanding, sharing or identifying the nature of Mascha's pain and collapse, that distance may be construed as Schroeter's way of creating a small, tentative place in which we can respond as sympathetic witnesses, if not fully empathetic ones. It is part of his 'embrace'.

It may be argued that the object in Schroeter's text to be 'worked through' is too ill-defined, his homeopathic ghosts too unspecific, to work. But that openness is part of the strength, since it permits a wide range of emotional positions and responses as different 'pieces' of the past are introjected and performed for us. In the same way, I think that *The Bomber Pilot* creates the space for a variety of different spectators. In a similar way, the musical choices Schroeter makes create a certain liberty for the listener. While the Liszt at the beginning and the Verdi at the Bruckner concert drive home specific points, to be sure, often the sheer beauty of a quoted piece (Sibelius *Waltz Triste* at the Schroeter figure's death), or its ugliness (Carla's and Mascha's singing), or its anachronistic inappropriateness (Strauss), present us with an undirected series of sounds, what many commentators have associated with his drive towards 'pure expression'. (Concerned as I am with kitsch, I would reword that to 'impurely pure expressivity'.) Desire runs freely throughout his work, as do its frustrations and identifications – with divas, with regimes, with music, weaving indeterminate but passionately. Importantly, this is precisely what kitsch is not supposed to do: its power, as Friedlander and others have claimed, stems from its manipulation of cheap, predictable sentiment, like the pity we are supposed to feel for portraits of wide-eyed street urchins. Schroeter's non-judgemental attitude towards emotional expression is duplicated in his approach to kitsch, and his embrace of it. This is not to say he is unaware of it, or its dangers (Carla's story would have been otherwise impossible), but he is unafraid of its purported decadence, lies or cheapness, nor of the *Kulturscheisse* it represents. In short, he does not try to keep the negative alterity associated with kitsch at bay, but incorporates it homeopathically into his own work, at times finding it beautiful.

Schroeter's lack of fear of beauty is not trivial, particularly in the light of Broch's remarks about kitsch meaning doing something beautifully, though not well – and *The Bomber Pilot* could never be accused of doing things well. Unlike some Marxist approaches to aesthetics, beauty is not always already narcotising or transcendent – though Schroeter is equally aware that music has been put to those uses, whether in Nazi ideology or Romantic aesthetics. By bringing concepts like 'authentic feeling' and 'beauty' along with countless kitschy artefacts into his text, Schroeter refuses to leave them 'othered' or as products of the realm of 'non-art', to recall Kulka's position. In fact, he says as much: 'For me . . . there's no great divide between kitsch and art. It's just stupid to look for traditional values in art and culture – one should just try to find a vitality in them' (Courant 1982: 14). *The Bomber Pilot* thus offers an unusual brand of kitsch not only in its self-awareness but also in its unwillingness to view kitsch as a closed, outside system. Kitsch, so othered in aesthetic, gay and even political accounts, here is part of the German *Kulturscheisse* with which Schroeter, as a contemporary German artist, works and in which he is able to find beauty, political critique and tastelessness. Additionally, his work acknowledges the need for expression, the expression of need or desire – rather than plying us with fantasies of their fulfilment, which is impossible in the first place. *Bomber Pilot* demonstrates how kitsch in general, and music in particular, offers potential homeopathic encounters with undesirable elements of history, self, and nation. As Timothy Corrigan observes: '[For Schroeter], history becomes a recurring moment, where time and place are an almost arbitrary stage on which the individual releases emotion, where one chooses to enter history form outside in order to perform oneself as a spectacle of time' (Corrigan 1994: 172). Schroeter's kitsch, contrary to Kulka's formulation, opens up new, decidedly *un*formulaic kinds of emotion, the overwrought, tacky musical of expression of which is as historiographically compelling as it is generous and . . . beautiful.

Acknowledgements

Thanks to Michelle Lekas and Dan Cottom for comments on an earlier draft, to James Reel for research assistance, and to the Social Sciences and Humanities Research Council of Canada whose generous support made the writing of this essay possible.

Notes

1. My thanks to Dan Cottom for this and other insights into the nature of kitsch in reading an early draft of this essay.
2. Kulka goes on to say that 'The aim of kitsch is not to create new needs or expectations, but to satisfy existing ones' (Kulka 1996: 27).
3. Several details about the choice of *Lohengrin* warrant comment. First, as Adorno somewhat contentiously notes, after the 1850 opera 'Wagner actually banned authentic historical conflicts from his work' (Adorno 1981: 115) and moved into the increasingly complex phantasmagoria of myth (this is not to say that *Lohengrin* is bereft of myth; indeed, critics ridiculed the mythic, medieval dimensions of this 'Artwork of the Future'). Unlike Adorno, for instance, Anthony Arblaster writes, '*Lohengrin* is one of my favourites among Wagner's operas, but it is one of the least political of his works' (Arblaster 1992: 157).

   As Roger Hillman has compellingly argued, the reappearance of *Lohengrin* at the end of *The Great Dictator*, during which Chaplin's Jewish character makes his humanistic speech, undercuts the critical edge the piece had bestowed upon the earlier portion of the film. Here the music aspires to reclaim, for more democratic, humanitarian ends, to be sure, the same cultural connotations of German spirit and *Volk* so crucial to National Socialism. In this regard, and although Hillman refrains from using the term, the second appearance of Wagner is perhaps even kitschier than the first. See Hillman 1997.

4. For another insightful critique of the film's relation to history and politics, see Liebman 1999.

5. The film leaves this reading indeterminate; other critics, like Gary Indiana, have interpreted the scene depicting Carla at work in a pastry shop and not as part of her 'show'.

6. My thanks to James Reel for this observation.

7. Interestingly, *Nabucco* was performed in Nazi Germany – but not by a high profile company. On 4 April 1935, the Nazi-controlled *Kulturbund deutscher Juden* mounted it in Berlin. Goebbels used the (highly ghettoised) *Kulturbund deutscher Juden* as a publicity tool to deflect foreign criticism of the anti-Semitism of the regime. Membership and audiences were restricted to Jews; resources were modest. Goebbels's ministry had final approval on all programmes: the group was prohibited from 'appropriating' German works like *Fidelio* and instead relied on a repertory of largely foreign and Jewish music. They were permanently disbanded – and arrested – in 1941.

8. Contrast this detail to the manner in which Kluge withheld speech from the victims of the war, granting it instead to the military knee.

9. Dorris Doerrie's 1998 *Am I Beautiful?* also explores Germany's fascination with Latin escape. With Schroeter, it arguably culminates in *Palermo or Wolfsburg* (1980), particularly in the protracted courtroom sequence in which a young lower-class Italian *Gastarbeiter* is tried for the murder of two German youths.

10. Another exception was the work of Chopin (Levi 1994: 145). According to Erik Levi (1994: 40), Nazi officials tended to relax their rules banning Jews and mixed blood members in opera more than in any other area of professional musical activity. Even Bayreuth, as 'the confessions of Winifred Wagner' assert, admitted popular Jewish performers during the ban. It would seem that opera enjoyed a peculiarly privileged position within the German Reich, one which tried to assert its German-ness fully aware of the racial, ethnic or national otherness within it.

11. Preminger eventually ended the relationship out of concern for his career – clearly, the fear of Carmen's alterity had not diminished over the years. Even more interestingly, Dandridge, who portrayed Carmen Jones, was dubbed by a white singer, adding racial difference to the separation of voice from image so foregrounded in *Bomber Pilot*.

12. By librettists Viktor Léon and Leo Stein.

13. Loosely translated by Edward Cushing (c.1954 A. Cranz, Brussels).

14. Thanks to Dan Cottom for this observation.

15. Only for the purposes of analysing *The Bomber Pilot* am I singling out Strauss. Plenty of nineteenth-century composers closely associated with nationalist movements of various countries emphasised the link between 'blood and soil', though of course the Germans did this with special ferocity. Wagner's work offers the clearest and most infamous example of 'pure' blood; mixed blood resulted in the undoing of Amfortas (for succumbing to the tainted female charms of Kundry; Parsifal succeeds, by contrast, for not sleeping with her) and persisting throughout *The Ring*, from the oath of *Blutbruderschaft* between Siegfried and Gunther (which Hagen Alberich [whose clichéd Jewishness is hard to deny] declines,

saying 'my blood would spoil your drink, for my blood is not pure and noble like yours'). See Arblaster 1992 and others for a fuller discussion.

16. I am very hesitant to attribute emotions or goals to Carla or to any of the film's figures, and especially to psychologise them. But because of space limitations, my argument in these paragraphs leans somewhat on 'character', something *Bomber Pilot* actively discourages. The particular formal mechanisms by which the film deals with the homeopathic process, and specifically, its appeal to alterity, are addressed in a longer version of this essay.

17. Plotted across *Bomber Pilot* in so many details, racial integration articulates much the same structure as kitsch and homeopathy. But it is made from a white-dominant perspective – *Bomber Pilot* observes the German othering of blackness and its desire to encrypt, embrace and to 'integrate' it – but at one step removed, by placing blackness, and the entire issue of integration, on US soil. The white, German integration of the other, less privileged, black term is evident musically in choices such as *Carmen Jones*, and a tacky German pop song called *Black Angel*. With these examples, and especially with the revised Strauss, Schroeter makes emphatically clear that kitschiness is already contained within German whiteness.

Bibliography

Adorno, Theodor (1981) *In Search of Wagner* (trans. Rodney Livingstone). London: New Left Books.

Arblaster, Anthony (1992) *Viva la Liberté: Politics in Opera*. London: Verso.

Benjamin, Walter (1992) 'The Work of Art in the Age of Mechanical Reproduction' in *Illuminations*. London: Fontana.

Broch, Hermann (1969) 'Notes on the Problem of Kitsch' in Gillo Dorfles (ed.) *Kitsch: The World of Bad Taste*. New York: Bell.

Calinescu, Matei (1977) *Faces of Modernity: Avant-Garde, Decadence, Kitsch*. Bloomington: Indiana University Press.

Corrigan, Timothy (1981) Werner Schroeter's operatic cinema. *Discourse*, no. 3.

Corrigan, Timothy (1984) On the edge of history: the radiant spectacle of Werner Schroeter. *Film Quarterly*, vol. 37, no. 4 (summer).

Courant, Gerard (ed.) (1982) *Werner Schroeter*. Paris: Goethe Institute/Cinematheque Francaise.

Dorfles, Gillo (ed.) (1969a) *Kitsch: The World of Bad Taste*. New York: Bell.

Dorfles, Gillo (1969b) 'The Origins of the Word Kitsch' in Gillo Dorfles (ed.) *Kitsch: The World of Bad Taste*. New York: Bell.

Elsaesser, Thomas (1989) *New German Cinema: A History*. New Brunswick: Rutgers University Press.

Friedlander, Saul (1993) *Reflections of Nazism: An Essay on Kitsch and Death*. Bloomington: Indiana University Press.

Hillman, Roger (1997) 'Beethoven, Mahler, and the New German Cinema'. *Musicology Australia*, no.20.

Hoberman, J. (1999) Dreaming the unthinkable. *Sight and Sound*, February.

Indiana, Gary (1982) Scattered pictures: the movies of Werner Schroeter. *Artforum*, March.

Kulka, Tomas (1996) *Kitsch and Art*. University State Park: Pennsylvania State University Press.

Levi, Erik (1994) *Music in the Third Reich*. London: Macmillan.

Liebman, Stuart (1999) If only life were so beautiful. *Cineaste*, vol. 24, nos. 2/3.

Santner, Eric (1990) *Stranded Objects: Mourning, Memory, and Film in Postwar Germany*. Ithaca: Cornell University Press.

Sontag, Susan (1999) 'Notes on "Camp"' in Fabio Cleto (ed.) *Camp: Queer Aesthetics and the Performing Subject: A Reader*. Edinburgh: Edinburgh University Press.

Chapter 8

Performance and the Composite Film Score

K. J. Donnelly

Rarely is music as central to a dramatic film as it is to the British film *Performance* (1970). It is the key film concerned with late 1960s British pop music culture and its embracing of counterculture and the underground. The film is aptly named because its narrative fore-grounds 'performances', firstly those of the gangster Chas (James Fox) and later those of the reclusive rock star Turner (Mick Jagger). Chas intimidates businesses into paying protection money to gangster Harry Flowers, but when he kills an associate, the gangsters want him dead. He flees to the house of Turner, a rock musician who has 'lost his creative demon', where the two of them investigate each other's – finally converging – identities. *Performance* is rich in allegory and particularly suited to multiple interpretations. Music in the film is prominent and elucidates some of the semi-submerged discourses, such as the notion of British national decline and degeneration in the wake of foreign influxes and youth culture decadence. *Performance* is very much of its period, embodying these anxieties as well as the protean energy of the emergent culture itself. With the film being partially set in the pop music milieu, it displays many aspects of the counterculture and its music for the audience as attractions, almost as if the film were a documentary or travelogue. *Performance* portrays Turner's world as extraordinary, focusing on drug taking, troilism, playful idleness and music – where it consistently exhibits a catholic taste as well as a fine sense of pop music pedigree. Music in *Performance* fulfils its cultural and magical possibilities. It delineates a number of worlds and consciousnesses in the film, ultimately proving to be the portal for the entry to a transcendent world.

Performance presents a model of film music that arose as a particular aesthetic in the 1960s; it mixes music from disparate sources, utilising a number of popular and world musics as an assemblage or composite. This musical collage replaces the functions of the dominant tradition of using a single coherent orchestral under-score, displaying an overriding concern with musical timbre and rhythm rather than melodic cohesion and harmonic movement that was and is still a trademark of orchestral film music. Consequently, music has an elevated status, sometimes in *Performance* it occupies the foreground and articulates the image track in a reversal of the dominant patterns of film music use.

Although scholarly writings about the film ignore it, the music is clearly the film's *raison d'être*. Even before Jagger's appearance on screen the audience is regaled by a number of different pieces of music in widely differing styles. Popular culture of the time was driven by music, as was psychedelia which the film gleefully represents. *Performance* marked a new type of film, one that incorporated music into a dramatic framework, rather than allow itself to be premised upon music in the tradition of Hollywood film musicals. The late 1960s was a period of flux for music in the cinema; popular music and the desire for tied-in hits had been exerting a pressure upon film composers since the late 1950s. While there always had been occasional appearances of songs in non-musicals, such as in *Casablanca* (1942), that included *As Time Goes By* among other songs, and *The Man Who Knew Too Much* (1956), which showcased *Que Sera Sera*, the 1960s accelerated the process. It was with the advent of pop music as a replacement for film music in *The Graduate* (1967) and *Easy Rider* (1969) that the film music paradigm that had been weathered but had persisted since the 1930s was broken. While the musical aggregate in *Performance* is very singular, the film also provides an example of the kind of musical soundtrack that was appearing at this time.

Performance was released in 1970 after a troubled production period, with Warner Brothers holding up the film's release for two years and forcing re-edits on the film's co-directors Donald Cammell and Nic Roeg (Farber 1975: 161; Walker 1986: 417–19). While the film was nominally a mainstream production, it was conceived and executed more as an experimental film, perhaps more closely related to European art cinema or American underground films than to mainstream dramatic films.[1] The group of people who made it were largely acquaintances and friends, which suggests that it was less a 'professional' film production than a collaborative event. Producer Sandy Lieberson had become an artistic agent in the UK in 1965, representing the Rolling Stones as well as actor James Fox, writer Donald Cammell and cinematographer Nic Roeg. *Performance* was Lieberson's first foray into film production and he engaged Cammell and Roeg for their directorial debuts. Cammell had been a painter and was a friend of Mick Jagger, while Christopher Gibbs, the set designer, had decorated Jagger's flat (Andersen 1993: 52–3, 188–9; MacCabe 1998: 24). There was additional unofficial aid from another of Cammell's friends, the underworld-connected David Litvinoff, who also brought in ex-boxing promoter Johnny Shannon,[2] who ended up playing gangster boss Harry Flowers (Andersen 1993: 189). In addition to these connections, the film's composer Jack Nitzsche had worked with the Rolling Stones, and he assembled an impressive cast of rock and other musicians for the production of the film's highly adventurous music. The production team for *Performance* thus included a large number of people inexperienced in film-making yet unified through the interconnectedness of art and popular culture in the late 1960s.

Pop music was the nexus of the production and the film showcases British pop music culture of the late 1960s, principally through the presentation of Turner's 'decadent' lifestyle and his portrayal by Mick Jagger. Jagger's appearance and musical performances were obviously a central attraction for audiences and one of the obvious reasons why Warner Brothers bankrolled the project. While Mick Jagger would attract Rolling Stones fans, his public profile was prominent enough for him not only to be a general attraction, but also an international symbol of the decadence and licentiousness of psychedelic pop music culture. As a consequence of the centrality of pop music culture to *Performance*, the film foregrounds the pop music milieu, yet it does not utilise pop music as its sole musical element. In fact, a wide variety of musical genres appear in the film. While British pop music culture was showcased, much of the music was not British at all: the film starts with American singer and composer Randy Newman singing a blues rock song, *Gone Dead Train*. This is quickly superseded by dissonant and futuristic electronic music, still within the title sequence. The body of the film includes more blues and rock, Indian sitar music, Middle Eastern santur music, an echoed piano theme as non-diegetic 'score', what seems to be commercial 'muzak' or easy-listening music and what might be 'improvised' music (consisting of guitar, jew's harp and wailing).

As already noted, the musical regime in *Performance* is radically different from that of the classical cinema, the text being a space for the conjugation of radically different musics, and with the musical discourse functioning coherently as a composite score and as one of the film's principal processes of unification. Instead of using an orchestra and repeating and varying musical themes, the common approach in underscores since Hollywood's heyday, it focuses firstly on the sound qualities of each form of music and secondly their broad associations within Western culture. Sound quality is exploited for its particular effect, such as the kinetic blues rock that accompanies Chas disguising himself by putting red paint into his hair. The cultural associations of the different types of music in the film are evident in the ethnic music, associated with the exotic and hippie interest in India and the Middle East, making it an integral part of the exotic décor of Turner's house. So the importance of the music in the film is beyond its materiality, beyond the particulars of its melody and harmony. Its function across the film is through the use of 'readymades': readily recognisable musical forms with specific qualities and associations for Western audiences.

Performance uses a composite score, comprising an aggregate of disparate musics, culled from the diversity of the world's cultural library. This makes the film a site for the union of a wide variety of musics from differing cultures and traditions. The nature of the composite film score is to wrest music from these traditions and attempt to homogenise it through subordination to the film's requirements. It lacks the organic unity of the traditional, especially written orchestral scores, despite the fact that most of *Performance*'s music was performed by a 'team' under Jack Nitzsche's direction. The music is often 'generic', representative of certain musical 'types' rather than being specific, while its relationships with other musics in the film are premised upon generic difference and tone colour rather than more 'pure' musical elements such as melodies. This form is related to the music library; these abounded at that time and are still heavily used for cheap film and television productions, and the principle has been used by films that recontextualise music such as *2001: A Space Odyssey* (1968), *American Graffiti* (1973), and Quentin Tarantino's films.

There is a tendency to articulate music as large pre-existing blocks rather than a coherent unity weaving through the film. If it is easy to see the film's music in the light of the 1960s tendency to 'plunder' other cultures, also evident in the film's design and oriental references, the film's theme of England's degeneration is related to the past of colonial glory – with some of the music as part of that imperial plunder. Chas is from an Irish family and works with Jewish and gay gangsters, intimidating Indian businessmen amongst others; Turner is England gone decadent and surrounded by foreigners and black men. This ethnic undercurrent is thrown into relief by the film's articulation of different musics to underline the idea of the swamping of Englishness and English culture by the exotic and foreign, accelerated by hippie culture. A good example of this was the rise in popularity of Indian music among Western audiences in the late 1960s, personified by sitar player Ravi Shankar who appeared at Woodstock. While the film's foregrounding of pop music culture motivates the variety of musics in circulation within the film, pop music culture conceives of other musics as a zone for 'miscegenation', where pop music plunders ethnic and other musics to create hybrids and pastiches, or simply relocates them within the pop music context of usage. Examples include the consumption of African pastiche pop songs such as the perennial *The Lion Sleeps Tonight* and Paul Simon's LP *Graceland* (1986).

Early reports spoke of 'Mick Jagger's score for *Performance*' (Cooper 1968: 12). This was erroneous; the film's music is credited to Jack Nitzsche. Nitzsche, who had been heavily involved with the world of pop music, wrote much of the music and assembled it into a coherent 'score'. In 1964, he had co-written The Searchers' hit *Needles and Pins* with Sonny Bono (later of Sonny and Cher fame). He had also worked with producer Phil Spector, Bobby Darin, Buffalo Springfield, and later Neil Young and The James Gang. Momentously, Nitzsche worked with the Rolling Stones from 1965 to 1969, arranging choirs and ensembles while playing the piano and harpsichord.[3] Although his film career had started inauspiciously with *Village of Giants* (1965), *Performance* led to the later successes of *The Exorcist* (1973) and *One Flew Over the Cuckoo's Nest* (1975).

For the film, Nitzsche assembled an impressive cast of musicians, most of whom were Los Angeles-based session musicians and friends. They included singer Buffy Saint Marie, who was Nitzsche's wife, and guitarist Ry Cooder who had played with Captain Beefheart; Randy Newman, synthesiser player Bernhard Krause, bass guitarist Bobby West (who had worked with Buffalo Springfield and Frank Zappa), Russ Titelman on guitar, singer Merry Clayton, percussionist Milt Holland, Amiya Dasgupta, guitarist Lowell George and drummer Gene Parsons who had been in The Byrds. The success of this unit of musicians is testified to by their reassembly for Buffy Saint Marie's 1971 LP, *She Used to Wanna be a Ballerina,* which included Nitzsche on piano, Clayton, Cooder, Titelman and Bobby West; while Randy Newman's *Sail Away* (released 1972) included Cooder, Parsons, Titelman and Holland. After the shoot of *Performance,* yet before its release, Nitzsche, Cooder and Clayton appeared on the Rolling Stones' album *Let It Bleed* in 1969.

Prominent among the musicians performing Jack Nitzsche's score is slide-guitarist Ry Cooder who, during the sequence of Chas going to Turner's house at Powis Square, plays a brief musical passage that was later to reappear intact in Cooder's acclaimed score for the film *Paris, Texas* (1984). Cooder later claimed that Nitzsche did not write a score for much of the film, but asked musicians to improvise and develop their own material (Romney 1995: 42). This underlines that Nitzsche's music for *Performance* is a diverse assemblage, not constructed in any way that resembles the through-composed especially written scores traditional to dramatic films. In place of an especially written orchestral underscore, the film pulls together a wealth of heterogeneous musics, which change status between being diegetically motivated and non-diegetic. The specifically non-diegetic music includes two repeated themes consisting of a thin texture of echoed piano, reminiscent of twentieth-century art piano music in that it contains dissonance that goes unresolved, yet also contains melodic configurations common to blues, jazz and rock music, and is thus a hybrid form. Despite only appearing twice, this embodies the nearest thing the film has to traditional non-diegetic underscore with its minimally repeated themes providing some unity.

Electronic music appears from outside the diegesis in the film's opening sequence while some later electronic music is motivated within the diegesis added to the rhythm and blues-inspired pop music. The rhythm and blues song in the title sequence, *Gone Dead Train,* likewise makes a later diegetic appearance as a record played in the kitchen at Turner's house, and returns to its non-diegetic status at the closing titles. The situation of this song is testament to the functioning of music across the film, where musical themes and genres cross regularly between diegetic and non-diegetic status. *Gone Dead Train* functions as a dominant figure for the film, marking the audience's entry and exit while breaking into the diegesis in the middle of the film to emphasise the theme song's status as a privileged signifier (Frith 1984: 78). In spite of this, the words are difficult to hear, suggesting that the overall sound of the music itself is more important, as blues and rhythm and blues are prominent in the film as a musical style. Diegetically motivated music includes the performances by Turner (playing on audience knowledge of Mick Jagger, as he rediscovers the Rolling Stones' musical origins in the blues), the first a guitar-accompanied blues and the second, resembling a song sequence in a classical Hollywood musical. The latter is remarkable for its rendering: it retains diegetic motivation of the music as the film moves away from the diegetic 'reality' it has established into 'fantasy'.

The opening sequence of *Performance* functions as an establishment of the film's stylistic regime more than as a foundation for the narrative. It includes footage of Chas and a woman engaging in sado-masochistic sex, intercut with a chauffeur-driven limousine driving on the open road. While it is possible to see the opening as inaugurating the narrative through the introduction of Chas and sado-masochism, and the car of the lawyer whom Chas threatens, both elements are only of retrospective value for the narrative and their relationship is highly ambiguous, so the opening sequence amounts to a number of disconnected incidents that may be retrospectively motivated, but are unified almost solely by the music track.

The construction of the sequence's visual track is based on a precise dynamic, crosscutting between two different spaces, establishing the principle of visual parallels that appears throughout the film and underpins the positioning of the two central characters, Chas and Turner. The shots of sex (sexual 'performance') and the aerial views of the car on the road are intercut with increased rapidity, becoming virtual flashframes until the point where the title of the film appears on the screen, interceding and freezing the action. The sequence ends by cutting from the car door being shut to the closing of a wardrobe door in Chas' flat. This seemingly synchronic connection has no apparent motivation in the diegesis, but it is a principle that appears continually throughout the film.

Gone Dead Train fades out quite quickly and some electronic music fades in; it consists of sounds like mechanical air blasts added to a deep drone that culminate in a climactic chord at the point of the appearance of the film title. The use of synthesiser music was extraordinary, with Bernhard Krause playing a Mini Moog prototype. The opening sequence contains no diegetic sound and elevates the non-diegetic music to a position of total dominance, a position that it retains at a number of significant points across the film. *Gone Dead Train*'s chord progression, which provides its inner structure, only partially follows the standard for blues and rhythm and blues, incorporating unexpected chord changes. These occur largely at the point where the rhythmic impetus stops and the words of the song's title are enounced. Although the song is relatively typical of the genre, it has a couple of untypical points that effectively emphasise the sinister undertone of its title, so as the introduction to the film, the song announces the film's rock content, while its words give an intimation of the ominous flavour of what is to follow.

The radical juxtaposition of the two musical genres (blues rock and electronic) in the opening sequence establishes the relationship of the music in the film, which presents heterogeneous musics in succession or mixed to form hybrids. The musical processes aid unification across the film, with the relationship of the musical components converging and providing a continuity for the audience in the face of potential confusion in the fragmented image track. The muzak machine in Harry Flowers' office provides the closest thing the film has to the traditional Hollywood underscore. The music's function initially seems to follow that of the traditional orchestral score, but it moves from the background into the foreground, explicitly articulating the image track and defining the logic of the sequence. However, the sequence does not follow simple temporal continuity. The gangsters are all in their office base, and the ensuing conversation is fragmented, not only by the interposing of non-diegetic insert shots related to what is said, but also by seemingly discontinuous dialogue. The sequence starts as a conversation between the gangsters present, but culminates in a filmic regime of heightened subjectivity – space is articulated around Chas and his point of view. Throughout the sequence, the music provides a fabric – from the initiation of the scene, where it is hardly audible, to the point where its volume is raised in the diegesis, to its final position in the subjective section, where it has marginalised diegetic sound and taken on some obtrusive distortion.

In *Unheard Melodies*, Claudia Gorbman likens the music of classical cinema to muzak (1987: 56–9). She points to their shared functions: both ease our anxieties and enable us to be more easily manipulated. In films, background music enables our suspension of disbelief, making us more willing to believe what we see on screen. Like muzak, the traditional underscore is, in the vast majority of cases, not meant to be heard in a conscious manner. The muzak that appears in this sequence in *Performance* is indeed reminiscent of some of the 'filler' music that can be found under dialogue in many classical films. But here we have what I would argue is a parody of the scores in classical films. It has the soupy string-dominated orchestral sound, but is purposely banal. If it were in the mould of the classical film score, it would follow the dynamics of the action, instead of which it forces the dynamics of the action conform to itself.

The music consists largely of a string section and a piano, playing a strong but simple, almost prosaic melody, accompanied by well-defined harmonic movement in the bass and chordal background. There is little real point in describing the melody – which is pleasing enough really – as its relevance is largely rhythmic only. While the pitches of the melody change, in rhythmic terms, much of it comprises a repeated cell of two notes, leading to further but nevertheless simple development as it runs to its conclusion. The timbre (instrumental sound) is more important than the melody and the harmonic movement (the chords) are aligned firmly to the temporal structure.

A sound dissolve brings the music to the fore – as part of this highly aestheticised sequence of audio-visual effects. This involves music being distorted as well as being loud, allied to changes in image tonality and continuity. The regularity of its structure becomes a skeleton upon which to hang the visuals.

Time as the regular visual succession of most mainstream films is confused. In addition, our impression of chronological time is distorted and fragmented. In its place, regulated musical time provides the logic of the sequence – supplying continuity, and with its own integrity, the integrity of musical logic. The piece of music is based on a regular rhythmic formation; and a short two-bar phrase structure, with chords changing at this regular interval. These two aspects regularise the music. Its structure is based on an eight-bar block that is repeated – this block explicitly marks out the 'subjective' section towards the end of the sequence, where the music and the montage coalesce at the critical point, each climaxing in an almost 'balletic' turn.

The sequence includes a succession of shots of Harry Flowers from increasing distances, while the music and his voice distort on the soundtrack, through phasing and removing high and low pitches to sound as if it is being fed through a telephone. The 'balletic turn' sees Flowers turn in his chair at the point where the sound distortion disappears and the music has reached its climactic point. The stylistic wildness of the image track is held in place by the regulated musical time of the piece of 'muzak', in a singular sequence where the image is 'treated' with distorting effects much like the sound which defines the sequence.

This sequence is taken as the basis for the film's climactic scene, being radically restructured and rewritten into an alternative form by the impetus of the music. *Performance* contains one full song sequence – for *Memo from Turner* – which is in certain ways reminiscent of song sequences in the classical musical. It varies its visual content as a direct result of its musical structure and is reminiscent of the more experimental pop promo films that existed at around this time.

Memo from Turner is the culmination of the film and provides the audience with what they probably expected: Mick Jagger performing a pop song in his customary manner. It resembles a classical musical, yet has been set within the confines of a primarily mainstream narrative film, although the film is premised upon music and employing as much as it possibly can. As in classical musical dances, the music of *Memo from Turner* structures the visual action. Heightened points of the song structure cause a concentration upon the figure of Turner, while the instrumental breaks cue a suitable variation in the consistency of the image track. *Memo from Turner* was released as a tied-in single in November 1970 at the same time as the film, while the soundtrack LP was released in September 1970; these were both tied to the film's cinematic release, although they had been recorded two years earlier and Jagger's subsequent film, *Ned Kelly*, had already been released in July 1970.

The narrative motivation for the song sequence is that it is an extremity of Chas' subjectivity: it is 'inside his head'. This is amplified by his drugged state, but Turner has already declared that it is his intention to enter Chas' mind, and he appears literally to do so. This allows for the elaborate visual rendering, although *Performance* has a consistently baroque visual style anyway. Following a lengthy initial sequence of diegetic music, the camera seemingly enters Chas' ear and proceeds to the space of Harry Flowers' office, which seems to figure an entry to Chas' consciousness. In that room, he beholds Turner as the head gangster, replacing Flowers in the same office and scenario, and containing much in the way of elements from the foregoing sequence. In fact, it is a total reinscription of elements that made appearances earlier, even including dialogue. The whole earlier scene is rebuilt around the new addition of the rock song.

The sequence marks a symbolic unification or superimposition of

the two worlds of the diegesis. The scene's basis as a reinscription of
the earlier part of the film places Turner as the leader of the gangsters
in a complete reorientation of the film's representations around a
point of the intersection of the two principal characters, seemingly
inside Chas' head. This is the point of union between Chas and Turner
and is something of a climax in the film, however it is also a conclusion
of the process of interaction between the two and is static in narrative
terms, the narrative drive being disengaged for a spectacular interlude
driven by the music.

At this point, the film is reinserting the Mick Jagger persona into the
film, reminding the audience of the connections between diegetic
acting performances and reality. The spectacle is of Mick Jagger,
the Rolling Stones singer, performing as himself rather than acting.
Indeed, it is arguable whether he was acting at all in the film. 'As for
his actual performance in *Performance*, Jagger was instructed not to
act at all, but to simply "be you". Marianne [Faithfull, Jagger's
girlfriend] urged him to reject his director's advice "You've got to
imagine you're poor freaked-out, androgynous, druggie Brian"'
[Jones] (Andersen 1993: 190). While Jagger may well have been
basing his persona upon Brian Jones, the Rolling Stone who left
the band in June 1969 and died a month later under highly suspicious
circumstances (Rawlings 1994), Jagger retained elements of this
character in his public image which suggests that he was becoming
a hybrid of himself and Jones, perhaps in reality as well as in the film.
Jagger, though, commented: 'I think Turner is a projection of Donald
[Cammell]'s fantasy or idea of what I am' (Jagger 1975: 169).

The initial music of the sequence, before the song sung by Jagger, is
Poor White Hound Dog, featuring the soulful vocals of Merry
Clayton. The reel-to-reel tape recorder that is rolling in the background motivates it as ambient diegetic music, guaranteeing the
diegetic 'reality' of the music and underlining its centrality to the
move from the film's diegesis to Chas' subconscious. While one of
Turner's lovers, Lucy, dances, Turner makes a succession of booming
sounds on his Mini Moog synthesiser.[4] These electronic sounds cue
Chas into moving in time to the music, and the camera begins wild
movements as an attempted visual equivalent to the music and Chas'
drugged state of mind. The rhythm of *Poor White Hound Dog* is
similar to *Memo from Turner* and the two segue seamlessly at the
point where the visuals move through Chas' ear to Flowers' office. The
synthesiser is the key. Its 'unnatural' sounds mark it as a 'magic'

device, opening the portal to Chas' mind and inaugurating the song sequence.

As I have already noted, the song sequence bears a distinct resemblance to the pop promo format that was still young at the time, as it utilises a micro-narrative structure tied to the song to provide unity. The conclusion of the sequence is the conclusion of the song itself; it stops abruptly, accompanied by a static long shot of the naked gangsters all lying dead in the room. The *Memo from Turner* sequence plays with the familiar and the unfamiliar. While it is based upon the previous scene at Flowers' office and reuses snatches of dialogue and shots, it adds other elements, such as Turner replacing Flowers and the gangsters removing their clothes. Turner then performs the song, which interpolates image and dialogue 'readymades' from the previous scene, such as one of the gangsters shouting 'It was Mad Cyril!'[5]

The music occupies the foreground and is the principal determinant upon the sequence itself. It emphasises the status of Jagger as pop star, and as such sounds as much like the Rolling Stones as is possible. *Memo from Turner* is a rhythm and blues-style song with a strong rock backbeat. The texture of the music is a product of Jagger's singing, and the classic rock instrumentation of drums, bass guitar and two guitars. In fact, the style of the music is very close to that of the Rolling Stones; it features their guitarist Keith Richard, using his characteristic syncopated guitar style that is particularly evident in the stuttering chords during the verse. There were difficulties over the recording of the song, as Jagger and Keith Richard fell out over Richard's girlfriend Anita Pallenberg, who plays Turner's lover Pherber in the film. Finally Jagger got his friends Steve Winwood and Jim Capaldi from Traffic to Olympic Studios and they reworked the song before handing it over to Jack Nitzsche to finish (Andersen 1993: 92–4). Despite its distinctive Rolling Stones sound provided by Richard, the screen credit for *Memo from Turner* is only for Jagger.

Memo from Turner's structure comprises traditional verses and choruses, where the verse has simple harmony (the alternation of primary chords I and IV), and the chorus repeats words and has more harmonic movement, culminating in a 'drop out', where the emphasised rhythm of the words halts the flow of the instrumental backing before it resumes. This provides the temporal dimension for the sequence, with key points like the start of the verse and the chorus cueing closer views of Jagger mouthing the words. As the words are not specific and only obliquely related to the film's action, the musical impetus and structure take on further importance for the scene. Musical structure defines visual rendering. The instrumental breaks from the singing (the guitar solos) provide the cue for visual variation from Turner's direct address to the audience. The first break allows him to order the gangsters to remove their clothes while the second (longer) instrumental break sees a temporary change to Turner, no longer dressed as a gangster but in his previous apparel, apparently dancing within the same scene.

The status of the music is diegetic, in that it continues from the previous scene before the camera's entry into the ear and is remotivated as originating on the muzak system (Jagger repeats Flowers' statement: 'I like that, turn it up'). The music has, in effect, changed status from diegetic 'reality' to diegetic 'fantasy'. Rick Altman's description of the musical's song sequence being cued by an audio dissolve from non-diegetic to diegetic music (Altman 1987: 110) materialises in a different form in that *Memo from Turner* is a backing-track to which Turner sings while the status of the diegesis itself has changed, with the music enabling our entry to a transcendent world. In formal terms, this rendering looks backwards, appearing like the 'bursting into song' of traditional integrated musicals, yet it also looks forward to the aesthetics of pop promos which wanted to have more dynamic visuals than simply groups performing as if on stage.[6]

In conclusion, *Performance* illustrates the heterogeneity of music that can converge as a structural unity within a film and it displays little of the melodic and harmonic concern and development characteristic of the dominant musical form for mainstream cinema, the especially composed orchestral underscore. The film's composite of disparate world musics and popular musics goes some way towards replacing the functions of traditional non-diegetic music and yet is in no way tailored to the requirements of the film's momentary dynamics. Pop music culture is the point of unification for the ethnic and 'modern' musics, while the film presents those disparate musics and then re-presents elements of them to create hybrid forms as a homogenising and unifying process across the film. The musical regime in *Performance* is radically different from that of most contemporaneous films, illustrating the variety of possible uses to which music can be put and demonstrating the possibilities for integration of pop music with a dramatic film. Indeed, the major impetus for the elevated status of the music discourse in *Performance* is the film's foundation in the pop music culture of the time (specifically psychedelia) and the showcasing of a famous pop star as a guarantee of its credentials. The diversity of musics that the film unifies are also to some extent 'on display' in that they have a prominent position in the film and at times determine the organisation of key sequences. Colin MacCabe wrote that '*Performance* does not refuse . . . classical rules but cuts to other rhythms which suggest new connections between vision and knowledge; that what we get is far more complicated than what we see' (MacCabe 1998: 57). Yet this ignores what we hear and the very apparent fact of musical rhythm and musical logic dictating much of the film's format.

Notes

1. The film's fragmented style includes a brief and obscure flashframe shot of Borges at the shooting of Turner, while earlier at Joey's shooting, a brief shot of boys from the film *Odd Man Out* (1947) inexplicably appears.
2. MacCabe (1998: 42) notes the importance of Shannon's voice, yet ironically the 1997 video release of *Performance* in the UK uses the US version of the film, where his voice was overdubbed by another actor.
3. Nitzsche had also made a few solo LPs, including *The Lonely Surfer* (1963), *Hits of the Beatles* (1964) and *Chopin 66* (1966).
4. Although Robert Moog had been selling modular synthesisers since 1965, the Mini Moog (the prototype appearing here) was not widely available until 1970 (Wright 1994: 33).
5. It is testament to the pop cultural status of the film that a sample of this and other dialogue was used in the Big Audio Dynamite song *E=MC2* and inspired songs by the Happy Mondays and Coil.
6. Sean Cubitt points to *Memo From Turner* as a key song sequence of influence for later pop promos (1996: 46).

Bibliography

Altman, Rick (1987) *The American Film Musical*. London: BFI.
Andersen, Christopher (1993) *Jagger: Unauthorised*. London: Simon and Schuster.
Cooper, Rod (1968) Production. *Kinematograph Weekly*, vol. 629, no. 3240.
Cubitt, Sean (1996) *Timeshift: On Video Culture*. London: Routledge.
Farber, Steven (1975) '*Performance* – The Nightmare Journey' in David Dalton (ed.) *The Rolling Stones*. London: Star.
Frith, Simon (1984) Mood Music. *Screen*, vol. 25, no. 3, May/June.
Gorbman, Claudia (1987) *Unheard Melodies: Narrative Film Music*. London: BFI.
Jagger, Mick (1975) 'Jagger on *Performance*' in David Dalton (ed.) *The Rolling Stones*. London: Star.
MacCabe, Colin (1998) *Performance*. London: BFI.
Rawlings, Terry (1994) *Who Killed Christopher Robin?: The Truth Behind the Murder of Brian Jones*. London: Boxtree.
Romney, Jonathan (1995) 'Tracking Across the Widescreen' [interview with Ry Cooder]. *The Wire*, issue 138, August.

Walker, Alexander (1986) *Hollywood, England: The British Film Industry in the Sixties*. London: Harrap.

Wright, Steve (1994) The museum of synthesiser technology: Dr Robert Moog. *Making Music*, no. 102, September.

Chapter 9

Sound and Empathy: Subjectivity, Gender and the Cinematic Soundscape

Robynn J. Stilwell

When George Lucas remastered and reissued the *Star Wars* trilogy in 1997, most of the media attention was given to additional scenes and improved special effects; yet in interview after interview, Lucas reiterated that the improvement in sound reproduction was the driving force behind his desire to revisit the films released twenty years earlier. Similarly, Wolfgang Petersen's director's cut of *Das Boot* (1997) not only restores scenes cut from the television mini-series for the original film release, but also has an extensively revamped soundtrack, including all-new sound effects and a new digital underlay of the musical score. Examples like these are proof in action of an extraordinary thing about the film soundtrack – the gap between its importance to the cinematic experience and the development of its technology, and its relative neglect in the reception and study of cinema.

Even the term 'soundtrack' is misunderstood. For most people, 'soundtrack' means a film's musical score. Yet music is only one of three main constituents of the film soundtrack: the others are speech (generically termed dialogue) and sound effects. Like the red, green and blue which combine to form the process colour of the film's image, dialogue, sound effect and music together form the film's soundscape, an inclusive term I prefer to use because of this misunderstanding of 'soundtrack'. It also lays a connotative substrate for the geography of cinematic sound, while shifting emphasis from the technological to the perceptual, which is the focus here.

Although the study of film sound has been slowly gaining ground in the past twenty years and several useful anthologies have appeared (*Yale French Studies*, no. 60 [1980], Weis and Belton [1985], Altman [1992]), alongside several scholarly books on sound's specialised subset, music (of which Gorbman [1987] is the first and still most important), the position of sound within the field of film studies is still marginal. It is still possible for undergraduate and even post-graduate courses to ignore sound with impunity, and sound is often missing from general texts on the subject (although this is improving year on year). Even more narrowly focused studies of genres or individual films may omit sound and/or music while still making some claims to comprehensiveness. At major international film conferences, with multiple sessions over several days, papers on sound – let alone music – can be completely absent, and few people even notice. Having dedicated sessions may improve visibility, but it also reinforces marginality by being separate and easy to skip.

My purpose is not to argue primacy of the aural over the visual experience, or even equality, but an importance that is easily the equal of such components as lighting, design, camera angles and editing and therefore needs to be integrated into the study of film as these other elements have been. In the chapter that follows, I would like to bring sound back from the margins of film studies, at least for the moment; sketch the ways in which sound, subjectivity and gender are mutually implicated (though rarely overtly) in psychoanalytic film theory; and take a look at a particular film, *Closet Land* (Radha Bharadwaj 1990), in which these factors are unusually foregrounded.

The Marginality of Sound

While no one would consider separating the image into red, green and blue for study, the separation of dialogue, sound effect and music is marked in film literature. Undoubtedly that analogy is exaggerated; there are fundamental phenomenological reasons why sound is segregated into dialogue, effect and music. Although all of them are the product of acoustic waves, just as colour is the product of light waves, they are in some ways less divisible into their constituent parts than colour: red light has a different wavelength than blue light, while a violin, a human voice and a police siren may all occupy the same range of acoustic wavelengths. They may be distinguished by amplitude (volume), direction, timbre (tone colour) and duration. While the first two of these may be erased by the cinematic apparatus – reproduced sound can be manipulated in volume and projected from whichever speaker in the auditorium[1] the sound engineer desires – it is in the continuity of sound, its rises and falls in pitch (wavelength), and its harmonics (the subsidiary vibrations that give a sound its particular timbre) that we identify the source as a musical instrument, a voice or a police siren. As human beings learn to listen to and comprehend sound, not merely receive (hear) it passively, we learn to distinguish and hierarchise sounds. The effect is sometimes referred to as the 'cocktail party' effect – amid the din of voices, clinking glasses and music, we can concentrate on the voice of the person talking to us, or even cue into someone across the room who mentions our name or a subject which interests us.

A similar process allows us to interpret the cinematic soundtrack. Typically, we prioritise the dialogue, as a bearer of the narrative, but the occasional sound effect may catch our attention with new information. Music tends to remain a subliminal signal for most audience members,[2] as is intimated by the title of perhaps the most significant book yet on film music, Claudia Gorbman's *Unheard Melodies*. In reality, of course, the music is not really unheard: it is merely not apprehended with the same semantic precision as dialogue or even sound effects.[3]

The tripartite division of the soundscape is replicated academically, as the methodologies are quite divergent: music is the domain of the musicologists (when they bother); sound effects are usually taken up by those interested in the technology of sound reproduction in film; speech can be split into dialogue (taken on by scholars of narrative or other literary or drama-based approaches) and the voice itself, which is primarily the province of film theorists of a psychoanalytic bent. Very few scholars have taken on the entire soundtrack (Weis [1982] was an early exception), and even the most prominent of those, sound theorist Michel Chion, has devoted separate books to his study: *Le Voix au Cinéma*, *Le Son au Cinéma*, and *La Musique au Cinéma*.

Although Chion's theories are flexible enough to encompass the entire cinematic soundscape, the scholarly division of labour has tended to perpetuate the segregation of the various sound components. And it is also true that in some cases, particularly in classical cinema, the way that a film's soundscape is constructed makes this segregation logical, or at least practical. In the past couple of decades, however, with the rise of the sound designer as a key technical contributor to the overall effect of a film, sound has become more integrated and interrelated in some films than others, and with the advances in sound recording and sound reproduction, sound becomes an increasingly important factor in the experience of 'seeing' a movie:

hence the attention of directors like George Lucas and Wolfgang Petersen, among many others, for the soundscape.

Subjectivity, Gender and Sound

Subjectivity is a complex concept, composed of multiple overlapping meanings, all of which bear, to some degree or another, a cultural coding as 'feminine', if only because of the deeply ingrained binarisms of Western culture that force gendered identifications of opposing terms. The multiplicity of 'subjectivities' can in itself be regarded as a 'feminine' trait because of these binarisms. Subjectivity is the opposite of 'objectivity', the prized goal of scientific, scholarly activity (historically associated with masculine endeavour). Objectivity prizes fact: it is unitary, there is only one right answer; subjectivity, in one of its most basic meanings, is what one feels or understands about something: it is contingent, and there is no such thing as a 'right answer'.

In a more philosophical and psychological sense, subjectivity is an individual's awareness of his or her own identity, a sense of self that encompasses what one thinks and feels. It also encompasses those characters, emotions and thoughts with which one identifies (that is with which one feels some affinity, a recognition of similarity or complementarity). This is the basis of one's experience as a spectator/auditor of a film, though this subjectivity can be (in reality, always is) shaped by the construction of the film itself.

In experiencing a film, the viewing/listening subject is invited to take a position with regard to the film text. Film theorists Christian Metz (whose writings through the 1970s are collected in Metz 1982) and Jean-Louis Baudry (1974–75; 1975) turned to psychoanalysis to describe this positioning, positing the experience of film as analogous to dreaming; in classical cinema, therefore, the technical aspects of film that reminded viewing subjects (and for these theorists, the subjects were almost always exclusively *viewing* subjects) that they were watching a film – editing, for example, and camera angles – were naturalised to a high degree.[4] Following from this came one of the most influential of film texts dealing with gender, Laura Mulvey's 'Visual pleasure and narrative cinema', which theorised the 'male gaze' of cinema 'that the camera creates a male subject position for the viewer, whether biologically/psychologically male or female, through the ego-gratifying identification with the male hero and the libidinal spectacularisation of the female body (Mulvey 1975). One need not even buy the psychoanalytic trappings of such an argument to recognise the camera as an extension of male directors and male cinematographers working for an audience in which the male perspective is not just presumed but assumed to be the norm. The heterosexual division of labour which equates the male with activity and the female with passivity allows the paradox that in a narrative about or image of a woman 'in which she is the subject (that is, the agent) of the narrative or image' she can become an object the moment she becomes passive, or even just still.

Sight is a means of exerting control; what we look at is an active choice. This is an illusion in film, as we are being guided to see what the author(s) of the film text wish us to see; as Mulvey argues, the 'real' gazes of the pro-filmic look of the camera (the camera's framing of the real people [actors], scenery, props and so on being filmed) and of the audience at the screen are collapsed with the gaze of the characters at each other within the diegesis. Sound, on the other hand, forces a surrender of control; we cannot turn away. Closing our eyes only serves to intensify our experience of the sound because of lack of interference from visual input; putting our hands over our ears rarely shuts out the sound completely. The equation of active sight with masculinity and passive sound with femininity is uncomfortably easy, reinforced by the domination of sight over sound in culture and especially film.[5]

Psychoanalysis, and therefore the film theory based upon it, allies sound with the feminine through another route, again a gendered binary of male = rational/female = irrational. In what follows, I am not suggesting that there is any discernible, essential truth in the psychoanalytic theories under discussion, or even that I believe that they illuminate the psychological effects of film spectatorship (in fact, I have serious reservations about both propositions); what I am interested in is the gendered discourse around sound and subjectivity. Often, the gendering is incidental to the overall argument the theorist is making, but these peripheral word choices are sometimes the most revealing of the persistence of certain gender stereotypes in Western culture, most of which go back at least as far as the Enlightenment.

According to Freudian theory, the male voice is that of the law; the female voice is reduced to meaningless babble, incoherent sound or – significantly – music. Mary Ann Doane (1980) uses the metaphor of the womb in describing film sound, a 'sonorous envelope' surrounding the spectator. Doane draws on French psychologist Guy Rosolato, who draws on Lacan, who is in turn based in Freudianism. The terminology changes, but the female-identification of the features associated with sound remain.

The womb metaphor is key in much psychoanalytic writing, extending the real, biological organ which envelops and nurtures the infant to the metaphoric post-natal stage before the child realises its separateness from the plenitude and wholeness of the mother's body. In addition to its warm, comforting qualities, however, the womb also threatens smothering and entrapment, even castration, all of which (particularly the latter) give priority to male experience as the subject struggles toward individuation.[6] This symbolic (and I use the term in its common rather than pyschoanalytic meaning) womb is also noisy: not just in the mother's body's sounds or her post-natal baby-talk and lullabies, but even in its theoretical abstractions: Julia Kristeva, for instance, theorises a space which is 'chaos': multiple, without reason (terms commonly associated with femininity), but also, paradoxically, ordering the infant's basic drives and manifesting flashes of energy and rhythm.[7] Kristeva calls this the 'chora', a term she borrows from Plato, yet in our present context it is hardly an 'innocent' choice; she chooses a word loaded with musical meaning from its earliest known usage. The term meant a space, but more specifically one where a chorus was trained or where a choral dance was performed.[8] Music, therefore sound, is already inscribed in the space.

The psychoanalytic feminine, even in its most benign form, is always shot through with violently negative feelings and irrationality; it is also associated with sound. From biological womb sounds to the mother's voice (replete with music, nonsensical baby-talk and lullabies), to film sound, feminine sound is elided similarly to the way Mulvey describes the collapse of the male gaze. Yet the experience of a film is still dislocated in space, split between the visual image projected on the screen at some distance from us, and the sound which envelops and even literally touches us as the air vibrates in sympathy with the speakers to transmit the acoustic waves which give us 'sound'.[9] This split reinscribes the visual as masculine and the aural as feminine, and this welter of gendered factors works to overdetermine a close relationship between sound and female subjectivity.

The Subject Position and the Geography of the Soundscape

Experiencing a strong identification with a character in the film places us in another's subject position, creating an emotionally empathetic response. Film has many ways of coaxing the audience into that position, from character development, narrative discourse and events, to the more 'visceral' point-of-view shot composition and sound design.

Despite the privileging of sight as active and the collapse of the pro-filmic, audience and diegetic gazes, the cinematic spectator is rarely put exactly in the subject position. The literal point-of-view shot, in which the camera takes the position of the character with whom we are asked to identify, is rare, often not very extensive, and frequently (over and above the Mulveyan equation of the camera with the male gaze) male-identified. Examples like the virtual-reality stalking and rape sequence in *Strange Days* (Kathryn Bigelow 1995) or the television comedy *People Like Us* (BBC 1999)[10] only serve to prove how 'unnatural' such a position is in mainstream narrative media. The more usual point-of-view shot is established by the shot/reverse shot structure which Baudry postulates was the means by which the spectator was 'sutured' into the narrative, and is inexact and implied.

Because of its intimate relationship to our real, physical bodies, via the vibrating air, sound seems more immediate. It does not need the same structuring composition as the image, which is not to say that it is without structure. In a modern cinema, the sound literally surrounds us with speakers all around the auditorium, 'reconstructing' a naturalistic acoustic picture which has direction that can even be partially reproduced by a moderately good home theatre system. But even before the cinematic apparatus was so adept at creating this acoustic picture, experience of the real world allowed the audience to construct a simulacrum via the image.[11] As Chion has pointed out, the coming of synchronised sound created space beyond the depicted image, by creating a space 'off' from which sound may emanate even if we do not see it within the frame (1994a: 83–4).

While vision creates a 'there', locating an object in space separate from (though obviously in relation to) one's own subject position, sound creates a 'here', or rather a 'there' + 'here': two points in space, the object and the subject, both separated and connected by the vibrating medium which transmits the sound. We create a geography of sound with our subject position always at the centre; to make an analogy to the visual, it is our 'point of audition'.[12] Chion makes the distinction between the spatial and subjective senses of this term, and points out that it is often impossible to speak of a precise 'spatial' point of audition (he proposes a 'place' or a 'zone' of audition [1994a, 89–92]), but the exploitation of the point of audition in film is perhaps more common than the point of view, though it is usually just as intermittently used. It is commonly called 'subjective sound', and is frequently associated with female characters. The classic examples cited by most historians are both from Hitchcock. In *Blackmail* (1929), a young woman who stabs a man who tried to rape her hears only the word 'knife' in an innocuous kitchen conversation; in *Psycho* (1960), the audience eavesdrops on the voices in Marion's head as she drives away from the scene of her crime. Once again, while point-of-view puts us in the subject position of a character in control, point-of-audition puts us in the subject position of a character who has lost or is losing control. The possibility for unease is far greater than with point-of-view (except possibly in such cases as that of *Strange Days* in which we are forced to identify with a person committing a horrible crime) because we must relinquish even the illusion of control. It is perhaps significant that *Closet Land*, a film about a woman struggling with a man for emotional and psychological control, is so dependent upon sound for its effect on the audience. It is also a film in which the spatial point of audition is unusually precise and reinforced by the extensive use of subjective sound; the two types collude to place the audience in the woman's physical and emotional subject position.

Closet Land

Closet Land has been criticised for being 'uncinematic':[13] by that, the critics mean that it seems too much like a photographed play. After all, it all takes place in one room (or does it?); and it has only two characters (or does it?). It is highly stylised, taking place in a nameless country at a nameless time, the characters merely identified as 'the Woman' and 'the Man'. Despite this abstraction, the film seems to have a profound effect on the viewer.[14] I would like to propose that one reason for this is the subject position constructed by the soundscape.

The soundscape is unequivocally cinematic; this is a 'filmed play' that could never take place in real space, because there is only one space that the audience can inhabit, and that is the Woman's place. Except for one brief moment, the entire soundscape of the film is generated from the female lead character, both from her psychological subject position and her physical point of audition. The power of this positioning may even undercut the psychoanalytically theorised visual spectacle of the passive Woman, which is further undermined by her appearance. Small, delicate, her dark hair pulled loosely back in a braid, her feet bare, she has a Madonna-like[15] quality, accentuated by her simple white cotton nightgown; the high waist minimises the curves of her slight figure, freezing her in pre-pubescence, a symbol of her arrested sexual development.

As the opening credits are printed in white on a black screen, we are plunged into her physical place by the sound. From the ambient room tone and the echoes of steps and voices, we can hear that it is a large room, empty and hard, probably cold; an electrical hum testifies to fluorescent lighting. The Woman is being handed over from a rough, gruff guard to the officer in charge. They are on either side of her, as the stereo effect makes quite clear, even though we will find out that this is an impossibility; an apparently 'realistic' sound is manipulated to deceive us as well as to force us into an unusually close identification with the Woman. The first visual image is also from her point of view: as her blindfold is removed, the light flares in her unaccustomed eyes – a sound of ringing crystal provides an aural homology to this blinding flash, momentarily overpowering other sounds – and gradually the face of her elegantly-clad interrogator resolves into focus. This visual/aural effect is repeated halfway through the film when she is blindfolded again.

Designer Eiko Ishioka created a high-tech interrogation room with classical columns, replete with optical illusions (the room is diamond-shaped rather than square, the columns do not extend all the way to the ceiling, the floor tiles appear to have holes in them, the lighting is indirect and hidden). Everything, including the clothing, is in cool shades of black, white and grey – everything, that is, but for the brilliant blue lining of the Man's overcoat, which becomes a telling marker. Outside, a thunderstorm is audible throughout the film.

These are just some of the many symbols in *Closet Land*, a film that virtually demands a semiotic decoding. The film is itself a deconstruction of the act of deconstruction. The Woman is being accused of 'subliminal indoctrination' because her interrogator interprets the children's books she writes as politically subversive. 'Do you object to my interpretation?' he asks; 'No', she replies, 'but that's all it is, your interpretation. I can't control the messages people choose to find in my stories. There are people who get turned on by passages in the Bible.' When she suggests that her story 'Closet Land' is merely a fairy tale in which the usual element of horror – a witch, a dragon, a monster – is replaced by an everyday object – the closet – the Man laughs in disbelief, retorting, 'It's not a simple word, is it?' and proceeds to delineate the myriad possible meanings of the closet.[16] He is right: the closet is not an everyday object in the story, but he has got the interpretation wrong. The stereotypical male = public/female = private split is realised in their interpretations: the story that he has interpreted politically is in fact symbolic of the Woman's sexual torment, brought on at the hands of one of her mother's literary friends when she was five years old and he used to molest her in the coat closet.

This revelation emerges as the two joust intellectually, occasionally physically, and the power gradually shifts. From the outset, the Man lets her know in no uncertain, if poetic and patronising, terms that he is in charge:

> I am a small part of a large mechanism; that goes for you, too, but together we must seek the truth. I will help you to the best of my ability, but the brunt of the responsibility lies with you. Deliberate deceit will not be tolerated, although personally I may find your lies charming; inadvertent blunders will be treated with firm kindness, and you must trust me to determine the ratio of firmness to kindness. Your best hope would be to depersonalise what follows and not to look upon me as a foe, or yourself as a victim. Remember, we are both seekers of truth, and in this quest, I am your friend, philosopher and guide.

He is polite, even friendly, offering her some broth and his suit jacket for warmth; but he also plays cruel tricks on her, calmly taunting her with a cigarette after telling her about prisoners being burnt by cigarettes and playing a tape secretly recorded at her mother's deathbed. As he plays the tape, the sound of an agitated heartbeat pulses like an underscore, abruptly ending when he explains such procedures are 'government policy' – it is as if her heart stops when she realises how much trouble she is in. When she reacts by crying, the sound is unnaturally loud, acoustically 'wet' and reverberant, as someone crying would hear within her own head.

Richard Einhorn's underscore is minimal, both stylistically and in the time it takes up in the soundscape. The minimalist style helps create a musical texture which blurs the borders between 'music' and 'sound effect', creating an empathetic depiction of the Woman's emotional and physical states. The first musical fragment, which occurs as the Woman enters the room and offers her wrists to the Man for her handcuffs to be removed, is not highly distinctive melodically, as in a classical film score, but is both a source of musical gestures used throughout the film and almost a physical description of the Woman's sensations (see Fig. 9.1). A light heartbeat rhythm provides the bassline; a slightly syncopated arpeggio figure (which might seem accompanimental but which is used thematically in the underscore) may reflect an agitated state of mind, the jangling of nerves; the long-held notes of the flute's descending line create tension, intensified by the long, dissonant suspension of the A flat, finally but briefly resolved.

Fig. 9.1: Opening empathetic cue

During the initial stages of the interrogation, the bursts of under-score are what might be described as 'heightened sound effects'. They are more obviously subjective, or empathetic, than the relatively neutral opening music. When the Man asks the Woman if she is menstruating, she is shocked, then outraged and refuses to answer; he calmly swoops in to kneel at her side, pinning her against the chair with one arm, and feels clinically beneath her nightgown. An outbreak of Taiko (Japanese)-style drumming provides an excellent outward expression of her panic and kinetic mimicry of her pounding heart and racing thoughts. Later, when he boxes her ears, a nauseating con-coction of chimes, their ringing bent and spacially displaced through recording manipulation, gives a realistic aural depiction of the phy-sical effects of having your ears boxed but is musically created.

But the Man's true deviousness is revealed when he blindfolds her for the second time and 'sends in' the gruff-voiced guard to knock her around. The gruff guard is merely another guise of the officer, as is the frightened fellow prisoner tossed at her feet to convince her to talk to the sensitive interrogator, the one who used to be a university professor, the one who plays the piano – the Man.

He can play all these parts because he is adept at manipulating sound. All three of his personae have distinctly different voices, different accents and different ways of moving. The guard has a rough bass voice and a slow drawl of indeterminate provenance; he wears heavy boots and moves like a bull in a china shop. The prisoner has a quavering, breathy tenor with a strong working-class London accent; he has no shoes and moves by dragging himself across the floor because he has been crippled by his torture. The officer has a clear baritone and a cultured (but not aristocratic) English accent;[17] he is light on his leather-shod feet, at times moving as gracefully as a dancer. To the blindfolded Woman, they sound like clearly differentiated individuals. In one sequence, he is both the guard and the prisoner engaged in a brutal interrogation, swiftly turning from one position to the other (and moving strikingly in and out of a key light which strikes the prisoner like the clichéd lamp in a third-degree but leaves the guard in shadow); in another, he even has a tape of the prisoner being tortured so that he can talk to her in the guise of the guard over the recorded cries and whimpers. Heightening his deception is the technical manipulation of the soundtrack at the beginning of the film, to which I have already referred. As the blindfolded woman is escorted to the interrogation chamber by the officer and the guard, their voices are clearly spaced in the stereo picture – the Woman in the centre, the voices of the 'guard' and the 'officer' on either side. For all the sound tricks in the film, this is the only one which, in retrospect, is impossible; the Man simply could not have moved from one side of the Woman to the other quickly enough – and more importantly, silently enough – to fool her; but it does have the effect of putting the audience off the scent and more importantly, plunging them into her subject position.[18]

Michel Chion has theorised the *acousmêtre*, or acousmatic being, who is heard but not seen; these characters often have striking 'powers' or 'gifts' because of their acousmatic existence: they see all, know all, are omnipotent and ubiquitous. Most acousmatic characters are revealed at some point during the narrative, as are Dr Mabuse, the Wizard of Oz, and Norman Bates' mother; in each case the revelation is highly dramatic, but also results in a defusing of their acousmatic powers (1994a: 129–31). In *Closet Land*, the security guard and the officer are acousmatic characters to the audience as well as to the woman, while the prisoner is acousmatic only to the woman. *Closet Land* may be the exception in which the character's power seems to grow – at least to the audience – with each new revelation, for we come to realise how all-powerful – at least over the Woman – the Man is.

There are other acousmatic characters who are never revealed: when the Man knocks the Woman out and leaves her alone, someone dresses her in a black bra and panties and paints her face in a clown's impression of a woman's makeup; against this parody of a 'sexy image', her hair is put into two hasty, child-like asymmetrical dog-ears and she is taunted with a tango, over which a man makes crude remarks and reveals that her stunted sex life has been under surveillance.[19] These sounds originate from outside the room, we never even see the speakers, and two spotlights shaped like cat's eyes follow the skimpily-clad woman around the darkened room like the projection of a voyeur's gaze. This voice is not the Man's, though 'the guard' chimes in with 'olés' in the tango. Later, when the Woman is drugged and strapped to the desk-cum-torture table, we hear two other male attendants talking casually about their children as latex-gloved hands clean the mask of makeup from her face; when they open the drawer to get a syringe, we see torture implements as well as pots of makeup, suggesting that these same, pleasant-sounding men we never actually see are the same ones who put her in such degrading clothes (although, to be fair, the plain satin lingerie could have been far more revealing than it is). And another prisoner, who has had his tongue cut out to keep him from shouting encouragement to other prisoners, whistles a simple rising fourth signal from time to time, bolstering the Woman.

The Woman's strength in resisting the Man's interrogation techniques begins to wear him down. As she resists, her words ring in his ears; the one moment in the film in which the point of audition shifts from her to him, he experiences an auditory flashback while we momentarily see him outside the room, driving in his car in the rain. Distantly, he hears a male voice, possibly (one of) his, echoing her words, hinting that he had once been in her situation and had not only been broken but turned, something to which 'the prisoner' had already alluded.

The Woman has psychological walls forged by her experience as an abused child. She can escape his torture into the fantasy worlds she had created then that now provide the inspiration for her children's books, which in turn have brought her to the attention of the authorities. These escape sequences are depicted as animations that look like the illustrations for such books, and the ambient sound changes to delicate wind chimes and soft insect and bird sounds all very quiet, but creating a definite sense of a change of space. That the Man is making some breach in her defences is indicated in an animation of her character 'the cat with green wings'; as he unfurls his protecting arms to enclose her, the cat's face is suddenly transformed into a fang-encrusted snarl and the insides of his wings turn to electric blue – the same colour as the Man's coat lining. But as she senses that the Man is breaking down, her defences are reinforced, and when the Man pulls out one of her toenails, she is able to call upon the cat, once more with comforting green wings, to fly down and carry her away through a portal that looks like the *trompe l'oeil* tiles in the floor.[20] Unnerved by this escape, the Man drags the Woman into a closet off the main interrogation room. A particularly loud thunderclap emphasises the opening door, and a distinct shift in the ambient room tone changes our perception of the size of the space 'we' are in.

The Man hopes to break her, but in fact he reveals himself, again through sound, by singing a nasty children's taunt ('Here comes the candle to light you to bed, and here comes the chopper to shop off your head').[21] The nursery gothic of the chant resonates with the woman's assertion that children's tales all have an element of horror in them. As the Woman recognises the tune (see Fig. 9.2)[22] and its implications, a man's voice is mingled with the tune played on orchestral chimes, and the whole is put through extensive electronic distortion, echoing and looping, creating an intensely subjective picture of the Woman's reeling mind. It is also the explanation for the flashes of a closet image, the distant sound of a man's voice and the similar playing of the 'chopper tune' on tubular bells during the earlier auditory maelstrom when the Woman's ears are boxed; this time, it is merely emotional shock that brings on the effect. She recognises the Man's singing voice as that of her literary molester, the man whose tortures on the child produce the resistance that the Woman uses to defeat the Man.[23]

Fig. 9.2: 'Chopper' tune

In the end, on the verge of tears, the Man begs her to sign the confession to save herself. She takes the confession and rips it up, the white pieces showering over them both in slow motion after she tosses them into the air. As dawn lights the strip of windows above the columns, the Man opens the door for her and ushers her out, handcuffed, presumably to her execution. She may be the one to die, but he is the one whose spirit is broken.

Although the Woman is the undisputed hero of *Closet Land*, the Man is not an unequivocal villain, as we have seen. The sounds, even when they are empathetic to the Woman, have sympathetic vibrations with the Man. The fact that he, too, is under surveillance is hinted at when, early on, he lowers his voice and murmurs 'The walls have ears'; the ambient sound expands dramatically, blended with the decay of a gong and low piano strings. We are suddenly aware of that space 'off' from which the watchers are watching. He even participates in the one traditional musical theme in the film, a tune connected with *Closet Land*, but more precisely with escape (see Fig. 9.3). The theme is first heard on flute just before the woman is knocked out, when she imagines herself as 'the closet child', 'glid[ing] out of hell' down a luminous hallway; the theme is repeated later when he asks about 'Closet Land' and she describes it for him. But between these two appearances, the moment comes when he blindfolds her for the second time and she protests. He quietens her by whispering intimately in her ear, 'They're watching me, too', and slips out of the room to the 'escape' tune, mirroring her 'glide out of hell'. Later, when she reveals to him the story of her molestation and the creation of 'Closet Land' as an escape, the theme forms the basis of the musical cue, decorated by chimes when she mentions the Sunday church bells. When he says, more in shock than admiration, 'I wonder if you know – really know – the strength of your mind? . . . You've escaped from us on the back of a flying cow and a cat with wings', the flute theme is doubled by a French horn, an orchestration that seems to suggest his sympathy with her. At the end, she glides handcuffed down the luminous corridor, now shown to lead off the interrogation room, to a triumphantly building minimalist texture under the escape theme played double time on the flute, once again a solo voice.

Fig. 9.3: 'Escape' theme

Preliminary Conclusions

Sound – particularly hearing – is historically associated with irrationality and emotion, traits magnified by its subset music; irrationality, emotion and music have all been associated with the feminine, making the equation of sound and femininity implicit in our culture. This alliance is woven deeply into psychoanalytic theory, with positive but also profoundly negative implications for female subjectivity, and therefore into psychoanalytic film theory. Yet these associations, like the recognition of sound in the field of film studies, are almost always oblique and marginal to the main argument – much in the way femininity exists in the gaps and margins of masculinity in these theoretical constructs.

Probably because sound in film exists largely in a liminal (even subliminal) position, it can have an uncanny effect on an audience – uncanny in that the 'spectator' is usually less able to recognise and articulate that effect than a visual one. This is particularly true in the case of music, though the cinematic soundscape as a whole has an effect on the audience which is rarely considered. Because most of the major work on sound in academic film scholarship has concentrated on the technology or technological history of sound, or on the abstract, usually psychoanalytical theory of sound on the (viewing) subject, and because music, sound effects and dialogue have tended to be methodologically segregated, we do not have many examples of studies which bring these disparate items together (Weis [1982], as mentioned above, and Fischer [1977] are two notable exceptions) and begin to illustrate how we actually experience a film. Although we may discern and hierarchise the elements, and some people may in fact be more perceptive of various elements than others as a result of proclivity and training, we do all receive film sound acoustically and then phenomenologically as a dynamic soundscape, interacting within itself and with the images and narrative trajectory.

In the film industry, sound seems to be of greatest concern to those who produce big movies; we have come to expect teeth-rattling explosions and bombastic scores in modern blockbusters. However, sound can be even more intensely felt in intimate, quiet films, where the slightest whisper or silence can have a marked effect. *Closet Land* is such a film, a political allegory in which the sparse but complex soundscape highlights subjectivity in its multiple meanings, both internally and externally to the film text, and particularly regarding gender and the geography of the cinematic soundscape.

Closet Land is a rare film in which the soundscape is equal, if not superior to, the visuals in constructing a subject position for the audience. As it happens, that subject position is quite atypically female. The soundscape is unusual, too, in the considerable overlap in the distinctiveness and function of two elements normally considered separate: sound effect and music. This elision creates sound effects more stylised than objective reality and more representative of subjective reality.

These conclusions are necessarily preliminary because the issues involved are so complex, crossing numerous disciplinary boundaries, from the acoustic to the psychological to the philosophical to the art-historical, and have so rarely been directly addressed. I am not so much interested in theoretical proof or 'truth' as the persistently gendered way in which sound (including music), subjectivity and the relationship between vision and audition are conceived. These are apparently so deeply ingrained in our culture that no amount of theoretical acrobatics can budge them, and thus must necessarily affect the way films are constructed and therefore the way we see and hear them.

Acknowledgements

My thanks to Peter Franklin, Nicholas Cook and Rachel Moseley for their helpful comments on earlier drafts of this chapter.

Notes

1. The terms of cinema reception, such as the place (auditorium) and the receivers (the audience), bear traces of an experience in sound, but have become so commonly reduced to the visual aspect (the screen) or allied to the social construction (the gender, socio-economic class, sexuality, age and so on of the people who go to see a film) that the words have lost some of their original specificity.

2. Something not always appreciated by non-musicians is the fact that musicians – even those of us with a keen interest in film music – may register the music just as subliminally as anyone else: actually *listening* to a film score is a feat demanding considerable concentration. Musicologists simply have two advantages in understanding the workings of the musical score: a heightened sensitivity to musical codes that allows them to be 'hailed' by a musical event (to have their attention drawn to the music, like hearing the person at the other side of the cocktail party talking about a subject in which one is interested), and a language that allows

them to conceptualise and describe the musical event and its effect on the audience.

3. A discussion of music and meaning is clearly out of the scope of this article, as it is one of the most intensely debated subjects in the field of musicology today. I shall therefore simply state my position: music does not have the same strong semiotic connection between signifier and signified that language does; however, there is a cultural consensus that music does have meaning, and there are enduring cultural connections between certain musical gestures and particular meanings, therefore it seems to me that although musical gestures may not have specific meanings, they often have a potential range of meanings that can be and usually are decoded by the listener.

4. Ironically, although these theorists ignored sound in this context, one of the abiding theories of why music has always been a part of the cinematic apparatus is that it psychologically softens the impact of technological tricks like editing, even lulling the viewer into a hypnotic state, an argument which might have bolstered their own psychoanalytic theories. See Gorbman 1987: 37–69 for a history and summary of this argument.

5. Curiously, perhaps even perversely, Mary Ann Doane (1982) excludes the soundtrack from her argument about female spectatorship 'primarily because it is the process of imaging which seems to constitute the major difficulty in theorizing female spectatorship' (1982: 10, 56).

6. Psychologist Carol Gilligan (1983) influentially argued that this goal-oriented striving toward an individual identity – of which separation from the mother is an important component – is not the way that girls develop psychologically (in the same white, Western, middle-class context in which Freudianism is also based, though without the same acknowledgement). Gilligan theorises that women do form an individual subjectivity, but through a spiral of relationships with others (and often at a later age than in men, who conversely tend to develop their connectedness with others at a later stage than women). Gilligan, however, says that this flaw in psychoanalytic theory – a lack of understanding of female psychology, or even a recognition that it was different from the male – became cast as a problem in women's development. This is, of course, a highly simplified overview of a complex psychological theory.

7. Kristeva also reinforces the feminine-musical-multiple-irrational elision so common in Western culture by describing how 'No text, no matter how "musicalized", is devoid of meaning or signification; on the contrary, musicalization pluralizes meanings' (1997: 52).

8. The original meaning is retained even more closely in Russian, in which the word *khorovod* still means a circle dance.

9. The issue of sound re/production is one that has caused some aggravation in film theory; James Lastra (1992) provides an excellent historical and theoretical overview of this debate between those who believe that film sound is reproduced, or essentially the same as the original sound produced (usually those of a more psychoanalytical tendency like Baudry and Metz, though including earlier film theorists like Béla Balasz and Stanley Cavell), and those who argue that sound is represented, or only a partial reproduction or even fabrication of the original sound (usually those who are interested in technology, like Rick Altman, Alan Williams and Tom Levin). While I agree wholeheartedly with the position that sound on film is representation, just as is the image (a position that seems confirmed by the fact that sound engineers will normally trade authenticity for legibility – or the perception of reality over the real), it remains that the vibrations of the transmitting medium (air) tend to create a greater *impression* of reality for sound than does the projected light for image.

10. The point-of-view carried throughout *People Like Us* is not even exact – the narrator, television reporter Roy Mallard (Chris Langham), is placed slightly beside his cameraman, and therefore sometimes his arm or shoulder or profile comes into shot. The series is shot through with desiring looks, both Roy/the camera lingering on attractive female interview subjects (a direct gaze); sometimes that gaze is returned, but obliquely because the woman is looking at Roy, not the camera.

11. One of the earliest explanations for the persistence of sound and music with respect to film was that it gave the two-dimensional images depth (both emotional and physical). See Gorbman 1987, Chapter 3.

12. There is also a conceptual geography of the soundscape that extends beyond the dialogue and the sound effect, even beyond the non-diegetic/diegetic/meta-diegetic construction articulated by such theorists as Gorbman and Chion. It is hinted at in the terminology with which we speak about the placement of elements of the soundscape: voice*over*, *under*score, *back*ground music. These conventional terms may have a perceptual reality (whether primarily or secondarily constructed) beyond their commonplace usage that I must pursue elsewhere because of space constraints.

13. See, for example, Daws (1991), Gilbert (1991) Honeycutt (1991), and Kehr (1991). Although most critics praise cinematographer Bill Pope for unusual inventiveness in lighting and shooting the single set, the sense of the story being 'hemmed in' and 'confined' underpins their critiques. *Closet Land* has, since its film release, been performed theatrically.

14. For strong anecdotal evidence, see the user reviews for *Closet Land* on the International Movie Database (http://www.uk.imdb/) to get an idea of the impact this film can have. I personally know of several ardent film fans who are unable to sit through *Closet Land* because of its intensity.

15. Perhaps not coincidentally, actress Madeleine Stowe's first acting job was as the Virgin Mary in the film *The Nativity* (1978).

16. Another musical homology – or at least, a simile – may be found in the score at this point: a pizzicato bassline in crochets creates a buffa-like underpinning to the man's rhythmic speech. After one musical period, the bassline is subdivided by upbeats, and after another period, the upbeats are further divided into semi-quavers, creating a full, classical accompaniment texture. Yet by layering the pizzicato strings in this way, the composer has laid bare the harmonic underpinnings and the rhythmic hierarchies of this stereotypical Alberti-bass pattern – ironically, deconstructing by constructing before our very ears.

17. One should perhaps not read too much into the Englishness of these accents; the actor is simply English. Had he been an American, accents with similar connotations might have been chosen: the guard might have had a 'redneck' or Brooklyn accent, for instance. After all, 'the Woman' has an American accent, even though they are supposedly from the same country.

18. One might argue that the actor, Alan Rickman, has one of the more distinctive voices in film and theatre, which resonates through the various disguises. This was, however, one of his earliest films, limiting his familiarity to the audience. Diegetically, the Woman would probably be too shaken by her experience to note the similarity between the two voices because the deception seems so improbable.

19. The tango is a famous comedy number, *Hernando's Hideaway*, from the Richard Adler and Jerry Ross' musical *Pajama Game*. The original lyrics (unheard here) are about a place for a secret lovers' rendezvous, an ironic juxtaposition to the Woman's situation.

20. Jarmila Potuckova, a Communist arrested for a Czech show trial in 1951, tells a remarkably similar story of escape: 'It was torture. They were shouting and swearing at me. I had to look into their eyes. At the beginning, I avoided this, but then I had to repeat their obscenities. Then I started to make up fairy tales for my son. I got into an imaginary world of castles and princes and animals. So when they shouted at me, I didn't have to answer them. I only looked into their eyes when I was making up those fairy tales.' The Cold War, episode 6, 'Reds-1948–1955', BBC2 transmitted 31 October 1998.
21. This refrain comes from the children's chant 'Oranges and Lemons' which cites the different church chimes in London. The remarkable specificity of this nursery rhyme seems quite out of character with the rest of this highly abstract text.
22. This tune is apparently composed for the film, as the refrain is spoken, or at most chanted on a single pitch or two, in all traditions which I have been able to determine. My thanks to the many members of the Arts Faculty of the University of Southampton who provided me with multiple versions of this nursery rhyme.
23. This too-neat closure marks the narrative's turn toward overt propaganda that actually undermines the power of the film, not least because there is only about ten years' difference between the two actors and therefore our perceptions of the characters – as a boy in his late teens, the Man could have been old enough to be the molester, but probably not old enough to be a member of her mother's literary circle. It might have been possible to use the twist with more integrity to the characters if the Woman had, in fact, been close enough to breaking down to collapse her two tormentors into one, and the Man, who is clearly intelligent and perceptive enough to do so, had played into her delusion. This may even be hinted at by the voice in the 'chopper' sequence, which sounds like none of the character's voices, nor does it sound like the actor at all (hence my distinction between the Man and the man).

Bibliography

Altman, Rick (ed.) (1992) Sound Theory Sound Practice. London: Routledge.
Baudry, Jean-Louis (1974–75) 'Ideological effects of the basic cinematographic apparatus'. Film Quarterly, vol. 28, no. 2 (winter).
Baudry, Jean-Louis (1975) 'The apparatus: metapsychological approaches to the impression of reality'. Cinema, Communications, no. 23.
Chion, Michel (1982) Le Voix au Cinéma. Paris: Cahiers du Cinéma.
Chion, Michel (1994a) AudioVision: Sound on Screen (trans. Claudia Gorbman). New York: Columbia University Press.
Chion, Michel (1994b). Le Son au Cinéma Cinéma. Paris: Cahiers du Cinéma.
Chion, Michel (1995) La Musique au Cinéma. Paris: Librairie Arthéme Fayard.
Daws (1991) 'Review: Closet Land' in Variety, 11 March.
Doane, Mary Ann (1980) 'The voice in the cinema: The articulation of body and space'. Yale French Studies, no. 60.
Doane, Mary Ann (1982) 'Film and masquerade: Theorising the female spectator'. Screen, vol. 23, nos. 3–4 (September–October).
Fischer, Lucy (1977) 'René Clair, le million, and the coming of sound'. Cinema Journal, vol. 16, no. 2 (spring).
Gilbert, Matthew (1991) Angst consumes: Closet Land. Boston Globe, March (http://kelclancy.tgsolutions.com/reviews/cl-bgl.htm).
Gilligan, Carol (1982) In a Different Voice: Psychological Theory and Women's Development. London: Harvard University Press.

Gorbman, Claudia (1987) *Unheard Melodies: Narrative Film Music.* London: BFI.

Honeycutt, Kirk (1991) Review: *Closet Land. Hollywood Reporter*, no. 316, 24 March.

Kehr, Dave (1991) 'Closet Land's politics and prurience'. *Chicago Tribune*, 8 March (http://kelclancy.tgsolutions.com/reviews/cl-ctrb.htm)

Kristeva, Julia (1997) in Kelly Oliver (ed.) *The Portable Kristeva.* New York: Columbia University Press.

Lastra, James (1992) 'Reading, writing, and representing sound'. Rick Altman (ed.) *Sound Theory Sound Practice.* London: Routledge.

Metz, Christian (1982) *The Imaginary Signifier: Psychoanalysis and the Cinema* (trans. Celia Britton *et al.*). Bloomington: Indiana University Press.

Mulvey, Laura (1975) 'Visual pleasure and narrative cinema'. *Screen*, vol. 16, no. 3 (Autumn).

Yale French Studies (1980) special issue: Cinema/Sound, no. 60.

Weis, Elisabeth (1982) *The Silent Scream: Alfred Hitchcock's Sound Track*. Rutherford, NJ: Fairleigh Dickinson University Press.

Weis, Elisabeth and John Belton (eds) (1985) *Film Sound: Theory and Practice.* New York: Columbia University Press.

Chapter 10

'Would You Like to Hear Some Music?' Music in-and-out-of-control in the Films of Quentin Tarantino

Ken Garner

> 'One of the things I do when I'm thinking about starting a movie, is, I'll go through my record collection and just start playing songs.'
>
> Quentin Tarantino interview,
> included on *The Tarantino Connection* (1996)

Music clearly means a lot to Quentin Tarantino. It also matters to the characters in his films. Even when they are not playing music, they like to talk about it, along with fast food, television and the rest of popular culture. Tarantino himself, as Mr Brown, opens *Reservoir Dogs* (1995) with a debate about the meaning of Madonna's *Like a Virgin*. In a scene written for *Pulp Fiction* (1995), but later cut during filming and replaced with another, Mia asks if Vincent Vega is related to Suzanne Vega 'the folk singer'; to which Vincent replies, 'Suzanne Vega's my cousin. If she's become a folk singer, I sure as hell don't know nothin' about it' (Tarantino 1994a). Bail bondsman Max Cherry asks the heroine of *Jackie Brown* (1998) why she 'never got into the CD revolution', to which she replies 'I can't afford to start all over again. I got too much time and money invested in my records.' 'You can't get new stuff on vinyl,' says Max. 'I don't buy new stuff that often,' says Jackie (Tarantino 1998).

But that last piece of dialogue also forms part of a scene of a type common to each of Tarantino's three major films (*Reservoir Dogs*, *Pulp Fiction* and *Jackie Brown*): a scene in which a central character is seen selecting music and then playing it, whether it be an LP record on a turntable, an audio-cassette in a car stereo, a reel-to-reel tape recorder, or by turning on and tuning a radio to a favourite station.

There is, of course, nothing original in having actors show the source of diegetic music, music from within the world of the film, in this way. Nor is it unusual for music that thus emerges from the hi-fi, car or radio to recur non-diegetically, on the soundtrack, playing over scenes from which it can't possibly be emanating. Film-makers have long used such techniques to either fill the world of the film with the affect of a carefully crafted composed score, or draw the audience into the emotional character or situation cues provided by diegetic music at crucial moments. What is different about the use of such diegetic music in Tarantino's films is that this act, the actors appearing to take control of the score, is explicitly celebrated. The process of music selection is foregrounded. It is the choice of this-music or that-music in these particular circumstances, its switching on and off – rather than just the music itself – which is made indicative of character or situation.

That scene in *Jackie Brown* where Max and Jackie discuss records versus CDs provides a good example. It begins with Jackie opening the door to Max and him walking in, the camera cuts to his point of view, and the first thing his gaze falls on is her turntable and pile of LP records in their sleeves. In between Max's saying 'You can't get new stuff on records,' and Jackie's reply 'I don't buy new stuff' we see an extreme close-up of the record needle dropping into the groove of the record. As the intro to The Delfonics' *Didn't I Blow Your Mind This Time* wells up, Jackie lights a cigarette, then performs a brief musical gesture with both hands in appreciation of the arrangement. He says it's 'pretty', asks her who it is, she tells him, 'it's nice,' he comments.

This use of music and music culture is the only aspect of this scene not present in chapter 12 of Tarantino's source for the film, Elmore Leonard's novel *Rum Punch* (Leonard 1998). Allowing for cuts, Tarantino's visualisation here is otherwise faithful to the spirit of the original. Not long after, we see an extreme close-up of a vertical rack of cassette spines labelled 'Best of the Delfonics', then Max going to the record-shop counter to buy the song he discovered from Jackie. Later, he mouths along to the lyrics while listening to *Didn't I Blow Your Mind This Time* in his car. He is still listening to this song on his car cassette player as he drives up to the Del Amo Mall to play his part in the plot's sting. Finally, and most comically, the song sweeps out of his car stereo once more, as tense Ordell, driving them to the dramatic denouement at Max's office where who-is-shafting-whom will finally be revealed, punches the cassette into the system. 'I didn't know you liked the Delfonics,' he says. 'They're pretty good,' says Max.

A fair conclusion from this example might be that this foregrounding of music control is wholly attributable to Tarantino, and a device of which he is particularly fond. It performs a number of functions. The film theorist in us spots the ease with which it enables a particular piece of music emanating from the diegesis to recur. Music fans can appreciate Tarantino's knowledgeable plundering of the back catalogue, here choosing a Philly sound hit from 1970, close enough to the era of the blaxploitation movies of the early 1970s, to which *Jackie Brown* is in part a homage, to provide aural consistency to the tribute. More importantly, however, the sound of *Didn't I Blow Your Mind* is given four new, different signifying functions within the specific context of this particular diegesis. As Jackie drifts into a brief reverie at its prompting, we cannot but see the song as signifying for Jackie general memories, probably of her youth. Secondly, her decision to play such a record to Max is itself a performative act of display of identity. To Max, the record and her reaction signifies to him that this is indeed a woman with a particular identity and past. Finally, Max's subsequent frequent replaying of the song in his car is a sign to the audience of his connection with Jackie.

It is this that makes its final recurrence simultaneously tense and comic. Surely Ordell will now realise the extent of Max's intimacy with Jackie, and realise he's being set up? But his question reveals that although thinking himself a cool guy, he, unlike us, does not realise how significant this song is. Instead, his black man's question merely draws attention for the first time to our preconception of the apparent absurdity of a middle-aged white man digging old Philly soul. We laugh with nervous relief, and at our own taste–culture prejudices.

What is noticeable about these various significations is that at no point is the song's meaning fixed. What it means precisely to Jackie and Max remains unclear. Clearly, what matters most about much of the music in Tarantino's films – all of it culled from existing records and movies – is the situational use his characters make of it. But before exploring further why this has helped his films' soundtracks touch a chord with young cinema audiences, it must be acknowledged that this is just one of the locations for music in his films of which there are three.

(i) Music for main themes and scoring

These are the records Tarantino selects to play over the main credits at the beginning (and end), as well as music that is played over certain scenes – in lieu of a composed score – which does not emanate from the world of the film. With the exception of *Reservoir Dogs*' use of the device of having almost all its music supposedly played on the radio station *K-Billy*'s 'Super Sounds of the Seventies Weekend', this music remains largely non-diegetic, outside the world of the film.

(ii) Unselected, incidental diegetic music

Occasional instances of music playing mainly in public places – shops, bars, coffee shops – which the leading characters have not chosen. Examples include Al Green's *Let's Stay Together* playing as Marcellus briefs Butch in his club, near the beginning of *Pulp Fiction*; and (*Holy Matrimony*) *Letter to the Firm*, by Foxy Brown, playing in the record shop as Max buys his Delfonics tape in *Jackie Brown*. These fill out and humanise these spaces; act as a caesura in the film's mood (the Al Green coming immediately after the opening execution scene in *Pulp Fiction*); and additionally enable Tarantino to offer a wider range of styles of music for inclusion on the soundtrack CD, than those which he selects for particular reasons for (i) above, and (iii) below. A unique exception to these common functions of unselected diegetic music is provided by the Jack Rabbit Slim's sequence in *Pulp Fiction*, as discussed later.

(iii) Diegetic music selected by characters

These scenes, as described above, provide the key, striking scenes in each of the three films under discussion; the scenes which if asked about Tarantino's use of music, most audiences think of immediately: Max's use of the Delfonics, as described above, in *Jackie Brown*; Mia, first, playing Dusty Springfield's *Son of a Preacher Man* as Vincent arrives at her house, then dancing to Urge Overkill's *Girl, You'll Be a Woman Soon* before overdosing, in *Pulp Fiction*; and Mr Blonde' slicing off the cop's ear to Stealer's Wheel's *Stuck in the Middle with You* on the radio in *Reservoir Dogs*.

All the music Tarantino chooses for his main themes and scoring shares three common characteristics: it is old; it is referential to distinct musical, film or media genres; and the opening credit music features what Richard Middleton (1984), developing the ideas of Philip Tagg (1982), has called musematic repetiton, rather than discursive, or melodic repetition of longer phrases. In other words, Tarantino chooses records for his opening credits whose first few seconds are characterised by repetition of short rhythmic units, or 'riffs'. Middleton says the effects of such repetition are 'epic-recursive', 'achieving a resonance with primary energy flow, setting it in motion'. In addition, this repetition in each theme is played by a unique instrument or voice, unmistakably expressive of a singular musical personality.

This last quality explains a lot. If his credit themes were only characterised by their age and referentiality, it would be tempting to see his use of music as exclusively post-modern in effect. By deliberately not choosing contemporary recordings for his themes for films set in the present, he eschews not only current pop-soundtrack standard practice (assemble a selection of new recordings that target the film's audience demographic), but also the approach of such directorial masters of appropriation of past records to locate their film's action or characters temporally, culturally or psychologically, as Scorsese, Kubrick and Allen. What he offers instead, a dated musical style, perhaps referring to film genres, might suggest the audience is intended to lean back and smirk at his knowingness.

But these undeniable characteristics are both limited in their effect by the degree of popular music and film expertise of the audience (not everyone knows the records, or what genres or movies this music comes from), and held in balance by the sheer 'epic' energy of the credit themes' musematic repetition, a quality Tarantino acknowledges he strives for (*The Tarantino Connection*, 1996: track 1, interview). For example, it is possible – if unlikely – to be familiar with soul legend Bobby Womack's career; to recognise the opening credit music to *Jackie Brown* as his theme song for the 1972 Barry Shear American thriller *Across 110th Street* (1972); and to sense that the film will therefore be in part a homage to blaxploitation movies of those years; and yet become wholly involved in this particular story from the moment Womack starts singing.

His is the first voice of the film. As light fades up on the 1970s wall mosaics inside Los Angeles airport, he moans a wordless, descending figure, twice, with a slight variation. Its melodic fall, in two successive triplets, is expressive of endless lament. It says, in effect, 'bad things will always happen, and they're about to happen again'. Then the verse, the main melody, begins as Jackie Brown appears; and the camera (tracking Jackie's progress along the travelator), the narrative and the lyric all start to move simultaneously. But her mature, blank face is still. It is thus inevitably connected with Womack's voice at the centre of the soundtrack's stereo imaging, a fixed point in the midst of his trademark chattering rhythm guitars and clavinet keyboard. The details of the lyric don't quite fit, but when he sings 'You don't know whatcha do until you're put under pressure' we know this middle-aged woman is going to have to do something bad. But she has survived before, the sequence says, and she will again. The music's datedness thus serves to authenticate her identity. Far from offering post-modern irony, the homage lays the foundation stone of Jackie's character. In the film *Across 110th Street* Womack's song had accompanied shots of a large black Cadillac driving through rough-looking areas of New York before arriving in Harlem, establishing the environment and world of the film. Tarantino, however, sharpens its focus onto a single character, drawing on the music's cultural associations to locate both his actress' performed past, and her character's background.

Something rather different is happening with the music in the opening credit sequence of *Reservoir Dogs*. The fact that K-Billy's 'Super Sounds of the Seventies' has already been mentioned – and praised – in the opening, pre-credit scene, means when the voice of Steven Wright as the DJ is heard as the screen fades to black as the men get up to leave the restaurant, we know the music we hear and its source has some meaning in the lives of these characters. The George Baker Selection's *Little Green Bag* is not so much a detached, authorial commentary on these men, as a musical emanation of the world as they hear it.

Tarantino himself has spoken of his intent to use the 'sugariness, catchiness, lightness' of early 1970s bubblegum pop singles throughout this film to either 'lighten up' some scenes, 'making it funnier', or to make the torture scene 'even more disturbing' (Dawson 1995: 79–81). Elsewhere he has been quoted describing this as providing 'ironic counterpoint' to the visual action (Ciment and Niogret 1998: 21), a conventional terminology which other critics have been happy to seize on to explain the function of the *Reservoir Dogs* soundtrack (Barnes and Hearn 1996: 102). However, Claudia Gorbman has persuasively pointed out the limitations of this critical description of narrative/music relationships in film studies, restricting music's function to providing either 'parallelism' or 'counterpoint': these notions 'erroneously assume the image is autonomous' (Gorbman 1987: 15).

She offers instead 'mutual implication'. This too implies commentary, but crucially, reciprocity between visuals and music. The film sound theoretician Michel Chion goes further, arguing that genuine 'audio-visual counterpoint' is rare in film, because 'sound and image fall into different sensory categories', so to apply the term at all is 'an intellectual speculation rather than a workable concept' (Chion 1994: 36). He goes on to suggest that what most film critics actually mean by 'counterpoint' is merely a contrast, which he defines as 'audiovisual dissonance, counterpoint-as-contradiction' (Chion 1994: 37–9). Counterpoint, however, in its strict musicological meaning, refers to two or more independent melodic lines that have independent musical life, each with its own rhythm; when individual notes in each line meet at the same point in time, we call that harmony (see Cummings 1995: 139; Burt 1994: 6; Chion 1994: 36). The writer and film composer George S. Burt argues that film and music can interact contrapuntally, with each medium perceived independently, but combining to 'make a statement that is larger than each of the component parts' (Burt 1994: 6). It is perhaps this kind of audio-visual harmony which characterises the main titles of *Reservoir Dogs*.

The images of the *Reservoir Dogs* titles sequence are hardly autonomous, because they are very obviously manipulated by Tarantino to fit the music. Why is everything in slow motion? Why are the men shown walking from right to left together, then towards the camera individually, then in longshot from behind walking away together? An obvious, practical answer to the first question is that slowing the sequence down means it's long enough to allow a full hearing of both the main themes of *Little Green Bag*. This is not as cynical as it might sound. Under Steven Wright's DJ announcement and the fade-to-black we hear the first statement on solo bass guitar of the first theme, or riff, of *Little Green Bag*, with tambourine. Over the repetition, now with drums and extra half-notes within the bass riff, seeming to up the urgency to double-time, we see the group from side-on, moving into shot in slow motion from screen right. But from the start of the vocal, we move to a sequence of slow motion head-on shots of the cast, with each actor getting two bars exactly of credit-time each: the edits fall on the first beat of every other bar. These shots of the eight players consequently neatly fill the entire sixteen bars of the complete statement of this theme. With the jump to the second, more melodic and light hearted seeming theme, played over a swinging Latino *La Bamba* rhythm, the image jumps to the long shot, from the rear, of the men walking away, with the film's title scrolling up. At the end of the vocal statement of this theme, the screen goes black and the remaining credits scroll up over its instrumental repetition.

The music's rhythmic and thematic structure is thus foregrounded throughout by the visual editing. Chion has categorised such 'synchronous cuts in both sound and image track' as examples of what he calls 'synch-points', which are 'salient moments of an audiovisual sequence during which a sound event and a visual event meet in synchrony' (Chion 1994: 58–9). With visuals and music locked together at the beginnings and ends of musical measures, song-parts and different points-of-view shots, then perhaps we can for once – acknowledging Chion's warning – apply counterpoint as a metaphor. The two independent melodic lines in this composition are the slo-mo men's legs, faces and backs; and George Baker's two-part song. The harmony between audio and visual lies in the synch-points.

As Tarantino rightly acknowledges, credits are frequently the only 'mood-time' films allow themselves (*The Tarantino Connection* 1996: 1). Slow motion here, then, encourages us to linger a moment, really look at these men, perhaps hinting that it's our last chance to see them all together. Indeed, the pre-credit scene, in which they argue violently over Madonna's *Like a Virgin* and attitudes to tipping, has already revealed the tensions within the group. The first theme of 'Little Green Bag' is another distinctively individual solo voice, this time on the bass guitar, playing an 'epic' riff which seems to set the action in motion. But its recursive nature, going over the same small musical territory time and again, combined with slow motion and the close-up for two measures on each face, suggests the self-absorption of these men, each individual bound up in an image of himself as a black-suited, sunglass-wearing villain. Then the second musical theme reveals the track's initial grooviness as phony, replaced as it is by a pale, third-hand imitation of Latino sophistication.

Combined with the long shot of the men's backs, a mundane reworking of a Hollywood cliché – the heroes walking off into the setting sun – it's hard not to suppress a smirk. The film has hardly begun, and we are being invited to wave these men goodbye. The story is already over, this sequence says: stay watching only to find out how it ended. Factor-in the lyrics about an absurd, paranoid search for lost drugs, and the comedy is complete. Look at these losers, says Tarantino, just listen to their music. Again, this credit sequence does not so much use music as 'ironic counterpoint', but as part of a synchronic – and thus harmonic – narrative whole, a mini audio-visual pageant.

So the music in the opening credits of both *Jackie Brown* and *Reservoir Dogs* is drawn from the diegesis, and is used to say something about character: at the end of *Jackie Brown* we see her driving away in Ordell's car, mouthing along to the Bobby Womack song, so the connection with her character is made explicit. By contrast, despite its impact on *Pulp Fiction*'s soundtrack CD sales (up to June 1999, *Pulp Fiction: Music from the Motion Picture*, had sold over 1 million copies in the UK alone, compared to *Reservoir Dogs*' 300,000, and *Jackie Brown*'s 100,000, according to MCA Records and Maverick/ Warner; and *Pulp Fiction* has sold more than 3 million copies in the USA [Smith 1998: 195]). Dick Dale's surf guitar instrumental *Misirlou* is used in a more straightforward way, to make a directorial statement of intent about the tone and mood of the film as a text or experience. This is sustained by the use of other surf instrumentals throughout the film. The characters do not – with one exception – listen to surf music themselves; it is not meant to represent their taste. Instead, as Tarantino says, it functions as 'rock n' roll Ennio Morricone music, rock n' roll spaghetti western music' (Dargis 1998: 69). It supplies a distinct kind of musical intensity of style, to complement the film's verbal and visual exaggeration.

This is especially true of the opening. Pumpkin and Honey-Bunny discuss the idea of robbing the coffee shop, with liberal use of the 'f' word. As they begin the robbery, Honey-Bunny screams 'Any of you fuckin' pricks move and I'll execute every motherfuckin' last one of you!' To underline the extreme language, at this moment the action freeze-frames on their outstretched, pointing guns, and Dick Dale's unique electric guitar sound surges in for the main titles.

In this case, unique is the right word. As his followers, the 'Dick-heads' know, Dale's sound was formed by the experimental demands he made of the legendary American guitar and amplification engineer Leo Fender in the early 1960s. These led to the production models eventually known as the Fender Dual Showman amplifier and the Fender Reverb unit, but these models never recreated the exact parts and construction methods of Fender's prototypes for Dale, which the guitarist still uses. There is also the matter of the very heavy string gauges Dale prefers, with a '16 thou' for the top E string, for example (most guitarists use 8–10 thou). The tune Tarantino chose, the one he personally told Dale he could not do the film without, *Misirlou*, was Dale's first recording with this exact technical configuration of Dual Showman and Fender Reverb prototypes, in March 1962 (see Dale 1996; Blair 1989; Blair 1996; dickdale.com 1999).

Misirlou itself was a Greek standard of the 1940s, which remains popular at slow tempi for dancing the tango. Dale had learnt it from his Lebanese father. To say the tune has an epic, recursive quality is an understatement. In Dale's performance, it is not just recursive melodically, but also as an extreme, minimalistic performative gesture. Dale had incorporated the tune into his live act when a fan challenged him to play a tune on one string only (Blair 1996). As anyone who has seen him perform live can confirm, and as attested by a recent tablature analysis of his fingering (tomwbell 1995), he plays the tune once through on the open, bottom E string; and a second time, with the same fingering, two octaves higher on the open, top E string. An electric guitar had never been fingered or sounded like this before, and no other has since: Dale is 'King of the Surf Guitar'.

Cinema audiences may have become used to extreme language and exaggerated visuals, but very few were aware of Dick Dale before *Pulp Fiction*. It is not therefore unreasonable to suggest that, thanks to the unique style of Dale's guitar, it is the musical communication code of *Pulp Fiction* that is the most distinctive of the film's three such codes, dialogic, visual and musical. Subsequent uses of three other famous surf instrumentals as scoring over later scenes – as well as three rock instrumentals – are carried along in the wake of Dale's opening onslaught, without quite ever matching its impact. The Tornadoes' *Bustin' Surfboards* seems to be playing when Vincent visits his drug dealer Lance, but its diegetic status is fluid, fading in and out without any obvious sign of a source. It is perhaps useful as a mood bridge between Al Green (over Marcellus and Butch) and what follows, the brief pop-video-like sequence – edited to *Bullwinkle pt II* by The Centurions – comprising extreme close-ups of Vincent shooting-up, cut with the immediate effect: his driving to Mia's while obviously high. After this sequence, surf/instrumental rock music only recurs briefly towards the end of the film: The Revels' *Comanche* plays over Maynard and Zed's rape of Marcellus – although Tarantino originally wanted The Knack's *My Sharona* (Mooney 1994: 73) – and The

Lively Ones' *Surf Rider* plays Vincent and Jules out of the diner and then over the end credits. Tarantino is using it as a simple code, its extreme reverberation, spartan instrumentation and epic melodies serving as a musical equivalent of visual action that dwells on bodily abuse and excess. The surface texture of surf music – its electro-acoustic dynamics, its tempo, its sheer volume – is intensely arousing; but its melodic recursiveness allows no lyrical, narrative development or commentary function. So in the surf music-scoring of *Pulp Fiction*, unlike a film with an original composed score, Tarantino makes no comment on the particular emotional content on screen. The music only communicates the degree or intensity of emotion present in the abstract. He merely wishes to elevate the audience to the heightened state of arousal of his characters. This is why the shooting-up-to-The Centurions sequence is simultaneously exciting and uncomfortable to watch, an attempt at audio-visual emulation of a narcotic experience. Our intense level of arousal is outwith our control.

A less disturbing but remarkably accomplished piece of scoring-with-records is constructed by Tarantino for the 'Money Exchange – For real this time' twenty-four-minute sequence in the third reel of *Jackie Brown*. The mood and narrative is opened and sustained by the extensive use of three tracks from Roy Ayers' soundtrack to one of Tarantino's favourite blaxploitation films, *Coffy* (1973), also one of star Pam Grier's most famous roles (Ayers 1973; Keough 1998). But these recontextualised, non-diegetic pieces – *Aragon*, *Escape* and *Vittroni's Theme/King is Dead* – are interspersed with three diegetic tracks listened to by the characters in their cars as they drive up to the Mall to play their role. Jackie, for example, is playing Randy Crawford's version of The Crusaders' *Street Life*. Technically, the frequent return to the Ayers riffs achieves several things. They give the sequence a feeling of coherence and organic drive: at first viewing, most, like me, will not consciously spot that they are different tracks at all. The fact that they stop and start again at key moments and after other diegetic songs have been heard embodies on the soundtrack the recursive temporal sequencing: we see what happens over a few minutes that afternoon from several characters' perspectives, one after another. The main two pieces – the funky brass riff of *Aragon*, and the edgy bongos of *Escape* – are used for precise, specific scoring functions: *Aragon* is an opening and ending theme, associated specifically with the object of the sting – the money – playing while Jackie hides the money under the towels, and when Max calmly walks out with the bag near the end; while *Escape* is the mood piece for tension, whether Jackie's or Ordell's. Finally, these pieces collectively serve as another homage to Tarantino's blaxploitation models for the films. But they are structurally prevented from seeming dated or too self-conscious by the integration of the snatches of diegetic music from various styles and periods. It is as if all this groovy music just might be found in one person's eclectic record collection.

The one noteworthy scene in the three films under consideration when diegetic music not specifically selected by the characters has more than passing influence is the extended 'Jack Rabbit Slim's' sequence in *Pulp Fiction*. It is not simply that the playing of 1950s rock n' roll records in the retro-theme restaurant is a natural sound for the diegesis. But, just like Mia and Vincent's dialogue (they teasingly call each other 'daddy-o' and 'kitty-cat', 'cowboy' and 'cowgirl'), the art direction (1950s cars, lurid primary colours) and costume (Vincent's bootlace tie, Mia's tail-fin cuffs, the waiters dressed as 1950s film and music stars), the performance of the music is another piece of dressing-up, playing with possible identities. Ricky Nelson impressionist Gary Sharelle is doing a passable imitation of the star's hit *Waitin' in School* as Mia and Vincent enter. As they eat, we hear Ricky Nelson's record of *Lonesome Town* and two classic Link Wray guitar instrumentals, *Rumble* and *Ace of Spades*. Coming after Sharelle's performance, these oldies are clearly located as emanating from the scene; and for the only time in the film, the sound of loud guitar instrumentals – elsewhere used solely as arousing scoring – is heard as offering a possible taste choice in the characters' own world, as immediately available sounds to stimulate their arousal, not ours. This function is made explicit by Mia and Vincent's stylised dancing to Chuck Berry's *You Never Can Tell* in the Jack Rabbit Slim's Twist Contest. In word, image and music, the entire sequence is an elaborate, masqued ritual, in which self-image for the purposes of sexual display is made both possible and yet safe, by being lifted piecemeal off the cultural shelf or record rack.

But all this takes place within the context of the precise emerging relationship between the characters of Mia and Vincent, which is what this whole section of the film is about. Jack Rabbit Slim's is merely the comic centrepiece of this story, the middle-eight of a twenty-minute sequence set to almost continuous pop music, in which the first verse-and-chorus and reprise form two of the most striking, memorable uses of music by characters in Tarantino's work: Mia watching Vincent arrive on closed-circuit TV as she listens to Dusty Springfield's *Son of a Preacher Man*; and, later, after their date at Jack Rabbit Slim's, dancing and then overdosing, to the accompaniment of Urge Overkill's cover version of Neil Diamond's *Girl, You'll Be A Woman Soon*.

Both scenes, in an alluring reversal of established gender roles in hi-fi history (see Keightley 1996), foreground the central female character's music selection and control of the aural environment, by featuring extreme close-ups on her music technology: the needle lifting from the groove of Mia's copy of the *Dusty in Memphis* LP; her finger pressing rewind then play on her reel-to-reel tape recorder. Tarantino's original script had the Dusty album more plausibly being played from a CD (Tarantino 1994a: 45), but the stopping-and-starting of a CD's internal laser cannot be shown as a physical, fetishised act. The scene as edited emphasises Mia's desire to exercise remote control over her and Vincent's first meeting. She selected and is playing Dusty's LP; she watches and directs Vincent's movements from another room by closed-circuit security camera. Her only words to him in person are imperative: 'Let's go'. Like Vincent, the audience is not permitted to see Mia's face. The extreme close-ups – Mia's razor blade and mirror as she snorts cocaine, Vincent's grasping the whisky bottle, Mia's hand guiding the camera joystick, the turntable needle – present music as just another social stimulant, depressant or technology for taking the up-close tension out of sexual encounters. The fact that we see these images of detachment while Dusty is singing about 'looking into the eyes of' her lover, 'stealing kisses' and 'learning from each other' is amusing and yet arousing. The music, the only direct manifestation of Mia's character and mood that Vincent and the audience are granted at first, is explicitly suggestive of illicit sexual relations, in both its lyrics and performative style. It is not certain, but the 'son of a preacher man' in the song might well be a black man. We already know from previous scenes that Mia is married to a jealous black gangster and Vincent is fearful of getting involved. In the circumstances, what more provocative a come-on record could Mia possibly have played? If we could only shut out the melodic and rhythmic drive of the record, offering tantalising glimpses of sexual fulfilment and narrative closure ('yes, he was, he was, oh yes he was'), we might find it easier to laugh or be concerned by Mia's detached, control-freak mentality. But like Vincent's blood, the music is booming too loud in our ears. In total, the scene suggests this is how sexual and power relations are conducted today: remotely, under the influence of narcotics. Mia appears to be playing a sophisticated game, surfing her own scene on a wave of cocaine and funk.

When they return from Jack Rabbit Slim's, things go very differently. Playing Urge Overkill's straightforward cover of Neil Diamond's hit *Girl, You'll Be A Woman Soon* on her tape recorder, Mia launches into a solo, self-obsessed dance while Vincent is in the bathroom. In his coat pocket she discovers what she imagines is cocaine, overdoses and collapses into a coma. The song fades out to silence, the screen fades to black. Like *Son of a Preacher Man*, Mia's second chosen song also lyrically promises female maturity and fulfilment. But much as any of us might in private, she also mimes along with the epicly recursive, three-note falling guitar riff (preserved from the original) which punctuates the chorus title line: 'Wow, wow, wow,' she wails on her air guitar. It acts like a new drug to get her started.

It is precisely at this moment of *Pulp Fiction* – Mia's near-death – that the real, moral action of the story begins. And it is noticeable that whereas most of this story 'Vincent Vega and Marcellus Wallis' Wife', occupying from twenty minutes to one hour into the film, is set to music, rising in concentration and intensity to Mia's overdose (fifty); by contrast, after this, there is no music whatsoever for thirty minutes, and it only recurs at all in the remaining eighty minutes of the film as two brief fragments of diegetic car-radio music, and two scored scenes. Just as Mia is snapped out of drug-induced coma, so is the audience rudely awoken from its musical haze. Suddenly everyone realises that all actions have consequences. In visual terms, an equivalence is established between the extreme close-ups of Vincent's heroin injection, Mia's turntable arm and needle and the adrenalin shot Vincent administers straight to Mia's heart. The only truly penetrating experiences available here are drugs, music and more drugs. Each seems to offer control of one's environment, and the ability to assume any desired sexual identity. But just as Mia takes too much of one, the audience is made to overdose on the other.

The potency of these foregrounded music-selection scenes for audiences is not simply a result of their shocking outcomes on screen. Tarantino is also dramatising the dominant music situational-use practices of his youth audience. As the music psychologist John A. Sloboda has argued, 'Music listening is . . . intensely situational. One cannot begin to give a full account of the cognitive, affective, or aesthetic response of a listener, without paying detailed attention to the reasons why the person is listening to that particular music at that particular time'. His review of recent findings suggests that most music listening accompanies domestic, solitary activity; and listening behaviour is 'ranged along a particularly important dimension, that of control, related to choice and autonomy . . . listeners must make very definite choices about the precise track to accompany activities'. The younger the listener, the more domestic activities there are which are accompanied by self-chosen music (Sloboda 1999). Several other studies confirm that music listening is the most popular leisure activity of older adolescents, used by them most commonly to alter mood and enhance emotional states; and that this listening is primarily a solitary activity (see for example Zillman and Gan 1997; Christenson and Roberts 1998: 33–53). Young audiences watching Tarantino's films are seeing adults in their rooms and cars doing what they themselves do with music; but, excitingly, seeking to project their private mood-enhancement on to other characters as well.

These psychological studies might even partly explain why the infamous scene in *Reservoir Dogs* in which Mr Blonde slices off a cop's ear to Stealer's Wheel's *Stuck in the Middle with You* is so disturbing. On one level, it is Mr Blonde's self-absorption in the music and detachment from the brutality of his treatment of the cop which is so shocking. If most of us turned on the radio while preparing to do some housework and heard *Stuck in the Middle with You*, we might perhaps turn it up a bit to 'moderate our arousal' in keeping with the low complexity of the task at hand, according to the theories of Konecki (see the summary of his work in Hargreaves and North 1997: 84–103). But other studies have shown that in some activities we deliberately choose continuously arousing music (arousing most likely by virtue of its volume, rather than its complexity) – a good example being for aerobics classes. North and Hargreaves sum this up by suggesting 'people prefer typical musically-evoked levels of arousal which help them to achieve a particular situational goal' (see Crozier 1997; Hargreaves and North 1997). We know Mr Blonde's goal is to torture the cop for fun; perhaps his conduct is so disturbing because we see him self-consciously topping-up his high state of arousal, dancing around to the music, much as we might in executing more innocent tasks. This characterises our everyday use of the radio for arousal purposes as a morally neutral act: arousal doesn't know what it's for, only we do.

There's something else this psychological perspective might help clarify: why Tarantino's soundtrack albums have sold so well. Among respondents to a mass observation mailing on music in 1997, those who reported more mood-enhancing functions for their self-chosen music also reported 'greater levels of liking' of music in public places. This is a promising indication, says Sloboda, that 'patterns of music use in high-control contexts have implications for attitudes towards music in low-control contexts' (Sloboda 1999). Watching a movie at the cinema must qualify as 'low-control'. You cannot alter the film music, no matter how annoying. If cinema audiences are comprised mostly of that youthful section of the public for whom solitary, mood-enhancing musical use is most important, they are likely not only to recognise the way Tarantino's characters use music, but also to discover something they like on his soundtracks. 'The use of music as a cue to reminiscence is the single most frequent use reported', says Sloboda. The person who buys and puts on a Tarantino soundtrack CD in the privacy of their room is taking pleasure in reminiscing over acts which transgressed the normal patterns of musical arousal. To do so is to act a bit like Tarantino's characters: in control enough to choose; yet choosing music which just might drive you out of control.

Bibliography, Filmography, Discography

Across 110th Street Soundtrack (1997) Rykodisc/MGM Entertainment RCD 10706.

Ayers, Roy (1973) *Coffy: Original Motion Picture Soundtrack*. Polydor Records PD5048.

Barnes, Alan and Marcus Hearn (1996) *Tarantino A to Zed: The films of Quentin Tarantino*. London: Batsford.

Bernard, Jami (1995) *Quentin Tarantino: The Man and His Movies*. London: Harper-Collins.

Blair, John (1989) Sleeve notes to *King of the Surf Guitar: The Best of Dick Dale and His Del-Tones*. Rhino Records CD R2 75756.

Blair, John (1996) Sleeve notes to *Cowabunga! The Surf Box Rhino Records* 4-CD set of surf music 1960–1995. R2 72418.

Burt, George S. (1994) *The Art of Film Music*. Boston: Northeastern University Press.

Chion, Michel (1994) *Audio-Vision: Sound on Screen* (trans. Claudia Gorbman). New York: Columbia University Press.

Christenson, Peter G. and Donald F. Roberts (1998) *It's Not Only Rock & Roll: Popular Music in the Lives of Adolescents*. New York: Hampton Press.

Ciment, Michel and Hubert Niogret (1998) 'Interview at Cannes' [1992] in Gerald Peary (ed.) *Quentin Tarantino: Interviews*. Jackson: University of Mississippi Press.

Crozier, W. Ray (1997) 'Music and social influence' in David J. Hargreaves and Adrian C. North (eds) *The Social Psychology of Music*. Oxford: Oxford University Press.

Cummings, David (ed.) (1995) *The Hutchinson Encyclopedia of Music*. Oxford: Helicon Publishing.

Dale, Dick (1996) Foreword to sleeve notes to *Cowabunga! The Surf Box Rhino Records 4-CD set of surf music 1960–1995*, R2 72418.

Dargis, Manohla (1998) 'Quentin Tarantino on *Pulp Fiction*' in Gerald Peary (ed.) *Quentin Tarantino: Interviews*. Jackson: University of Mississippi Press.

Dawson, Jeff (1995) *Tarantino: Inside Story*. London: Cassell.

.dickdale.com (1999) http://www.dickdale.com/history.html, 'The Official Dick Dale Homepage', downloaded 27 June 1999.

du Gay, Paul, Stuart Hall, Linda Janes, Hugh Mackay and Keith Negus (1997) *Doing Cultural Studies: The Story of the Sony Walkman*. London: Sage/Open University.

Gorbman, Claudia (1987) *Unheard Melodies: Narrative Film Music*. London: BFI.

Hargreaves, David J. and Adrian C. North (1997) *The Social Psychology of Music*. Oxford: Oxford University Press.

Jackie Brown: Widescreen special edition (1998) Miramax Home Entertainment, D888016 PAL/VHS.

Jackie Brown: Music from the Miramax Motion Picture (1997) Maverick/A Band Apart, 9362-46841-2.

Keightley, Keir (1996) 'Turn it down! She shrieked: Gender, domestic space, and high fidelity, 1948–59'. *Popular Music*, vol. 15, no. 2.

Keough, Peter (1998) Press conference on *Jackie Brown* [1997] in Gerald Peary (ed.) *Quentin Tarantino: Interviews*. Jackson: University of Mississippi Press.

Leonard, Elmore (1998) *Rum Punch* (film tie-in edition, first published 1992). London: Penguin.

Middleton, Richard (1984) 'Play it again Sam': Some notes on the productivity of repetition in popular music. *Popular Music*, vol. 3.

Mooney, Joshua (1994) Interview with Quentin Tarantino, in Gerald Peary (ed.) *Quentin Tarantino: Interviews*. Jackson: University of Mississippi Press.

North, Adrian C. and David J. Hargreaves (1997) 'Experimental aesthetics and everyday music listening,' in David J. Hargreaves and Adrian C. North (eds) *The Social Psychology of Music*. Oxford: Oxford University Press.

Peary, Gerald (ed.) (1998) *Quentin Tarantino: Interviews*. Jackson: University of Mississippi Press.

Pulp Fiction: Special widescreen edition (1995) Touchstone Home Video, D400172 PAL/VHS.

Pulp Fiction: Music from the Motion Picture (1994) MCA Records, MCD 11103.

Reservoir Dogs (1995) Polygram Filmed Entertainment, 6379523 VHS/PAL.

Reservoir Dogs: Music from the Motion Picture Soundtrack (1992) MCA Records, MCD 10793.

Sloboda, John (1999) Everyday uses of music listening: A preliminary study' in S. W. Yi (ed.) *Music, Mind and Science*. Seoul: Western Music Research Institute.

Smith, Jeff (1998) *The Sounds of Commerce: Marketing Popular Film Music*. New York: Columbia University Press.

Tagg, Philip (1982) Analysing popular music: theory, method and practice. *Popular Music*, vol. 2.

Tarantino, Quentin (1994a) *Pulp Fiction*. London: Faber and Faber.

Tarantino, Quentin (1994b) *Reservoir Dogs*. London: Faber and Faber.

Tarantino, Quentin (1998) *Jackie Brown*. London: Faber and Faber.

The Tarantino Connection (1996) MCA Records, MCD 80325.

—— tomwbell (1995, rev. 1997), 'Miserlou tablature', members.aol.com/tomwbell/music/Miserlou.html, downloaded 27 June 1999.

Woods, Paul A. (1996) *King Pulp: The Wild World of Quentin Tarantino*. London: Plexus.

Zillman, Dolf and Su-Lin Gan (1997) 'Musical taste in adolescence' in David J. Hargreaves and Adrian C. North (eds) *The Social Psychology of Music*. Oxford: Oxford University Press.

Contributors

Michael Allen lectures on film, television and digital culture at Birkbeck College, University of London. He is the author of *Family Secrets: The Feature Films of D.W. Griffith* as well as several articles on the history of media technologies. He designs multimedia programs for film studies use and is currently writing a book on modern US cinema. He lives quietly in London with his wife and cat.

James Buhler is assistant professor of music theory in the School of Music at The University of Texas at Austin. He is editor with David Neumeyer and Caryl Flinn of *Music and Cinema* (Wesleyan University Press 2000) and is currently working on a book on mass culture and the dialectic of enlightenment.

Alfred W. Cochran is Professor of Music at Kansas State University. His research focus has included the life and music of Gail T. Kubik, as well as film music of the 1930s–1960s, especially that of Aaron Copland, Gail Kubik, Virgil Thomson and Leith Stevens.

K. J. Donnelly is a lecturer in film, television and radio studies at Staffordshire University. He was once a professional musician and has published a number of articles concerned with music and the moving image. He is at present adapting his doctoral research on pop music and British cinema for publication by the British Film Institute.

Caryl Flinn is an associate professor of Women's Studies and Media Arts at the Universtiy of Arizona, USA. She is the author of *Strains of Utopia: Gender, Nostalgia and Film Music* and co-editor of *Cinema* *and Music.* Her articles on film sound, music and gender have appeared in a variety of anthologies and journals.

Peter Franklin is Reader in Music at the University of Oxford, where he is a Fellow of St Catherine's College. His published work includes *The Idea of Music: Schoenberg and Others* (1985), *Mahler Symphony no. 3* (1991) and *The Life of Mahler* (1997); he also writes on early twentieth-century opera and Hollywood film music.

Ken Garner is a lecturer in the Division of Language, Media and Journalism, part of the Caledonian Business School at Glasgow Caledonian University. He is the author of *In Session Tonight: The Complete Radio 1 Recordings* (BBC 1993). He has also published on the film music of Woody Allen, sound styles in contemporary British radio drama and the radio broadcasting of the new Scottish Parliament. He is also a journalist, and is currently radio critic of the *Sunday Express*.

David Neumeyer is Professor of Music Theory in the School of Music and Leslie Waggener Professor in the College of Fine Arts, The University of Texas at Austin. He taught formerly at Indiana University, Bloomington.

William H. Rosar is the founder of the Society for the Preservation of Film Music and the International Film Music Society. He has lectured in film music history and analysis in the 'Scoring for Motion Pictures and Television' program at the University of Southern California in Los Angeles and is the editor of the forthcoming *Journal of Film Music*.

Robynn J. Stilwell is Lecturer in Music at the University of Southampton; her research involves the interaction between music and movement (including dance film, and music video), music and narrative and cultural processes.

Index